EVALUATING LANGUAGE ASSESSMENTS

Evaluating Language Assessments offers a comprehensive overview of the theoretical bases and research methodologies for the evaluation of language assessments and demonstrates the importance of a fuller understanding of this widely used evaluative tool. The volume explores language assessment evaluation in its wider political, economic, social, legal, and ethical contexts while also illustrating quantitative and qualitative methods through discussions of key research studies. Suitable for students in applied linguistics, second language acquisition, and language assessment and education, this book makes the case for a clear and rigorous understanding of the theoretical and methodological underpinnings of language assessment evaluation in order to achieve fair assessments and just institutions.

Antony John Kunnan is Professor of Applied Linguistics in the Department of English at the University of Macau. He is a specialist on language assessment, and his research has focused on fairness and justice, statistical analysis, and ethics and public policy. He was the founding editor of *Language Assessment Quarterly* and is currently Editor-in-Chief of the *Journal of Asia TEFL*.

New Perspectives on Language Assessment
Series Editors: Antony J. Kunnan, University of Macau; and James E. Purpura, Teachers College, Columbia University.

Headed by two of its leading scholars, this exciting new series captures the burgeoning field of language assessment by offering comprehensive and state-of-the-art coverage of its contemporary questions, pressing issues, and technical advances. It is the only active series of its kind on the market, and includes volumes on basic and advanced topics in language assessment, public policy and language assessment, and the interfaces of language assessment with other disciplines in applied linguistics. Each text presents key theoretical approaches and research findings, along with concrete practical implications and suggestions for readers conducting their own research or developmental studies.

The Diagnosis of Reading in a Second or Foreign Language
By J. Charles Alderson, Eeva-Leena Haapakangas, Ari Huhta, Lea Nieminen, and Riikka Ullakonoja

Talking About Language Assessment: The LAQ Interviews
Edited by Antony John Kunnan

Evaluating Language Assessments
By Antony John Kunnan

EVALUATING LANGUAGE ASSESSMENTS

Antony John Kunnan

Routledge
Taylor & Francis Group

NEW YORK AND LONDON

First published 2018
by Routledge
711 Third Avenue, New York 10017

and by Routledge
2 Park Square, Milton Park, Abingdon, Oxon, OX14 4RN

Routledge is an imprint of the Taylor & Francis Group, an informa business

Every effort has been made to contact copyright-holders. Please advise
the publisher of any errors or omissions, and these will be corrected in
subsequent editions.

Library of Congress Cataloging-in-Publication Data
A catalog record for this book has been requested

ISBN: 978-0-415-89776-1 (hbk)
ISBN: 978-0-415-89777-8 (pbk)
ISBN: 978-0-203-80355-4 (ebk)

Typeset in Bembo
by Apex CoVantage, LLC

To my family:
Ignatius John Kunnan, Mary John Manjali
Suchitra Sadanandan, Minnal John Kunnan

CONTENTS

ILLUSTRATIONS

Figures

Tables

SERIES EDITOR PREFACE

Language testing began in the late 19th century with assessments of foreign languages (French, German, and Spanish mainly) in the U.S. and English as a second language at Oxford and Cambridge in the U.K., along with a range of language assessments in France (*le Baccalauréat*) and Germany (*der Abitur*). Most scholars, however, consider the birth of modern language testing as a field of study dating back to 1961 with the publications of Robert Lado's book *Language Testing* and John Carroll's chapter on the *Fundamental Considerations in Language Testing*, coupled by the earliest efforts to organize what is known today as the *Test of English as a Foreign Language* or the *TOEFL iBT (Internet-based TOEFL)*. In the last 50 years, the field of language assessment has developed into an interdisciplinary enterprise, influenced by both the broad field of applied linguistics (concerned with the nature of language as well as its relation to acquisition, use, pedagogy, and policy) and synergies with the fields of educational measurement and statistical modeling; the sciences of thinking and learning; teacher education and professional development; computer and telecommunication technologies; and more recently, sociology, philosophy, ethics, and the law. It has also been influenced by a need to carve out its unique identity through the development of its own theories, research, and practices.

This series hopes to capture this burgeoning field by offering a cogent and comprehensive state-of-the-art coverage in the following areas:

(1) The development of language assessments to understand performance in large-scale or instructional contexts (e.g., diagnostic assessment, placement assessment, young learners' assessment, integrated skills assessment, task-based assessment, language for specific purposes assessment, or more specifically, assessments of pronunciation or pragmatics) and the use of these assessments in decision-making

(2) The development and use of language assessments to understand and promote learning in large-scale and instructional contexts (e.g., learning-oriented assessment, scenario-based assessment, formative assessment)

(3) The development of language assessments related to new or renewed areas of concern: assessments for intercultural communication; translation and interpretation; language certification in professional contexts (e.g., aviation); or the use of corpora, eye-tracking, or brain-imaging techniques in assessments

(4) The innovative use of computer and telecommunications technologies in the construction, delivery, scoring, and use of technology-mediated assessments (e.g., new tools for advancing the design and implementation of assessments, speech recognition, and automated scoring of L2 production)

(5) The use of quantitative and qualitative research methods for conducting validation research related to assessment (e.g., the use of psychometric models and methods or the use of protocol analysis, conversational analysis, or ethnographic analysis for test validation research)

(6) The development of language assessments for immigration, citizenship, asylum, and schooling

The primary purpose of this series is, thus, to provide theory, research, and practice-informed academic texts for addressing some of the most compelling contemporary questions, issues, and concerns in fields that involve, directly or indirectly, the use of language assessments. The scope of the series is designed to be broad enough to include books that examine questions in the past with fresh eyes, that explore new technologies and the affordances they provide for examining new constructs, and that describe various methods for conceptualizing and implementing assessment research.

This series should be of interest to students and teachers of language assessment in undergraduate and graduate programs; language and mainstream educational assessment researchers; language assessment businesses; and officers in education, government, and the military agencies involved in assessment. Faculty and researchers in other fields of applied linguistics (e.g., SLA, language pedagogy, L1 literacy, discourse analysis, and communications), as well as those in psychology, mainstream education, measurement, and research methods, should also find value in the series.

The series will experiment with different formats, including authored and edited books on topics of interest (e.g., diagnostic assessment of reading, pragmatics, or pronunciation assessment), books devoted to a single author's scholarly work, or books profiling the life and work of prominent assessment experts through in-depth interviews. In sum, the series aims to cast a wide net in addressing various topics of interest in language assessment.

In the current book, *Evaluating Language Assessments*, Antony John Kunnan begins by describing how over the years a number of high-stakes assessments, used in the context of civil service, literacy, immigration, and schooling, have displayed dubious records in terms of fairness, and have, as a result, not only failed to benefit society, but in many cases have caused harm. To avoid the repetition of these circumstances, Kunnan argues that the decision to use assessments needs to be guided by a rigorous process of evaluation, where systematic and meaningful analyses rooted to an overarching framework can provide a robust evidentiary basis for the selection and principled use of assessments. With this backdrop, Kunnan addresses two critical questions in his book:

(1) How do we determine if an assessment, potentially to be used for high-stakes decision-making, has the qualities needed to ultimately provide fair, just, and beneficial assessments to the community that it aims to serve?
(2) How might we challenge violations to fairness, justice, and beneficence when encountered?

Kunnan begins by describing several contexts in which assessments and assessment practices have led to unfairness and injustice, and suggests that had there been a regular process of evaluation in place, the institutions would have had more incentive to rectify their practices. Kunnan then reviews two current approaches to assessment evaluation (the standards-based and argument-based approaches) and argues that neither has succeeded in fully addressing the issues of fairness and justice. To address this gap, Kunnan invokes the work of moral philosophers to provide an intellectual background for the formulation of principles and sub-principles related to fairness and justice in the context of assessment. He further argues that these principles can be used to help guide reasoning as to whether an assessment is fair or not and justification as to whether an institution is behaving in a just manner. After proposing this framework, Kunnan describes how Toulmin's approach can be used to build an argument to support the principles and sub-principles of fairness and justice. In the following four chapters, Kunnan explores claims, sub-claims, warrants, and backing as a means of building an argument that can be used to evaluate assessment and assessment practices in terms of fairness and justice. These four chapters focus on the concepts of (1) Opportunity-to-learn, (2) meaningfulness, (3) absence of bias, and (4) the consequences of test use and how information from these concepts can contribute to the evaluation process. Finally, Kunnan introduces the concept of "ethical thinking" and provides a thorough discussion of how to apply ethical thinking to the evaluation of assessments and assessment practices.

This volume makes a major contribution to the field of language assessment in that it provides an in-depth discussion not only of how to conceptualize assessment evaluation in terms of fairness and justice, but also how to think through the justification process so that these arguments might eventually become part of the public discourse surrounding assessments and assessment practices.

James E. Purpura
New York City

PREFACE

Why pursue fairness? Because fairness is an essential component of justice. And, *Homo sapiens* is so constituted that unjust treatment offends not just its victims but its bystanders as well. Only in a setting where fairness prevails can we manage to live satisfying lives.

—*Nicholas Rescher (2002)*

I think the first duty of society is justice.

—*Alexander Hamilton (1755–1804)*

Imagine that your son or daughter was required to take a test in Grade 6 (at age 12 or so) as part of a primary school leaving examination system. But the principal of the school and the examination authority did not have any research evidence that the examination was fair so that they could assure parents regarding the fairness of the assessment. Or imagine we were asked to take a language assessment as part of our immigration or citizenship application, but when asked about the quality of the assessment, our instructor said she did not know if the assessment was fair. Also, imagine further that there were no alternative assessments to these two assessments. In these situations, test takers have no options except to submit to these assessments and hope the assessments would be fair.

This is the situation most test takers face around the world, as there is most often a single mandated assessment with no alternatives and the fairness of the assessment is unknown. Given a choice, almost none of the test takers would voluntarily submit to take such an assessment. Further, in the case of most assessments, when there is unfairness, it is hidden or covered up. And institutions that conduct these unfair assessments are probably aware that if these assessments are evaluated, deficiencies would be identified and those would need to be corrected. But they do not conduct evaluations and improve assessments for a variety of reasons that include untrained staff, cost of revisions, disregard for fairness, consequences of an assessment, and the lack of pressure to design and develop fair assessments. This is why evaluations of assessments ought to be mandatory in order to safeguard the careers and life opportunities of students in schools, colleges and universities, and workplaces and applicants for immigration and citizenship.

The first step of this evaluation process would be to identify assessments that are unfair and to locate the source of the unfairness. In order to do this, assessment agencies need to chart a development and research agenda that puts fairness and justice in the center of their evaluation frameworks. It is not enough though to merely identify and record unfair assessments and unjust institutions; it is necessary to go beyond this. Thus, the second step would be to find ways to understand the causes of unfairness so that we can remove manifest unfairness and injustice and replace it with fair assessments and just institutions. Assessment agencies need to conduct carefully designed research studies from the perspective of fairness and justice could lead to fair assessments and just assessment practices.

This book in a broad sense, is about evaluating language assessments from the perspectives of fairness and justice. In the ten chapters that follow, three complementary procedures that are followed. First, there is a general identification and diagnosis of unfair assessments and unjust institutional practices. These examples are from school, college, and university examinations, as well as workplace and immigration and citizenship assessment contexts. Second, there is a brief excursion into the ethical or moral philosophical positions held by two deontologists (or duty-based ethicists), John Rawls and Amartya Sen, that help ground the principles that need to be formulated. Third, there is a presentation of Toulmin's argumentation model that is used to chart and diagram assessment claims and warrants and supply backing from research studies. Finally, there is a discussion of how to bring the different pieces of evidence together that support claims or rebuttals and how to decide that claims have been supported or not. Central to all these efforts is the need for public justification or public reasoning by assessment agencies of their assessments in a non-parochial global way. This critical aspect of public policy is emphasized in the later chapters as a necessary framework engaging all the stakeholders of assessments that include test takers, instructors, administrators, score users, and university or government policy makers.

What is central and important about the argument in the book is the pursuit of fairness and justice in the various contexts of language assessments. The key point made through these contexts is that fairness and justice are necessary everywhere language assessments are used—in schools, colleges, and universities; in the workplace; in immigration, citizenship, and asylum; in all countries, big, medium, and small; and in well-developed, developing, and slow-developing communities. For every test taker in the world—young or old; man or woman; white, black, yellow, or brown; with disabilities or otherwise—needs to experience fair language assessments and just assessment institutions throughout their lives. Such a global non-parochial approach should remind us of Martin Luther King's famous words written as a letter from a jail in Birmingham, Alabama, in 1963:

> Injustice anywhere is a threat to justice everywhere. We are caught in the inescapable network of mutuality, tied in a single garment of destiny. Whatever affects one directly, affects all indirectly. Never again can we afford to live with the narrow, provincial "outside agitator" idea.

If we language assessment professionals succeed in pursuing fairness and justice for all, we would make a substantial contribution to our communities.

Reference

Rescher, N. (2002). *Fairness: Theory and practice of distributive justice*. New Brunswick, NJ: Transaction Publishers.

ACKNOWLEDGMENTS

This book has been slow in coming. My first thoughts on fairness were presented at the Language Testing Research Colloquium in Tampere, Finland, in 1996. The key ideas that I presented at the Colloquium (Kunnan, 1996) were formulated in a not-so-large University Arms hotel room on Hills Road in Cambridge, England. My one-week visit to the University of Cambridge Local Examinations Syndicate (UCLES, for short; now Cambridge English Language Assessment) gave me the opportunity to consider ideas of fairness alongside validation. In numerous further visits to UCLES and keynote addresses and workshops at various Association of Language Testers of Europe meetings in Barcelona, Berlin, Budapest, Prague, and Sofia, the participants encouraged me to think further and refine my ideas. For these and other generous support, I must thank Mike Milanovic and Nick Saville for their faith and confidence in me and my ideas.

Fueled by these efforts, Mary Spaan and I co-organized the Language Testing Research Colloquium (LTRC) in Orlando, Florida, in 1997 with the theme of "Fairness in language testing." The opening and closing panels discussed various topics on fairness, including its overall usefulness and possible limits. I collected and edited these papers in a volume titled *Fairness and Validation in Language Testing* (2000).

In 1999 and 2000, I was privileged to teach two seminars to graduate and doctoral students at University of California, Los Angeles on validation and fairness. The students and I discussed in the seminars (many of them are faculty members at universities now) interrogated my positions on various aspects of validation and fairness. One "seminar student" who led the questions most often was Lyle F. Bachman, who actually invited me to teach the seminars and was then the chair of the Department of Applied Linguistics at the University of California, Los Angeles! These seminars gave me the opportunity to make forays into moral philosophy and relate ideas from utilitarians and deontologists to assessment. My memories of those argumentative debates, comments, and suggestions were very valuable, and I benefited substantially from them. My heartfelt thanks to Lyle for this opportunity.

Another seminar experience that I valued very much was at the University of Bologna and the University of Modena and Reggio Emilia from 2011–14. In this annual workshop and seminar series, Jim Purpura, Kirby Grabowski, and I presented our views on various aspects of language assessment. I took the opportunity to discuss my views on fairness, and I received interesting comments from language instructors, government officials, and, of course, from Jim and Kirby. I have to thank Jim Purpura and Marc Silver for making this happen for four years in a row despite financial difficulties at the university.

Invitations from other universities to speak on fairness and justice among other language assessment topics gave me new ways of articulating my position. I want to thank the following universities: Dubai Men's College; the American Universities in Cairo, Sharjah, and Armenia; the National University of Singapore, Nanyang Technological University, Singapore; Seoul National University, the University of Hong Kong, and Hong Kong Polytechnic University; the Central Institute of English and Foreign Languages, Hyderabad; Delhi University; Chulalongkorn University, Bangkok; Regional Institute of English, Bangalore; Tunghai University, Taichung and National Taiwan University, Teachers College, Columbia University; and the University of Macao. Various recent international conferences where I delivered plenary talks helped me understand new issues in countries with different resources. These conferences included the Teaching English as a Foreign Languages in Bali; Asia Teaching as a Foreign Language in Nanjing; New Directions for the British Council in Seoul; English Teaching Association in Taipei; Asian Association for Language Assessment in Bangkok, Bali, and Taipei; and LTRCs in Barcelona, Cambridge, Hong Kong, Princeton, Tokyo, Toronto, and Vancouver. The names of organizers and researchers at these seminars, meetings, and conferences are too many to list individually, but interactions with many individuals stand out. They are Priya Abeywickrama, Vivien Berry, Nathan Carr, Liying Cheng, Sara Cushing, Fred Davidson, Ardeshir Geranpayeh, Lianzhen He, Eunice Jang, Yong-Won Lee, Constant Leung, Hang Li, Rama Mathew, Gary Ockey, David Qian, Nick Saville, Yasuyo Sawaki, Sunyoung Shin, Natsuko Shintani, Barry O'Sullivan, Lynda Taylor, Jacob Tharu, Carolyn Turner, Elvis Wagner, Cyril Weir, Mikyung Wolf, Jessica Wu, Jirada Wudyathangorn, and Jin Yan.

When Lyle Bachman was given the Lifetime Achievement Award by the International Language Testing Association at LTRC in Temecula, California, in 2004, he gave an invited lecture in which he offered a new way of considering assessment claims and assembling evidence as a way of justifying a language assessment. In his lecture, Lyle applied Toulmin's argumentation model to the language assessment context. This pioneering paper was published in *Language Assessment Quarterly* in 2005. As you will see in Chapter 3 and beyond, this work influenced me greatly and I have tried to extend his thinking in these chapters.

I have also been fortunate that many researchers in the field have pioneered debates, books, and papers in which they have contested the claims of assessment agencies in the last 20 years. I am thinking of authors who have influenced my thinking in many ways: Charles Alderson, Carol Chapelle, Alan Davies, Glenn Fulcher, Tim McNamara, Jim Purpura, Elana Shohamy, Bernard Spolsky, Charles Stansfield, and Xiaoming Xi. I want to acknowledge and thank them for being there to pose a question, engage in a debate, provoke a response, or start a conversation.

I have benefited greatly from my former and current students—from their suggestions, critiques, and intellectual quality—in Los Angeles, Taichung, Hong Kong, Singapore, and Macao. I would like to acknowledge a few of them: Beryl Meiron, Carmen Velasco-Martin, Paoli Lee, Heejin Kim, Limei Zhang, Sha Liu, Hafeni Hamakali, Giang Hoang, Carol Darbarera, Yuyan Cai, Elizabeth Li, and Matthew Wallace. I want to specially thank Laura Staniute at the University of Macao for her work on checking references and indexes.

I need to also thank the people who read my first rough drafts—Lyle F. Bachman, J. D. Brown, Dan Reed, Matthew Wallace, Elvis Wagner, and Jim Purpura. They made excellent suggestions and queried me on many points. The chapters and the overall book have benefited from their questions and meticulous reading. But, of course, any and all deficiencies are mine.

I have had the good fortune of having kind editors at Routledge in New York who waited very patiently for the final manuscript. For their patience and their careful reading, Leah Babb-Rosenfeld, Kathrene Binag, and Rebecca Novack, I am most grateful to you. Of course, my final word of thanks has to go to my family, who have missed me on many occasions as I was lost in thought or busy working out an idea—particularly, my mother, who has been asking me for more than two years when the book would be finished.

Antony John Kunnan
San Gabriel, California
December 2016

1
THE NEED FOR EVALUATION

Introduction

Almost all of us from around the world have experienced an assessment of our language ability at one time or another. It could have started in an elementary/ primary school classroom where a teacher asked us to write the letters of the alphabet, or read a paragraph or recite a poem, or write a description or a story. Later in life, if we started to work as a bank employee, we would have had to read accounts and finance documents, or as a nurse, to read doctors' prescriptions to help patients with medications, or as a repair technician, to read a manual to repair a TV, or as an air traffic controller, to communicate with pilots. If we studied at a college or university, we would have had to understand lectures, discuss issues, write reports and essays, and respond to questions in quizzes and term examinations; all of these would be graded by the professor. If we were considering immigration or citizenship, we might have been asked to demonstrate our language ability of the new country or to take part in social integration programs. In all these activities and assessments, from elementary school to the workplace to being a new immigrant, language is the central component in our ability to succeed, whether it is by using our first/native or home language or a second or third language. And in all these contexts, a parent, a teacher, a supervisor, a professor, an examiner, or a standardized assessment system would have assessed our language performance. We may remember days when we received the results of our performances; at least for that day, the results seemed to define who we are and who we might become. Thus, we can say that assessments (particularly, high-stakes assessments) in modern times not only gather information about our abilities, but simultaneously define our self-image and ultimately control our potential careers and lives.

Now imagine if in any of these assessment contexts, the teacher, or the professor or the examiner, or the assessment system did not function in a *fair* manner with aspects of the assessment, such as constructs and tasks, access and administration, scoring and reporting or decision-making, and other lesser critical aspects (room, furniture, equipment, etc.). We might have then remarked that the assessment was *not* fair—in fact, recalling the event even today many years later would bring back that unsavory autobiographical episode vividly.

To be more specific, language assessments can be unfair in different ways: imagine if a teacher in a primary school systematically gave more marks or points for the same answers to boys than to girls; or one of the teachers in a high school had oral language assessments tasks for ten minutes for each student, but in another room, a teacher hurried through the tasks in five minutes; or a college entrance examination grader who always gave more points for essays when graded in the morning than he did when graded in the afternoon; or a college professor who asked more difficult questions in a question–answer session of immigrant students than he did of locally born students. Or one group of test takers was asked to respond to the questions using paper and a pencil, whereas another group was given computers to work with; or one set of test takers took an assessment at a test center under strict conditions of test security, whereas another group took it at a center with lax test security, thereby leading to fraud and cheating. Or much worse, in terms of overt discrimination, imagine if a government's immigration or citizenship policy required a high level of language ability designed in such a way so that a particular group of applicants would clearly fail. What is common in all these scenarios is the unfairness of language assessments.

Two researchers brought the issue of fairness to our attention more than two decades ago. Alderson (1988) was among the first to state in the title of his article "This test is unfair: I'm not an economist!" Similarly, Fulcher and Bamford (1996) said in their title "I didn't get the grade I need. Where's my solicitor?" These articles were among the first to document the issue of unfairness in terms of different aspects of assessment. Some of us may have expressed similar sentiments about assessments that did not display fairness although we may not have written articles about them. Therefore, even without having much documentation or research evidence on hand, we might agree that some assessments could be unfair, and when this happens, the outcomes are likely to be biased against some test takers. And if these assessments are high-stakes assessments (such that academic careers or life opportunities are determined by the assessment results), unfair assessments can have a lifelong impact. Thus, assessment institutions have the responsibility to use fair assessments with the best available knowledge and practices.

Revolutions and Legislations

A few illustrations from history regarding fairness and fair treatment in public life will be useful. *Egalitarianism* is a concept that people should be treated equally by society and laws. But as the history of nations has shown, there have been decades and even centuries during which "difference" between peoples was endemic to political and governmental institutions. For example, differences were created by colonizers of colonized peoples; by regional and sectarian groupings; by race, ethnicity and color, gender, religion, and immigrant status; and in terms of native language, accent, and conversation patterns.

Many political revolutions in the last two centuries have worked to remove such differential creation and treatment of people: the French Revolution of 1792 in terms of social class, feudalism, and Catholic dogma; the German Revolution of 1848 in terms of economic class; the U.S. Civil War of 1865 in terms of slavery; the U.S. Suffragist Movement of the 1920s and the Feminist Movement of the late 20th century in terms of gender bias in voting; the political de-colonization revolutions in the mid to late 20th century in Asia and Africa; the U.S. Civil Rights Movement of the 1960s in terms of race and ethnicity; the repeal of Apartheid laws in South Africa to end White dominance and White rule; the protection given to people with disability through the Americans with Disability Act of 1990; and most recently gay and lesbian civil and equal rights campaigns of the 21st century in the U.S. and Europe to end same-sex marriage inequality.

Legislative statements that emphasize this egalitarian viewpoint include the second sentence of the U.S. Declaration of Independence of 1776: "We hold these truths to be self-evident, *that all men are created equal*, that they are endowed by their Creator with certain unalienable Rights, that among these are Life, Liberty and the pursuit of Happiness" (emphasis added). And, the U.S. Pledge of Allegiance ends with the phrase "with *liberty and justice for all*" (emphasis added). Similarly, Article 1 of the 1948 Universal Declaration of Human Rights of the United Nations states that "*All human beings are born free and equal* in dignity and rights," and Article 7 states that "All are equal before the law and are entitled without any discrimination to equal protection of the law" (emphasis added), and the 19th-century French motto highlights *liberté, égalité, fraternité* (for liberty, equality, fraternity).

The European Union, too, has on its books equality between women and men: "The equal treatment of men and women has been a fundamental tenet of the European Union since its inception and the principle of gender equality is central to all its activities" (p. 1).[1] Similarly, the Racial Equality Directive 2000/43/EC is an act of the European Union concerning labor law:

> It implements the principle of equal treatment between persons irrespective of racial or ethnic origin. Since the Treaty of Amsterdam came into force in 1999, new EC laws, or Directives, have been enacted in the area of anti-discrimination, and this Directive complements other Directives on gender and age, disability, religion and sexual orientation.[2]

But despite all these efforts, political and governmental institutions in some countries continue to deny equality to all their citizens. This is the case in authoritarian states where the rule of law is not transparent, inequality in many forms is rife, and citizens cannot protest to bring about change. Such states are less likely to provide equality in public institutions like schooling and college admissions, workplace employment and promotions, housing rentals and purchase, health care and insurance, and retirement, to name a few. These states are also less likely to offer personal equality provisions in terms of gender, race, ethnicity, national origin, occupation, native language, religious membership, political affiliation, and sexual orientation. Further, such states are less likely to provide individual and media freedoms, such as freedom to express your ideas; to form associations; to vote for political parties that form government; to criticize institutions; to protest against policies, both governmental and non-governmental; to have a free press, radio, television, and Internet; to a transparent judicial process; and so on. Such policies could generally affect other public institutions, including educational and assessment-related institutions, which could choose to reflect the states' authoritarian ways and lack transparency in their processes, leading to unfairness and inequality for test takers.

Detrimental-to-Beneficial Scale

From the earliest known assessments like the Chinese Imperial Civil Service examinations, language assessments (like all educational assessments) around the world function in different political, social, cultural, educational, and technological contexts and, therefore. These assessments have often been used as instruments to remove patronage and privilege and to level the playing field and to offer opportunities for all students in schools, colleges, and universities. But assessments have also been used as a bourgeois or meritocratic device contrived to preserve the status of elite or dominant communities and to whom career and social privileges continue to be offered. They have also been used as political instruments to form the collective culture of nation-states such as civic nationalism and patriotism, or to provide empirical support for a public policy of social inclusion or exclusion. Therefore, assessments can be detrimental or beneficial, but it is best they are placed on a continuum of a detrimental-to-beneficial scale, with very few being horribly detrimental and very few being wonderfully beneficial, most being benign but not useful, or necessary but painful. Such judgments or evaluations of the benefits/detriments of assessments will depend on many factors, with the core factors being the purpose of assessment, the quality of assessment instruments (its content, scoring, reporting), the basis for decision-making, and the effect they have on the community.

To be more specific, any survey of assessments from the past to the present will show that some assessment agencies take great care to develop and use *fair* assessments in terms of (a) providing opportunity-to-learn the knowledge or skill that is going to be assessed; (b) selecting constructs and operationalizing them into appropriate tasks; (c) planning appropriate developmental processes (designing and writing tasks and scoring and reporting assessment performances); (d) conducting research activities that provide evidence regarding the quality of the assessments; (e) using administrative procedures to preserve anonymity, eliminate fraud, and eliminate cheating; and (f) providing assessments that contribute to the good of community. However, as one can expect, there would be other assessment agencies that do not pay attention to these matters, resulting in *unfair* assessments and detrimental effects on test takers.

These assessment agencies may not have the planning, the motivation, the trained staff, or the infrastructure to develop and use fair assessments and fair assessment practices. Such agencies may use assessments that are (a) irrelevant or inappropriate for the purpose of the assessment; (b) not piloted or pre-tested or reviewed; (c) not fair in terms of providing opportunity-to-learn knowledge or skills; (d) not fair in terms of providing adequate access such as cost or accommodations for test takers with disabilities; (e) biased in terms of the content of test materials that favor wealthier test takers or specific gender, age, class, nationality, native language, or sexual orientation group; (f) blatantly unjust as they are designed to fail (or pass) most, if not all, of the test takers; and (g) generally harmful or detrimental to the communities where they are in use. These practices can certainly lead to unfair assessments and, therefore, these agencies can be called *unjust* institutions causing detrimental effects to test takers.

As mentioned earlier, most assessments are not likely to be entirely beneficial or detrimental, but they are likely to have some desirable qualities along with some harmful or undesirable qualities. In order to illustrate this, descriptions and evaluations of a few language assessments from different contexts (civil service examinations, literacy tests, and school-level assessments) are presented next. These assessments are meant to show that even with the best intentions, many intervening factors influencing assessments could lead to unintended consequences and in some cases result in unfair assessments that cause harm to test takers and to the community.

Civil Service Examinations

Service Examinations in China

Arguably, the first examinations in the world were the Imperial Civil. Generally speaking, these examinations were supposedly created to reduce the power of the aristocracy and to create a bureaucratic class that was obedient to the emperor. The examinations were promoted and interpreted as a way of identifying merit and capability and offering equal opportunity, thus making social mobility possible. Much later, similar examinations for the civil service were introduced in the 19th century in the U.K. for service in England and India.

The Chinese Imperial Civil Service Examination

Description

It can be argued that the prehistory of the large-scale assessment system started with the Chinese Imperial Civil Service examination system instituted in China as early as the Sui (581–618 CE), Tang (618–907) and Northern Song (960–1127) and continued into the Ming (1368–1644) and Qing dynasties (1644–1911). In ancient China, power was in the hands of a landed aristocracy where official recommendations and kinship relations were the only way to enter the social and political elite class. The introduction of the examination system effectively disrupted this continuity (see Figure 1.1). According to Yu and Suen (2005), the examination system started in 606 CE and officially ended in 1905.

EXTRACT 1.1 FLOW CHART OF CIVIL EXAMINATIONS AND DEGREES DURING THE MING AND QING DYNASTIES

Apprentice tests (*Tongsheng*)
(Pre-school apprentice students educated at home)
↓
County, Department, and Prefectural Licensing Examination (*Tongshi*)
↓
Triennial Qualifying Examination (*Keshi*)
↓
Tribute Student (*Gongsheng*) or State Student (*Jiasheng*)
↓
Triennial Provincial Examination in the Fall (*Xiangshi*)
↓
Triennial Metropolitan Examination in the Spring (*Huishi*)
↓
Palace Examination (*Dianshi*)
↓
Palace Graduate (*Jinshi*; literatus presented to emperor for appointment)
↓
Optimus (*Zhuangyuan*)
↓
Palace, Capital, Provincial, or Local Appointment by Rank

From: Adapted from Benjamin Elman's (2013) *Civil examinations and meritocracy in late imperial China*

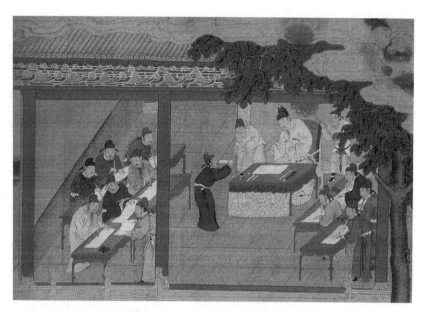

FIGURE 1.1   Palace Examination at Kaifeng, Song Dynasty, China

Image from www.chinasage.info/examinations.htm; available under a Creative Commons license

Examinations were held at the district, prefectural, qualifying, provincial, and metropolitan and palace levels. Extract 1.1 provides a flow chart of examinations in the Ming and Qing dynasties. An applicant would start with the Apprentice tests and then proceed to the County, Department, and Prefectural licensing examination and so on, and if the applicant was successful, he could go all the way to the Palace examination. The language of the examinations was written classical Chinese and spoken Mandarin (the official spoken dialect), and the examinations tested knowledge through quotations from the *Four Books* (Confucian Analects [*Lun Yü*], Mencius, The Great Learning [*Ta Hsüeh*], and The Doctrine of the Mean [*Chung Yung*], the *Five Classics* (the Books of Poetry, Documents, Change, Rites, and Springs and Autumns), and dynastic histories (Elman, 2013).

The ability to write was of supreme importance, as quotations from the Four Books and the Five Classics and judicial terms had to be annotated, and legal and policy questions had to be answered in the eight-legged essay form.[3] Other tests included writing poetry on given subjects using set poetic forms or rhymes and calligraphy (called the Imperial rescript or exact article reproduction without smudges). Thus, the examinations included classical erudition; historical knowledge; literary style; poetry; the esoteric art of calligraphy; and the infamous rigid, formulaic, parallel-prose style of the eight-legged essays. In preparation for these examinations, candidates had to memorize between 470,000 and 620,000 characters at the rate of 200 characters a day for six years in preparation for the examinations, according to Miyazaki (1976).

According to Cheng and Curtis (2010), many test response formats were used: oral responses for the question–answer portion; remembering missing lines from texts; passage summarization; poetry recitation; text elucidations (from the *Classics* and the *Books*); poetry composition; and free discussion on historical, political, and contemporary affairs. In the Ming Dynasty, although candidates had to "write poems, articles on state affairs, and essays on the Confucian classics . . . essays were required to be written in a certain fixed style" (Cheng & Curtis, 2010, p. 17) with a fixed character count of 500 to 700 in eight paragraphs.

The administration and grading practices of the examination system ensured honesty and fairness, according to Miyazaki (1976). Candidates were thoroughly searched on entering the examination compound and forbidden to leave during the examination process. The anonymity of candidates' written responses was guaranteed, as the facing page with the name of the candidates was covered and only the numbers of the candidates were visible for grading purposes. In addition, written responses were re-copied by copyists so that handwriting would not give away the identity of the candidates. According to Kracke (1967), responses were read by two evaluators and reconciled by a third reader. But despite these arrangements, collusion between candidates and graders sometimes escaped the safeguards; Chaffee (1985) reported that eight candidates who passed the metropolitan examination in 1156 were virtually illiterate.

The end of the Civil Service examination system started when ideas for educational reform and mass education were underway: Emperor Guangxu issued a decree that started the Jing Shi Da Xue Tang (Beijing University) and the teaching of Chinese classics along with Western sciences. A few years later, in 1905, the Civil Service examination system was abolished along with a plan for the growth of a system of primary, middle, and high schools. This ended the longest, almost continuous, examination system of 1299 years.

Evaluation

Primarily, the examination system was presented to the public as a means to identify meritorious and capable candidates with the idea of offering them employment, thus making social mobility possible. But most researchers now argue that social mobility remained elusive. Many classes of people like women, peasants, artisans, clerks, prostitutes, Taoists, Buddhists, and sons of merchants were excluded from the examinations as they were not considered to have sound morals. These restrictions immediately reduced the number of people who could be part of the social mobility. There were other forms of discrimination too, which included political credentials and family history to be affirmed by honorable witnesses. Further, although theoretically an adult male, regardless of his wealth or social status, could become a high-ranking official by passing the appropriate examinations, in reality the process of studying for the examinations was arduous and the costs involved in hiring tutors were high. Additionally, the use of Mandarin as the spoken language of the examinations and the use of archaic written classical Chinese created a further divide between the Mandarin-speaking northeast and other geographical regions. All this meant that most of the candidates came from a small group of wealthy land-owning families.

Elman (2013) commented on the haphazard rankings during the Ming and Qing dynasties' examinations as seen through inconsistent marking partly due to examiner incompetence or corruption. He provided examples of candidates who received different rankings at the three different examinations: in 1469, the optimus finished 240th on the metropolitan examination and 83rd on the provincial; in 1568, the optimus ranked 351st on the metropolitan examination and 83rd on the provincial examination.

In addition to the inconsistency of marking, there were the usual problems of cheating and plagiarism. Elman (2013) listed the various techniques of cheating during the Ming period: (1) impersonation (assuming someone else's name or sitting in someone else's cell), (2) passing essays composed by someone else to the candidate, (3) secretly carrying materials in one's clothing, (4) bribing the examiners, (5) signaling one's identity by leaving blank pages or including a secret code of a few paragraphs previously agreed upon, and (6) buying questions from the examiners or clerks.

In terms of the construct and the operationalized content of the examinations, we could ask questions regarding the relevance of the examined skills and knowledge and the ability to govern and be good civil servants. Was the examination system providing the emperor and the bureaucratic system useful civil servants at all levels? Otto Franke (1905, cited in Hanson, 1993) summed it up this way: "Instead of wise and morally outstanding representatives of government authority, the system supplied incompetent officials ignorant of the ways of the world; instead of an intellectual aristocracy, it supplied a class of arrogant and narrow-minded literati" (p. 191).

Elman (1991, 2000) and Chaffee (1995) argued that the examinations themselves were a masterpiece for the reproduction of the elite status. They persuaded all levels of society to buy in to a "Confucian Dream" that offered hope for social mobility even as it misrepresented the consequences of the system. Elman (1991) maintained that "despite shortcomings in fairness (in the examination system) . . . the civil service examinations remained the main avenue to wealth and power in late imperial China until the late 19th century" (p. 23).

In a chapter titled, "The Failure of Fairness," Chaffee (1995) outlined the failures of the examinations from the Southern Song onwards. He argued that the main causes were favoritism by examiners towards family or acquaintances and the role of privilege in the way special examinations were available for high-ranking relatives. He concluded:

> [T]he early emperors. . . had directed their policy of "fairness" (kung) at curbing the powerful and attracting the talented, especially from among

southern literati. Southern Song writers also appealed to "fairness," but the very different social conditions of that era gave the term a different meaning, one which emphasized the perception of fairness and not necessarily its reality. . . Thus, fairness was used to pacify the masses of literati who were threatening to overwhelm the examination system, even as the unfairness of special examinations continued unabated.

(p. 115)

The British Civil Service Examination

Description

The British Civil Service Commission, which grew out of the 1854 Northcote-Trevelyan report on the Civil Service[4] (although the report was not fully implemented for another 15 years) became the primary means of entry to the service through competitive examination rather than through patronage. The report argued for a recruitment entirely on the basis of merit by open, competitive examinations, with entrants recruited to a unified home service (in Britain) and an Indian Civil Service (ICS) and not to a specific department. This allowed for transfers between departments, and recruits could be placed into a hierarchical structure of classes and grades so that promotions could be based on merit and not on preferment, patronage, or purchase. The Commission was established to oversee recruitment to the Civil Service on merit, on the basis of fair and open competition based on the guiding principles of integrity, honesty, objectivity, and political impartiality. But its elite curriculum restricted the number of successful entrants to elite universities. According to Gilmour (2006), in 1859, of the 32 examinees who passed the ICS, Oxford and Cambridge supplied 8 each; Trinity College Dublin 5; Edinburgh 3; Aberdeen; King's College, London; and Queen's Belfast 2 each; and Cork 1.

The Civil Service only looked for young men "of superior education," although individual departments had different requirements. Although not all departments demanded that candidates must be unmarried and without family (a precondition for being considered for appointment as a Lieutenant of Revenue Police), most required high standards of attainment in arithmetic, English grammar and composition, history, and geography, along with excellent handwriting and spelling. To join the Treasury, candidates also had to be prepared to answer questions on the first three books of Euclid and translate a passage from Latin, French, German, or Italian (and later Spanish and Dutch). Ineligible persons included married men, money lenders, and women except in very exceptional circumstances and when no suitable man was available (Ministry of Labour Staff Code of 1927). Until 1939, to join the ICS, in addition to passing the written and *viva voce* examinations, the ability to ride a horse had to be certified by the superintendent of the Royal Artillery Riding Establishment at Woolwich.

EXTRACT 1.2   BRITISH CIVIL SERVICE SCHEME OF EXAMINATION QUESTIONS, 1855

Subjects	Marks
• *English language and literature*	
• *Composition*	*500*
• *English literature and history*	*1,000*
• *Language and literature of*	
• *Greece and Rome*	*1,500*
• *France, Germany and Italy*	*1,125*
• *Mathematics, pure and mixed*	*1,000*
• *Natural sciences*	*500*
• *Moral sciences*	*500*
• *Sanskrit language and literature*	*375*
• *Arabic language and literature*	*375*
Total	*6,875*

From: Allen's *Indian Mail*, London, April 2, 1855

In terms of the subjects assessed, according to Gilmour (2006), each year the commissioners of the Civil Service would announce the subjects and the procedures. Extract 1.2 shows the scheme of the examination in 1855. It was dominated by language and literature: English language and literature for 1500 marks, and language and literature of Greece and Rome for 1500 marks, and language and literature of France, Germany, and Italy accounted for 1125 marks, and language and literature of Sanskrit and Arabic for 750 marks, for a total of 4875 out of a possible 6875 (or 71 percent).

The examination was later modified as follows: 300 marks for compulsory subjects, 700 marks for elective subjects, and 300 for the *viva voce*. Chapman (1984) stated that

> Written examinations in academic subjects are a good test of intelligence and have stood the test of time. They are also widely regarded as fair, between candidates. The Commission do not seem to lay the old-time stress on the importance of manifest fairness as between candidates.

(p. 151)

The examinations were held in London (and in Allahabad in the early 20th century). Once the candidates had been selected to serve and finished their probation, they were posted to a province in India based on their ranking in the exam. There were about 1200 in number, and until the early 20th century, the civil servants were mainly British. They formed the administrative arm of the British Raj; they held all the key posts, surrounded the Viceroy, and dominated the provincial governments. They were the ones who were ultimately responsible for overseeing government activity in the 250 provinces that comprised British India.

Evaluation

As in the case of the Chinese Imperial Civil Service Examinations, the British and ICS examination was created to build a capable bureaucratic class that served the government, particularly in colonial India, Malaya, and East Africa. Once again, the ineligibility list of women, married men, and money lenders is a sign that fairness in terms of these candidate characteristics was ignored. Further, it is obvious that access and success on the examinations were restricted to wealthier candidates, as the examinations required knowledge of subject matter of a very specialized nature, the need to go to a crammer,[5] and the need to live in London for some time prior to the examination.

Chapman (1984) wrote that a certain Professor Kelsall in his published book in 1955 stated that there were enormous advantages if the candidates were from wealthier classes in society. For example, the test takers needed to stay in London for a month and study at a cram school like Wren's. He noted:

> cramming was more of a necessity than a luxury. The chances of success without one were apparently rated very low, even by Oxford and Cambridge men. In 1910, for instance, out of 33 successful Cambridge candidates, 21 were at Wren's[6] for six months or more, and three for seven weeks.
>
> (p. 155)

Again, we could ask questions regarding the relevance of the assessed skills and knowledge and its relationship to being good civil servants. What were the constructs and operationalized questions that were being assessed, and how were they relevant to becoming good civil servants? According to Gilmour (2006), Mathew Arnold, the poet and critic who was an examiner for a while, remarked that he would not have appointed the candidates he had awarded the highest marks because "they were crammed men not formed men. The 'formed men,' however, gained only low marks because they had not studied the textbooks on English literature" (p. 80).

The use of foreign language subjects gave an advantage to those who learned how to deal with this opportunity. As Chapman (1984) reported on a certain E. G.

(later St. Thomas) Compton, who joined the Civil Service in 1929: "I scored 70 out of 100 in Spanish as an *extra numerum* language, by a week's cramming of the language and without being able to speak a word of it" (p. 16).

Further, although the *viva-voce* lasted only 15 minutes, it was allocated 300 marks (along with 300 marks for compulsory subjects and 700 marks for elective subjects). Chapman (1984) commented on this: "One purpose of the interview seems to have been to test alertness, together with the candidates' general address, good manners, brightness, interest in various things and sympathy" (p. 155).

Another aspect of the ICS was that very few Indians were successful. According to Gilmour (2006), during the first 14 years of competition, of the 16 examinees who took the examination, only 1 was successful; in 1869, 4 were successful, but in the 20 years that followed, only 12 Indians were successful. These numbers should not be surprising, as very few Indians would have had the resources to travel to London and to study the subject matter (that they may not be familiar with) with the help of a crammer. Therefore, in response to the cry for simultaneous examinations in London and Calcutta, the government created the Statutory Civil Service, which was to award a sixth of the places for "young Indians of good family and social position" (p. 83). But by 1910, only 6 civil servants in every hundred were Indian, and in 1947 at the time of India–Pakistan independence, only 65 from India and 81 from Pakistan had served in the ICS. Chapman (2004), among others, concluded that the allegations of bias in the recruitment of the candidates to the service may not have been blatantly obvious, but as an institution, it condoned institutional cultural bias and inequality in practice.

Thus, we can conclude from the Chinese and British Civil Service Examinations, the main goal of identifying and employing merit-worthy candidates through a series of examinations was successful in a limited way as the examinations discriminated against many groups and excluded others through cultural or elitist bias. The main problems included (1) the relevance of some of the subject areas in the examinations, (2) the choice of an elite curricula that ensured the dominance of elite classes, (3) the restriction on women and many men from taking the exam, (4) bias in selection and decision-making process, and (5) whether reliance of subject matter knowledge of the two examination systems were the best way to identify and select civil servants. Overall, the question that can be asked is whether these two assessments could be considered *fair assessments* and whether the two institutions that developed and administered them were *just institutions*.

Literacy Tests in the U.S.

Literacy tests were used in the U.S. for assessing the literacy of prospective voters in the mid-19th century and for restricting immigration from Southern and Eastern Europe in early 20th century.

Literacy Tests for Voting Rights

Description

The 15th Amendment of the Constitution of 1870 gave Black men the right to vote, and the 19th Amendment of the Constitution of 1920 gave women the right to vote; however, Southern states[7] used literacy tests, among other disqualification tactics, to keep Black voters from the ballot box. Literacy tests were approved by state legislatures as part of the voter registration process, and they were used from the 1890s to the 1960s supposedly to assess the literacy in English of prospective voters prior to permitting them to vote. The first formal literacy tests were introduced in 1890 and were required of all, but White people were exempted if they

---

EXTRACT 1.3   SAMPLE QUESTIONS, LITERACY TEST, STATE OF LOUISIANA, 1960s

1.   Draw a line around the number or letter of this sentence.
2.   Draw a line under the last word in this line.
3.   Cross out the longest word in this line.
4.   Draw a line around the shortest word in this line.
5.   Circle the first letter of the alphabet in this line.
6.   Draw a line through the letter that comes earliest in the alphabet.
      Z V S B D M K I T P H C
7.   Cross out the number necessary when making the number below one million.
      10000000000
8.   In the line below cross out each number that is more than 20 but less than 30.
      31 16 48 29 53 47 22 37 98 26 20 25
9.   Spell backwards, forwards.
10. Print the word vote upside down, but in the correct order.
11. Print a word that looks the same whether it is printed forwards or backwards.

Taken from: www.slate.com/blogs/the_vault/2013/06/28/voting_rights_and_the_ supreme_court_the_impossible_literacy_test_louisiana.html

Bruce Hartford of the Civil Rights Movement Veterans (www.crmvet.org/) states on their website: "At one time we displayed a 'brain-twister' type Louisiana literacy test. We removed it from the website because it was quite atypical and was probably little used."

---

could show that they descended from someone who was eligible to vote before 1867 (when only Whites could vote). The test was usually administered by White local officials who had complete control over the pass–fail decision.

A sample of the state of Louisiana's version of the test (11 questions out of 30) is given in Extract 1.3. It states that the test is to be given to anyone who cannot prove a 5th grade education. There are 30 questions in all to be answered in 10 minutes without any errors. Jeff Schwartz (2010, p. 1) stated further that the test was graded and administered in an insidious manner:

> Check out (the) question which says: "Spell backwards, forwards." If a Black person spelled "backwards" but omitted the comma, he/she would be flunked. If a Black person spelled "backwards," he/she would be flunked. If a Black person asked why, he/she would be told either "you forgot the comma," or "you shouldn't have included the comma," or "you should have

---

EXTRACT 1.4 SAMPLE READING ALOUD TEXT, LITERACY TEST, STATE OF ALABAMA, 1860s

White applicants might be given:
SECTION 20: That no person shall be imprisoned for debt.

Black applicants might be given:

SECTION 260: The income arising from the sixteenth section trust fund, the surplus revenue fund, until it is called for by the United States government, and the funds enumerated in sections 257 and 258 of this Constitution, together with a special annual tax of thirty cents on each one hundred dollars of taxable property in this state, which the legislature shall levy, shall be applied to the support and maintenance of the public schools, and it shall be the duty of the legislature to increase the public school fund from time to time as the necessity therefore and the condition of the treasury and the resources of the state may justify; provided, that nothing herein contained shall be so construed as to authorize the legislature to levy in any one year a greater rate of state taxation for all purposes, including schools, than sixty-five cents on each one hundred dollars' worth of taxable property; and provided further, that nothing herein contained shall prevent the legislature from first providing for the payment of the bonded indebtedness of the state and interest thereon out of all the revenue of the state.

From: www.crmvet.org/info/littest.htm. Reproduced with permission of the Civil Rights Movement Veterans.

spelled "backwards, forwards." Any plausible response by a white person would be accepted, and so would any implausible response.

In the state of Alabama's version of the test, it was necessary to name all 67 county judges in the state, name the date on which Oklahoma was admitted to the Union, and state how many bubbles there were in a bar of soap. In a later form of the Alabama test, in Part A, applicants were to read aloud a section of the

---

EXTRACT 1.5   SAMPLE QUESTIONS, LITERACY TEST, STATE OF ALABAMA, 1965

1. Which of the following is a right guaranteed by the Bill of Rights? _____
   Public Education _____Employment _____Trial by Jury _____Voting.
2. The federal census of [the] population is taken every five years. _____
   True _____False
3. If a person is indicted for a crime, name two rights which he has.
   _____
4. A U.S. senator elected at the general election in November takes office the following year on what date? _____
5. A President elected at the general election in November takes office the following year on what date? _____
6. Which definition applies to the word "amendment?" _____Proposed change, as in a Constitution _____Make of peace between nationals at war _____A part of the government
7. A person appointed to the U.S. Supreme Court is appointed for a term of _____
8. When the Constitution was approved by the original colonies, how many states had to ratify it in order for it to be in effect? _____
9. Does enumeration affect the income tax levied on citizens in various states? _____
10. Person opposed to swearing in an oath may say, instead: (solemnly)
    _____
11. To serve as President of the United States, a person must have attained:
    _____25 years of age _____35 years of age _____40 years of age
    _____45 years of age
12. What words are required by law to be on all coins and paper currency of the U.S.?

From: www.ferris.edu/htmls/news/jimcrow/origins/images/al_literacy.pdf

Alabama Constitution taken from a loose-leaf binder. It is claimed widely that White applicants, if given the test at all, would be given an easy section to read, whereas Black applicants were given a hard section that was filled with legalese and had long convoluted sentences. An example of this is shown in Extract 1.4.

The registrar marked each word that in his opinion was mispronounced. In some counties, applicants had to orally interpret the meaning of the section to the registrar's satisfaction and copy out by hand a section of the Constitution. Even here, White applicants would be allowed to copy the text, but Black applicants had to take dictation of the section from the registrar. The registrar then judged whether the applicant was literate or illiterate; this judgment could not be appealed. In the 1965 version of the Alabama test, there were 68 questions addressing civics, history, and government; a sample of the questions is shown in Extract 1.5.

It was only with the passing of the Voting Rights Act of 1965 that literacy tests were suspended in all states or political subdivisions in which less than 50% of the voting-age residents were registered as of November 1, 1964.

Evaluation

An examination of the three extracts provides sufficient evidence that literacy tests in various southern states of the U.S., along with poll taxes and other forms of intimidation, were used to deny voting rights to Blacks or African Americans. The tests of literacy were clearly not about literacy at the 5th grade level (which was the standard set for voting rights), but a formal way to prevent Blacks from obtaining voting rights. The unfairness of the system is obvious when comparing the constructs and operationalized test questions and the level of the construct of literacy at the 5th grade level.

Several other pieces of evidence in terms of the speededness[8] of the test administration and grading show how biased the test practice was towards Black applicants. Further, the power of the registrar or White local officials to supervise, grade, and judge the applicants' responses without any appeal process is another example of unfairness. The fact that the local, state, and federal governments had allowed these arbitrary and capricious practices to continue for so many decades shows that it was not only the test and testing practice that was totally unfair, the whole institution of government in the Southern states was unjust.

Literacy Tests for Immigration

Background and Description

In 1895, the Immigration Restriction League (IRL) advocated a literacy requirement as a means to control and restrict immigration. In their document, "The

Educational Test as a Means of Further Restricting Immigration," they observed that the newcomers from Southern and Eastern Europe were "undesirables" as they were unable to assimilate into the political, social, and cultural fabric of the U.S. and adopt American values, unlike previous immigrants from England, Ireland, and Germany. They also associated new immigrants with problems such as crime, delinquency, poverty, labor unrest, and violence. Members of the IRL wrote books, pamphlets, and newspaper articles to alert the public about these dangers and hired lobbyists to pressure members of Congress to support their idea of a literacy test.

The literacy test bill, termed House Bill No. 1 and Senate Bill No. 112, received the support of many prominent leaders. In addition to the support in Congress for the test, there were endorsements from 186 newspapers from across the country and 101 workers' unions, businesses, associations, and chambers of commerce. The bill advocated "the exclusion of all persons between 14 and 60 years of age who cannot both read and write the English language or some other language." Congress passed the literacy bill in 1896, but President Cleveland vetoed it as he felt it was contrary to traditional American policy and values.

A brief in favor of the illiteracy test (as it was now called) was made available through the IRL's publications as Publication No. 56. In it, they claimed that whereas average illiteracy among Northern Europeans (Scandinavian, Scotch, English, Finnish, Irish, Dutch and Flemish, German, French, and Northern Italians) was 3.5 percent, average illiteracy among Eastern and Southern Europeans (Spanish, Slovak, Greek, Croatian and Slovenian, Hebrew, Polish, Russian, Portuguese, Bulgarian, Servian, and Southern Italian) was 42.1 percent. They also claimed that in 1909, over 60 percent of the total immigration was of these races. Statistics compiled by the Commissioner-General of Immigration showed that of immigrants admitted to the U.S. between 1899 and 1910, 53.9 percent (911,566) of Southern Italians (of 1,690,376 admitted over the age of 14) could not read or write, and the numbers for other races/peoples with high immigration numbers (of over 100,000) with 35 percent or more illiteracy were Croatian and Slovenian, 36.1 percent; Lithuanian, 48.9 percent; Polish, 35.4 percent; and Ruthenian (Russniak), 53.4 percent.

Senator William P. Dillingham (R, Vermont) introduced Bill No. 3175 in 1911 providing for an educational test for immigrants, the exclusion of those not eligible for naturalization, and other restrictive features. During the debate, Senator Dillingham, a Republican and chairman of the earlier Dillingham Commission on immigration reform, spoke in favor of the literacy test as more practical than a percentage plan as a means of limiting immigration. President Wilson vetoed the bill, but it was overridden by both the House (287 to 106) and the Senate (62 to 19),[9] and the Immigration Act was formally passed on February 5, 1917. The law required that all persons between 14 and 60 years of age had to demonstrate literacy in English or some other language. Exceptions were made

EXTRACT 1.6 U.S. IMMIGRATION TEST, 1920s

Class No. 4 Serial number 0730 Italian

Io dico: Che cosa 'e l'uomo, che tu ne abbi memoria? e che cosa 'e il figliuola dell'uomo, che tu ne prenda cura?
E che tu l'abbi fatto poco minor degli Angeli, e l'abbi coronato di floria e d'onore?

What is man, that thou art mindful of him? And the son of man, that thou visitest him?
For thou hast made him a little lower than angels, and hast crowned him with glory and honor

From: www.nps.gov/stli/learn/historyculture/history-of-ellis-island-from-1892-to-1954.htm

for wives, mothers, grandmothers, unmarried or widowed daughters, and fathers and grandfathers over the age of 55. An example of the mood of the nation at that time, in addition to the numerous debates and speeches made in support and in opposition in Congress, can be seen through the 18th annual contest of the Central Debating League. The University of Chicago team was declared the winners in the debate on the literacy test for immigrants against Michigan and Northwestern Universities held on January 21, 1916. The three Chicago pro-literacy affirmative speakers won over the three negative speakers from the other universities, resolving the question before them: *Resolved, That the United States should adopt a Literacy Test for all European Immigrants* (Delta Sigma Rho, University of Chicago Chapter, 1916).

Extract 1.6 shows an example of the literacy test in dual-language cards, here in Italian and English. Italian immigrants were expected to read aloud either the Italian or English text to the immigration inspector. Armenio-Turkish, Greek, Hebrew, Hindustani-Afghani, Punjabi, Russian, and Swedish (along with English) were other dual-language cards that were made available. According to Martin (2011), "immigration inspectors, under the direction of the Secretary of Labor, were to use uniform pieces of paper, each with no fewer than 30 [and] not more than 40 commonly used words, printed in plainly legible type, to test the immigrants" (p. 142) but there are no records to show such word lists.

The story of Ms. Friedman, a 23-year-old Yiddish-speaking native of Poland, who arrived in New York on March 17, 1923, captures best how the literacy test was put into practice:

> (She) was asked by the (immigration) inspector: "Do you read any other language than Yiddish?" "No," she replied. As part of her entry examination, her literacy was then tested using a printed slip in Yiddish, the English translation of which was: "Blessed is the man who walketh not in the counsel of the ungodly, nor standeth in the way of sinners, nor sitteth in the seat of the scornful." Although she was able to read a large majority of the words, she could not explain the meaning of them. Ms. Friedman was denied admission.
>
> *(Hing, 2004, p. 51)*

Evaluation

It is not difficult to see that the impetus for the literacy test for immigrants among members of Congress in the 25-year period (1895–1920) was racially motivated. Behind this notion was the idea that illiterate Eastern and Southern European immigrants would be a burden on society and that they would not become part of the American mainstream, speak English, and uphold the values of the country. In fact, the target of the bill was squarely on immigrants from southern Italy and Poland, both of whom had high numbers of illiteracy, but these immigrants were also targets in their own communities in New York and Chicago, respectively, in the build up to the bill.

That the literacy test was used as an instrument of public policy to exclude groups of people (mainly southern Italians and Polish) from the U.S. is obvious. The fairness of the test construct and the operationalized version with those dual-language cards can be questioned. In the extract provided, judging from the English version, there can be no reasonable claim that an average American-born resident would be able to read archaic language presented in the card. And, therefore, to expect an immigrant from countries where they have little or no opportunity to go to school is offering a pretense of a chance to succeed. The test is clearly stacked against such immigrants. Thus, we see an officially approved process (by Congress, no doubt) of biased actions against immigrants clothed in a literacy test. The institution of immigration, with all its attendant ministers such as Congress, newspapers, workers' unions, and chambers of commerce who supported the bill, was together unjust in this case.

The two examples of literacy tests in the U.S. were instituted with the specific intention of keeping out Black test takers from specific benefits rather than to select candidates from the pool of Black test takers. In terms of U.S. immigration tests, too, there is clear intent to exclude applicants from Eastern and Southern Europe through English language tests. Such blatant misuse of assessments to harm test-taking groups shows us once again why assessments must be examined and their intentions revealed.

Once again, the question that can be asked is whether these assessments could be considered *fair assessments* and whether the two institutions that developed and administered them are *just institutions*.

School-Related Assessment in the U.S.

The most widely used context for language assessments has been the classroom arena. These assessments are typically developed by teachers or groups of teachers and used for various purposes from monitoring growth and achievement to certifying levels of achievements. There are also state-mandated standardized assessments that are developed by assessment consortia or agencies (like Educational Testing Services, Princeton, or the WIDA Consortium, Wisconsin). The purpose of most of these assessments is certification, as they are end-of-course assessments; indirectly, these assessments could be used for school and teacher accountability. The Great City Schools report titled *Student Testing in America's Great City Schools* (Hart, Casserly, Uzzell, Palacios, Corcoran, & Spurgeon, 2015) categorized school-level assessments as follows:

(1) *Statewide tests.* These are typically administered to students in Grades 3 to 8 and once in high school pursuant to the No Child Left Behind (NCLB; now replaced by the Every Student Succeeds Act in December 2015) legislation. These assessments include (a) the Partnership for Assessment of Readiness for College and Careers (PARCC), (b) the Smarter Balanced Assessment Consortium (SBAC), (c) state-developed assessments based on previous standards (2013–2014), and (d) new state-developed assessments to measure college- and career-ready standards in 2014–2015.

(2) *End-of-course (EOC) assessments.* These assessments are mandatory and administered at the conclusion of a particular course of study, usually in middle and/or high school grades, and typically involve tests in such core courses as English language arts, math, science, and/or social studies. These assessments are used as part of student graduation requirements, but some states also use them to satisfy federal NCLB or school accountability requirements. The California High School Exit Exam (discontinued in January 2016) was an example of this assessment.

(3) *Formative assessments.* These assessments are often mandatory and include short-term tests developed by the PARCC/SBAC consortia, states, school districts, and commercial publishers. They are administered to students periodically throughout the school year to assess content mastery. The assessments are given every three to six weeks and cover one, two, or three instructional units per subject area.

(4) *Interim or benchmark assessments.* These assessments are administered two or three times during the school year to measure student progress. The assessments could be computer adaptive, as in the case of the Northwest Evaluation Association's *Measures of Academic Progress* (NWEA-MAP).

(5) *Nationally normed-referenced assessments.* These assessments are standardized measures that are commercially developed and designed to determine how students taking the tests compare with a national norm group. Examples include the Iowa Test of Basic Skills (ITBS), the Cognitive Abilities Test (CogAT), the SAT, and the Terranova test.

Examples of school-level classroom assessments and the NWEA–MAP will be discussed next.

English Language Assessments

Description

Teacher-made classroom language assessments in the U.S. have been in use for at least a century. Language teachers generally design, write, administer, and score assessments and assign grades to students. Some of these assessments could be unit tests, weekly tests, quizzes, and term tests in several skill areas such as listening, speaking, reading, and writing or in the language elements such as grammar and vocabulary. The assessments typically have a variety of task types, including selected response, limited production, and extended production; specific response formats could include sentence repetition, recitation, reading aloud, dictation, gap-fill tasks, reading comprehension, correction and transformation of sentences, essay and letter writing, organized elocution contests, storytelling, or creative

---

EXTRACT 1.7   ENGLISH ASSESSMENT, 8TH GRADE, SALINA, KANSAS, USA, 1895

Grammar (Time, One Hour)

1. Give nine rules for the use of capital letters.
2. Name the parts of speech and define those that have no modifications.
3. Define verse, stanza, and paragraph.
4. What are the principal parts of a verb? Give principal parts of "lie," "play," and "run."
5. Define case; illustrate each case.
6. What is punctuation? Give rules for principal marks of punctuation.
7–10. Write a composition of about 150 words and show therein that you understand the practical use of the rules of grammar.

From the original document on file at the Smokey Valley Genealogical Society and Library in Salina, Kansas, and reprinted by the *Salina Journal*.

writing tasks. The quality of these assessment tasks depends on the language teachers' ability to design and write suitable tasks, administer and score or grade them (perhaps with other teachers as raters or judges), and give feedback to students in the form of scores, as well as through more informal notes, comments in margins, or remarks at the end of a performance. Many of these tasks, typically delivered in the paper-and-pencil mode (although this may change), are low stakes in the sense that the scores or marks may not have a life- or career-changing effect, although the negative effects of receiving low scores on such assessments could have long-lasting effects in terms of reduced motivation and effort.

Extracts 1.7 and 1.8 are from school-level assessments, both from 8th grade, in 1895 from Kansas and in 1912 from Kentucky, respectively. These assessments were chosen as examples of assessments from an era when the English language (and maybe all languages) were taught and learned in the same way as history or biology—as a body of knowledge. The knowledge that was expected to be learned and mastered was the rule systems of grammar and spelling in these two assessments. In most countries and contexts today, these assessments would be

---

EXTRACT 1.8   BULLITT COUNTY SCHOOLS, 8TH GRADE EXAMINATION, KENTUCKY, USA, 1912

Spelling

Exaggerate, incentive, conscious, pennyweight, chandelier, patient, potential, creature, participate, authenticate, bequeath, diminish, genuine, vinegar, incident, monotony, hyphen, antecedent, autumn, hideous, relieve, conceive, control, symptom, rhinoceros, adjective, partial, musician, architect, exhaust, diagram, eneeavor (sic), scissors, associate, saucepan, benefit, masculine, synopsis, circulate, eccentric

Grammar

1. How many parts of speech are there? Define each.
2. Define proper noun; common noun. Name the properties of a noun.
3. What is a Personal Pronoun? Decline I.
4. What properties have verbs?
5. "William struck James." Change the Voice of the verb.
6. Adjectives have how many Degrees of Comparison?
7. Diagram: The Lord loveth a cheerful giver.
8. Parse all the words in the following sentences: John ran over the bridge. Helen's parents love her.

From: http://bullittcountyhistory.org/bchistory/schoolexam1912.html

considered anachronistic and out of place, but there are school assessments that are similar even today.

Evaluation

The grammar test in Extracts 1.7 and 1.8 would be typical of the late 19th century and much of the 20th century where knowledge of rules of grammar was considered to be a primary indicator of language ability. Much classroom-based language assessment of this type existed around the world in the past (and may still do). Further, the focus on these tasks is on memory of rules and definitions. Thus, a high score in such an assessment cannot inform teachers of students' ability in using language, but could be an indicator of metalinguistic knowledge or rule systems of the language. From newer perspectives of the communicative language ability movement (see Bachman & Palmer, 1996) and current conceptualizations of assessing grammar (see Purpura, 2004, 2014), these assessments obviously look out of place and mostly irrelevant in terms of what we value in assessing language ability (including language use). And, again, the question is whether these two assessments could be considered *fair assessments* and whether the two institutions that developed and administered them *just institutions*.

Measures of Academic Progress

Description

Northwest Evaluation Association's (NWEA) Measures of Academic Progress (MAP) program created a personalized assessment by adapting to each student's learning level so that students, parents, and teachers could have essential information about each student's abilities and what they were ready to learn—all within 24 hours. The MAP, developed by the NWEA, in Portland, Oregon, a not-for-profit organization founded by researchers and educators from school districts in the Pacific Northwest in the late 20th century, was to serve the role of formative assessment. More than 5200 school districts across the U.S. used data from the MAP to inform their teaching practice in reading, mathematics, and English language usage, tailoring instruction to meet the specific needs of the students in their classrooms. The MAP is a computer-adaptive assessment administered to Grade 3 to 10 students three to four times a year to provide cross-grade measurements of students who perform on, above, and below grade level. The subjects included English language reading, language usage, mathematics, and Spanish language mathematics. The assessments comprise 40 to 50 questions that can be completed in under 60 minutes per subject. It was reported that MAP had over 32,000 items in its test banks.

In addition to the assessment, the MAP program included teacher training and access to MAP resources on how to use data from these assessments to differentiate instruction. MAP assessments and training were used in nearly 20 percent of K–12 school districts in the U.S. and about a third of the Midwest states in the U.S. (www.nwea.org/support/article/1339). Recently, the MAP also morphed into the Common Core MAP that provided a new set of results tied to the Common Core curriculum that were enforced in some states in the U.S.

Evaluation

In the last few years, questions have been raised about MAP, its role in the classroom—particularly in terms of teacher evaluation—and its validity and value of tests.

An important research study titled "The Impact of the Measures of Academic Progress (MAP) Program on Student Reading Achievement" (Cordray, Pion, Brandt, Molefe, & Toby, 2012) was conducted with the following research questions:

(1) Did the MAP program (that is, training plus formative testing feedback) affect the reading achievement of Grade 4 students after year 2 of implementation, as measured by the Illinois Standards Achievement Test (ISAT) reading scale scores or the MAP composite test scores in reading and language use?

(2) Were MAP resources (training, consultation, web-based materials) delivered by NWEA and received and used by teachers as planned?

(3) Did MAP teachers apply differentiated instructional practices in their classes to a greater extent than their control counterparts?

(4) Did the MAP program affect the reading achievement of Grade 5 students after year 2 of implementation, as measured by the Illinois Standards Achievement Test (ISAT) reading scale scores or the MAP composite test scores in reading and language use? (pp. xi–xii)

The findings from the study were not very positive; the conclusion was that

the MAP program was implemented with moderate fidelity, but that MAP teachers were not more likely than control group teachers to have applied differentiated instructional practices in their classes. Overall, the MAP program did not have a statistically significant impact on students' reading achievement in either grade 4 or grade 5.

(p. xii)

In 2013, teachers at Garfield High School in Seattle, Washington, decided to boycott the MAP. By all accounts, the MAP had serious problems at Garfield as (1) the students were told the test would have no impact on their grades and, because of this, students tended to give little thought to the test and hurry through it; and (2) there was little overlap between what teachers were expected to teach (state and district standards) and what was measured on the test.

Based on these problems with the exam, the content, and the lack of statistical significance of the students' scores, Kris McBride, who served as academic dean and testing coordinator at Garfield, stated that their teachers felt strongly that this type of assessment is *unfair*. She stated:

> Our teachers have come together and agree that the MAP test is not good for our students, nor is it an appropriate or useful tool in measuring progress. . . . additionally, students don't take it seriously. It produces specious results, and wreaks havoc on limited school resources during the weeks and weeks the test is administered.

Since this initial announcement of a boycott by Garfield teachers, a number of other schools in Seattle joined the protest. Educators, professors, parents, and community members wrote in support of the boycott, and thousands of people signed an online petition to the Superintendent of Seattle Public Schools.[10]

In April 2014, Ann Arbor Public Schools administrators in Michigan announced that Ann Arbor Open will no longer administer the NWEA's MAP assessment to its students. An Ann Arbor parent, Heather Sullivan MacPhail said that "The NWEA MAP test doesn't test the content of what the teacher taught to the child. . . It tests random knowledge, not what's happening. I don't think it's a good measure of them understanding content."[11]

But in the state of Illinois, in 2015, school districts were considering whether to continue the MAP or to use the state-mandated PARCC (short for Partnership for Assessment of Readiness for College and Careers) assessment that is aligned to the new Common Core standards or the Illinois Standardized Achievement Test (ISAT). In an era of growing backlash to standardized testing and the time they take from instruction, Illinois' educators said that the MAP could be the preferred assessment as it could enhance instruction, whereas standardized assessments were not providing useful information.[12]

Common Core Standards Tests for New York

Description and Evaluation

The Common Core Standards tests for New York City schools are based on the new Common Core curricula. They are administered to students from Grade 3 to 8 or 11 in English language arts and mathematics. The Board of Regents in New York City adopted the New York P-12 Common Core Learning Standards in ELA/Literacy and Mathematics in 2010 in order that students will develop skills in close text analysis in reading and deep understanding in mathematics. Specifically, in the English language arts test, students have to read and understand texts, write short answers and brief essays, and answer multiple-choice questions. The mathematics test requires students to show their steps in getting to the answers and explain working out complex problems.

In 2014–2015, there was a huge outcry against the tests because of the problems related to test items. Here are examples from the English language arts test reported in New York newspapers:

(a) A third-grade reading passage was from "Drag Racer" which has a grade-level reading of 5.9 and an interest level of 9th to 12th grade.

(b) Fourth graders were required to write about the architectural design of roller coasters and why cables are used instead of chains.

(c) A sixth-grade reading passage was from "That Spot" by Jack London, which included words and phrases such as "beaten curs," "absconders of justice," "surmise," "savve our cabin," and "let's maroon him."

(d) The sixth grade test required students to read a passage on nimbus clouds and architecture; an extract is presented in Extract 1.9.

(e) The eighth grade test required students to read articles on playground safety. Vocabulary included bowdlerized, habituation techniques, counter-intuitive, orthodoxy, circuitous, risk averse culture, and litigious. An extract is presented in Extract 1.10; also see Extract 1.11 for previous problems with the test.

Quite obviously, the items show that the reading passages and vocabulary listed are mismatched in terms of grade level and familiarity. There is little doubt even without a detailed analysis that there is unfairness related to whether students have had the Opportunity-to-learn the material in the test (particularly for the vocabulary part). As a result of these problems, many schools and school districts in New York State have witnessed an outcry from many parents, according to

---

EXTRACT 1.9   COMMON CORE ENGLISH LANGUAGE ARTS FOR NEW YORK SCHOOLS, GRADE 6, READING PASSAGE. PEARSON TEST, 2015.

As a result, the location of the cloud is an important aspect, as it is the setting for his creation and part of the artwork. In his favorite piece, Nimbus D'Aspremont, the architecture of the D'Aspremont-Lynden Castle in Rekem, Belgium, plays a significant role in the feel of the picture. "The contrast between the original castle and its former use as a military hospital and mental institution is still visible," he writes. "You could say the spaces function as a plinth for the work."

From: www.smithsonianmag.com/science-nature/nimbus-clouds-mysterious-ephemeral-and-now-indoors-166627507/#zeVz8kE148bVkjqR.99

EXTRACT 1.10   COMMON CORE ENGLISH LANGUAGE ARTS FOR NEW YORK SCHOOLS, GRADE 8, READING PASSAGE. PEARSON TEST, 2015.

Paradoxically, we posit that our fear of children being harmed by mostly harmless injuries may result in more fearful children and increased levels of psychopathology.

From www.nytimes.com/2011/07/19/science/19tierney.html?_r=0

Carol Burris of the *Washington Post* (April 19, 2015). She wrote that more than 200,000 New York parents opted out of the tests based on Common Core. Opt-outs are a legal procedure that parents can use to keep their children out of the tests if they choose to do this; no reason is necessary.

In response, Governor Cuomo of New York State set up a task force to address these issues. In December 2015, the task force issued a report calling for changes to what New York students learn and how they are assessed. Illustrating public sentiment of the move, Kate Taylor of *The New York Times* reported in an article on December 11, 2015,[13] that one-fifth of the students did not sit for the exams.

EXTRACT 1.11   ADDITIONAL TEST PROBLEMS, COMMON CORE TESTS FOR NEW YORK, PEARSON TEST

1. The New York State Regents, Global history, 2006: A series of questions asked students to describe how Africa "benefited" from imperialism. Using this 150-year-old quote: "We are endeavoring. . . to teach the native races to conduct their own affairs with justice and humanity, and to educate them alike in letters and in industry," students were asked to name "two ways the British improved the lives of Africans."
2. The New York State Regents, Grade 3 reading practice test, 2006: The practice test used the example of African American tennis stars Serena and Venus Williams to ask children questions about tennis "doubles" and country clubs.

From:http://parentsacrossamerica.org/civil-rights-discrimination-standardized-testing/

Further, at about the same time in mid-2015, there was growing concern elsewhere in the U.S. that school assessments were taking up too much time and eating into teaching and learning. One important report supported this concern: Hart, Casserly, Uzzell, Palacios, Corcoran, and Spurgeon (2015) concluded in their report titled *Student Testing in America's Great City Schools* by the Council of the Great City Schools that

> the average student in these districts will typically take about eight standardized tests per year. Some of these tests are administered to fulfill federal requirements under No Child Left Behind, NCLB waivers, or Race to the Top (RTT), while many others originate at the state and local levels. Others were optional.
>
> *(p. 9)*

President Obama responded to the increasing opposition to frequent high-stakes testing in public schools by declaring that the push for accountability and proliferation of tests through assessments had gone too far. Kate Zernike of *The New York Times* of October 25, 2015, wrote that the Obama administration "called for a cap on assessment so that no child would spend more than 2 percent of classroom instruction time taking tests" (p. A1).[14]

In summary, this turn-around in the administrations of New York State and the U.S. government shows that the push towards frequent assessments through legislations such as NCLB and RTTP not only did not succeed, but backfired. In addition, the activities of researchers through investigations of assessments and parents through calls for collective actions and opt-outs (in the case of New York State) show that parents want assessments to be beneficial and not to be conducted as per legislation without much concern for students who take the test and the usefulness of the assessments for them. One important point to note here is that the state and national government administrations listened and understood the frustration of parents, students, researchers, and the communities involved. Thus, their action must be seen as a victory for political institutions that are democratic and offer the possibility of governance by reasoning and justification.

Once again, in all these school-related assessments, the overall question that can be asked is whether these assessments could be considered *fair assessments* and whether the institutions that developed and administered them are *just institutions*.

Conclusion

This chapter introduced language assessments from the different contexts of civil service, literacy and immigration, and schooling. General descriptions and brief evaluations offered a glimpse of the types of test items and the purpose for which they were used in the past and in the present. As we have seen in the example assessments, there are many reasons why assessments need to be evaluated.

First, although assessments may be part of imperial or government policy, as with the Chinese Civil Service and British Civil Service or the U.S. literacy tests both for voting rights and immigration, there are problems with fairness with such assessments and assessment practice that need to be investigated and addressed.

Second, assessments and assessment practice that are unfair are typically not challenged by test takers or by community members in which the assessments are used. There could be many reasons for this: One reason could be the general feeling that assessments are infallible as they are written or administered by experts, professors or teachers. So, how could they be wrong? Why would they write unfair assessments? Or indulge in unfair practices? Another reason could be that unfair assessments and assessment practices cannot be challenged as there are no paths for remedies. In some countries, a few remedies such as score retotaling, rescoring, or retaking may be available for a fee that is often too high. And challenging an assessment or assessment practice with a lawsuit maybe practically impossible as individual test takers may not typically have the resources to take on a government or a commercial agency. However, most countries even these remedies may not be available, and test takers have to hope the assessments they are required to take for education, employment, immigration, or citizenship are fair.

It is in this light that the protest against the NWEA's MAP and the New York Common Core assessments have to be seen. The complaints were regarding problems in test design and operations, as well as usefulness of the assessments to students, teachers, and the community. Public concerns aired through research and newspaper publications, radio and TV reports, and parent opt-outs and community condemnation resulted in a change of policy in the state of New York. All of this was possible as individual and media freedoms such as freedom to express ideas without fear of repercussion is available in New York and in the U.S.[15] This is in contrast to the period when the literacy tests were introduced in the U.S. Although there was widespread frustration regarding these tests then, legal challenges were not successful in changing the tests until the 1960s.

Thus, in contexts and countries where such freedoms are prohibited, grassroots movements (from students, teachers, and parents) may be restricted or nonexistent, and assessment agencies may not be asked to reason and justify their assessments in public forums. In these cases, the burden is on assessment agencies to step up their research and development efforts to provide fair assessments and assessment practice to their communities.

Therefore, as I have argued, assessments need to be evaluated on a regular basis so that the community (where the assessment is used) can be reassured of the fairness of assessments and assessment practice. In order for this to become a reality, a framework or structure that is systematic and meaningful needs to be available. Some of the questions that need to be the centerpiece of the evaluation of every single assessment are: Is the assessment fair? Is the assessment practice fair? Is the assessment beneficial to the community? Is the assessment advancing fairness and justice? Is the institution administering and approving the assessment a just institution? These questions will be elaborated on and discussed in the rest of the book.

Book Chapters

In the next chapter, past frameworks and evaluations of language assessments will be presented. Chapter 3 presents a fairness and justice framework and how to build a fairness and justice argument in the Toulmin model of argumentation. Chapters 4 to 8 illustrate arguments in support of claims regarding fairness and justice with associated principles, claims, warrants, and backing (and in some cases rebuttals). Chapter 9 focuses on the application of fairness and justice for training assessment agency professionals, university professionals, and researchers. Finally, Chapter 10 looks forward in terms of how to apply ethical thinking in the evaluation of language assessments.

Notes

1 Gender Equality in the European Union. Retrieved from: http://ec.europa.eu/justice/gender-equality/files/brochure_equality_en.pdf
2 Race Equality Directive. Retrieved from: https://en.wikipedia.org/wiki/Race_Equality_Directive_2000f
3 Elman (2013) identified the first formal appearance of the eight-legged essay genre to the Ming period. It had the following structure: (1) break open the topic, (2) receiving the topic, (3) beginning the discussion, (4) initial leg, (5) transition leg, (6) middle leg, (7) later leg, and (8) conclusion. This rigid approach led to topics that were severely limited and prevented creativity. In fact, Hu (1984 as cited in Hanson, 1993) remarked that the essays became "no more than stylistic frippery and literary gyrations" (p. 190).
4 The British and Indian Civil Service refer to government positions in various services such as civil, criminal, finance, and administration in Britain and India, respectively, from the late 19th century until Indian independence in 1947. The Indian Civil Service examinations continue annually even today with considerable modifications.
5 A crammer is like a modern-day tutorial or cram school.
6 Possibly a well-known tutorial or cram school.
7 Matthew Wallace (PhD student in Singapore; personal communication, 2016) writes that these Southern states were supported by "southern elites, comprised of male white land owners who tried to maintain their hold on political power by restricting voting rights through the use of biased tests, special requirements, intimidation, and other disqualification tactics to keep black voters from the ballot box."
8 A test is speeded when the purpose is to check whether test takers can respond to many tasks in a short amount of time; hence the test may feel speeded to the test taker.
9 The House and Senate are two elected legislative bodies in the U.S.
10 Scrap the MAP! Solidarity with Seattle teachers boycotting the MAP test. (2015, December 20). Retrieved from: https://scrapthemap.wordpress.com/about/
11 Biolchini, A. (April 24, 2014). Ann Arbor drops use of NWEA student progress test. Retrieved on December 20, 2015, from: www.mlive.com/news/ann-arbor/index.ssf/2014/04/ ann_arbor_open_school_drops_us.html
12 Adams, P. (May 2, 2015). NWEA MAP standardized test is the assessment of choice for many area educators. Retrieved on December 20, 2015, from: www.pjstar.com/article/20150502/NEWS/150509892

13 Taylor, K. (2015). Cuomo's panel calls for further retreat from Common Core Standards. Retrieved on December 30, 2015, from: www.nytimes.com/2015/12/11/nyregion/cuomo-task-force-signals-further-retreat-from-common-core-school-standards.html

14 Zernike, K. (2015). Obama administration calls for limits on testing in schools. Retrieved on December 30, 2015, from: www.nytimes.com/2015/10/25/us/obama-administration-calls-for-limits-on-testing-in-schools.html

15 It could be argued that this volume, with many examples of assessments from the U.S., is possible because of the free access to information and individual freedoms that I have living in the U.S. In most countries, documents (past and present assessments), legislations (debates, discussions), and legal remedies are not available or not permitted.

References

Adams, P. (2015, December 15). NWEA MAP standardized test is the assessment of choice for many area educators. *Journal Star*. Retrieved from: www.pjstar.com/article/20150502/NEWS/150509892

Alderson, C. (1988). This test is unfair: I'm not an economist! In P. L. Carrell, J. Devine & D. E. Eskey (Eds.), *Interactive approaches to second language reading* (pp. 168-182). Cambridge, UK: Cambridge University Press.

Bachman, L. F. & Palmer, A. (1996). *Language testing in practice*. Oxford, UK: Oxford University Press.

Biolchini, A. (2015, December 20). Ann Arbor Open drops use of NWEA student progress test. *Michigan Live*. Retrieved from: www.mlive.com/news/ann-arbor/index.ssf/2014/04/ann_arbor_open_school_drops_us.html

Burris, C. (2015, April 19). Educators alarmed by some questions on N.Y. Common Core tests. *The Washington Post*. Retrieved from: www.washingtonpost.com/news/answer-sheet/wp/2015/04/19/educators-alarmed-by-some-questions-on-n-y-common-core-tests/

Chaffee, J. W. (1985). Chu Hsi and the revival of the White Deer Grotto Academy, 1179–1181 A.D. *T'oung Pao, 71*(1/3), 40–62. Retrieved from: www.jstor.org/stable/4528332

Chaffee, J. W. (1995). *The thorny gates of learning in Sung China*. Albany, NY: State University of New York Press.

Chapman, R. (1984). *Leadership in the British Civil Service*. Oxford, UK: Routledge.

Chapman, R. (2004). *The Civil Service Commission 1855–1991*. London, UK: Routledge.

Cheng, L., & Curtis, A. (Eds.) (2010). *English language assessment and the Chinese learner*. New York: Routledge.

Cordray, D., Pion, G., Brandt, C., Molefe, A., & Toby, M. (2012). *The impact of the Measures of Academic Progress (MAP) Program on student reading achievement: (NCEE 2013–4000)*. Washington, DC: National Center for Education Evaluation and Regional Assistance, Institute of Education Sciences, U.S. Department of Education.

Delta Sigma Rho. (1916). *Resolved, that the United States should adopt a literacy test for all European Immigrants*. Central Debating League: University of Chicago Chapter.

Elman, B. (1991). Political, social, and cultural reproduction via Civil Service Examinations in late imperial China. *The Journal of Asian Studies, 50*, 7–28.

Elman, B. (2000). *A cultural history of civil examinations in late imperial China*. Berkeley and Los Angeles: University of California Press.

Elman, B. (2013). *Civil examinations and meritocracy in late imperial China*. Cambridge, MA: Harvard University Press.

Fulcher, G., & Bamford, R. (1996). I didn't get the grade I need: Where's my solicitor? *System, 24*, 437–448.

Gilmour, D. (2006). *The ruling caste: Imperial lives in the Victorian raj.* New York: Farrar Straus Giroux.

Hanson, F. A. (1993). *Testing testing: Social consequences of the examined life.* Berkeley and Los Angeles: University of California Press.

Hart, R., Casserly, M., Uzzell, R., Palacios, M., Corcoran, A., & Spurgeon, L. (2015). *Student testing in America's great city schools.* Washington, DC: Council of the Great City Schools.

Hing, B. (2004). *Defining America through immigration policy.* Philadelphia, PA: Temple University Press.

Kracke, Jr, E. A. (1947). *Family vs. Merit in the Chinese Civil Service Examinations During the Empire Harvard Journal of Asiatic Studies, 10*, 103–123.

Martin, S. (2011). *A nation of immigrants.* New York: Cambridge University Press.

Miyazaki, I. (1976). *China's examination hell: The Civil Service Examinations of imperial China.* (Translated by C. Schirokauer). New Haven, CT: Yale University Press.

Purpura, J. (2004). *Assessing grammar.* Cambridge, UK: Cambridge University Press.

Purpura, J. (2014). Assessing grammar. In Kunnan, A. J. (Ed.), *The companion to language assessment* (pp. 100–124). Malden, MA: Wiley.

Schwartz, J. (2010). *CORE's Freedom Summer 1964: My experiences in Louisiana.* Retrieved from: www.crmvet.org/nars/schwartz.htm

Taylor, K. (2015, December 11). Cuomo panel calls for further retreat from Common Core Standards. *The New York Times.* Retrieved from: www.nytimes.com/2015/12/11/nyregion/cuomo-task-force-signals-further-retreat-from-common-core-school-standards.html?_r=0

Yu, L., & Suen, H. K. (2005). Historical and contemporary exam-driven education fever in China. *KEDI Journal of Educational Policy, 2*, 17–33.

Websites

European Union Community Law and the Racial Equality Directive 2000/43/EC Retrieved on April 4, 2017, from: http://en.wikipedia.org/wiki/Racial_Equality_Directive

Council Directive 2000/43/EC of 29 June 2000 implementing the principle of equal treatment between persons irrespective of racial or ethnic origin. OJ L 180, 19.7.2000, (pp. 22–26). Retrieved on April 4, 2017, from: http://europa.eu/legislation_summaries/employment_and_social_policy/equality_between_men_and_women/

2

PAST FRAMEWORKS AND EVALUATIONS

Introduction

Formal assessments do have a long history, as we have seen in Chapter 1, but evaluations of assessments do not have as long a history. The main reason for this has been the erroneous belief that assessments are infallible because they seemed to be beneficial to society. This perspective is fueled by the perception that assessments have historically helped ensure equal opportunity for education and employment and attacked the prior system of privilege and patronage. There is also the belief that assessment institutions or agencies would not use assessments that are detrimental to test takers. Despite this, everyone who has taken an assessment knows that assessments are not always fair and that assessments and assessment practices need to be evaluated.

As language learners and test takers during our school years to later years, we may have had to face only a few occasions of irresponsible assessment use: when we believed an assessment was too difficult, not representative of the material that had to be mastered, that the administration was not conducted well, that the scoring or reporting was inaccurate, that the cut score used was inappropriate resulting in poor decision-making, or that someone, maybe the teacher, was deliberately biased against us. But as individual test takers, can we do anything about any of these situations given the obvious power imbalance between test takers and assessment institutions? The answer is no, unless the assessment institution has provisions for rescoring or retotaling and the cost and process were not too onerous. More often than not, we bury our disappointment and carry on with our lives, but we never forget the instances of unfairness.

To avoid such inequities, assessment institutions ought to be asked as a public requirement to submit their assessments and assessment practices to formal evaluations that may be conducted by independent researchers. Such public evaluations are already available when we want to buy household appliances, electronics, babies and children's products, garden equipment, or automobiles. Consumer magazines evaluate products in terms of their features, price, ratings, safety, and comparisons with other brands and offer their recommendations. For example, *Consumer Reports*,[1] a non-profit organization that publishes expert independent product reviews in the U.S., claims on the home page of its website that it is "an expert, independent, nonprofit organization whose mission is to work for a fair, just, and safe marketplace for all consumers and to empower consumers to protect themselves." Similar organizations like *Car Magazine*[2] or *Auto Car*[3] review cars of every type, size, and price and offer recommendations after reviewing the features as well their performance on the road. Such reports safeguard consumers against cars that might be lemons or accessories or products that might be harmful.

Although *Consumer Reports, Car Magazine*, or *Auto Car* may be the gold standard of evaluations, in the field of assessment (and language assessment), we have just begun to ask these questions—mainly about high-stakes examinations related to university entrance. In the vast majority of cases, test takers and the test score–using communities do not have all the information that magazines like *Consumer Reports* publish. For example, test reviewers do not have an actual assessment or assessment performance data supplied to them for secondary analyses; at the most they may have test manuals, reports, and newsletter information. Thus, unlike consumer reports of products or car reviews that are based on test trials, assessment reviewers write reviews without access to the actual assessment instrument and assessment performance data.

Despite these major handicaps, reviews of general assessments and language assessments have been conducted by many researchers for various journals and publications. The most well known is the *Mental Measurements Yearbook* (MMY) which has published general (and a few language assessment) reviews since 1936. According to the MMY website, the Oscar Buros Center for Testing (named after its founder), which produces the MMY,

> is an independent organization within the University of Nebraska–Lincoln that shares its expertise in assessment-related endeavors. We function as the world's premier test review center, as well as a provider of outreach efforts related to our mission to improve testing, assessment, and measurement practices through consultation and education, with special emphases in psychology and education.[4]

Their mission is to improve the science and practice of testing and assessment by providing timely, consumer-oriented test reviews and evaluative information to promote and encourage informed test selection. There is a telling quote on the MMY website from Buros in 1938 in which he encouraged test takers to demand evidence of test validity: "Test users have every right to demand that test authors and publishers present full particulars concerning the methods used in construct-ing and validating the tests which they place on the market."[5]

This point was echoed decades later by Cronbach (1988), a well-known inde-pendent psychometrician:

> The bottom line is that validators have an obligation to review whether a practice has appropriate consequences for individuals and institutions, and especially to guard against adverse consequences. You... may prefer to exclude reflection on consequences from meanings of the word validation, but you cannot deny the obligation.
>
> *(p. 6)*

Although Buros' and Cronbach's views are on the right lines, the MMY evalu-ations are severely limited in scope and thus they have had very little impact on the field of assessment. But, as noted in the previous chapter, there have been grassroots and community-organized protests of New York state assessments for public schools and the general outcry against the frequency of assessments by researchers, teachers, and community leaders in the U.S. leading the Obama administration to call for limitations on assessments.

This chapter briefly examines two main approaches to assessment evaluation (standards based and argument based) that have emerged in the last 50 years and how they have contributed to language assessment evaluations with a few illustra-tive reviews.

The *Standards*-Based Approach

The standards-based approach to assessment evaluation attempted to general and specific qualities in assessment development, administration, scoring, and decision-making over decades. These qualities followed by good practices among assess-ment developers and score users have come to be informally known as standards or standard practice.

The earliest U.S. institution that took a clear interest in assessment evaluation was the American Psychological Association (APA), in Washington, DC. It issued *Technical Recommendations for Psychological Tests and Diagnostic Technique* in 1954. A second docu-ment titled *Technical Recommendations for Achievement Tests*, prepared by two commit-tees representing the American Educational Research Association (AERA), and the National Council on Measurement in Education (NCME), was published in 1955. These documents focused on test development and the kinds of information test developers and publishers were to provide to test users, such as test manuals. A third document titled the *Standards for Educational and Psychological Testing* (*Standards*, hereaf-ter) was published jointly by AERA, APA, and NCME in 1966 and replaced the first two documents. It is the *Standards* document of 1966 that is regularly revised now. Extract 2.1 presents a summary of the landmark changes in the *Standards*.

EXTRACT 2.1 APA, AERA, AND NCME *STANDARDS FOR EDUCATIONAL AND PSYCHOLOGICAL TESTING;* KEY FEATURES

Standards (1954) on tests

Standards (1966) on testing

Standards (1974): Three types of validity: content, criterion related, and construct validity

Standards (1985): Includes Messick's unified view of validity

Standards (1999): Includes chapter on "Fairness in Testing and Test Use" with 12 standards for fairness

Standards (2014): Includes a foundational chapter on "Fairness in Testing" with 20 standards

---

AERA, APA, and NCME's *Standards*

The AERA, APA, and NCME's *Standards* (1966, 1974, 1985, 1999, 2014) movement has influenced educational and language assessment test development and research for many decades. Lado (1961), the first author in modern language assessment, mirroring the *Standards*, wrote about test evaluation in terms of validity (face validity, validity by content, validation of the conditions required to answer test items, and empirical validation, namely, concurrent and criterion-based validation) and reliability. Later, Davies (1968) presented a scheme for determining validity, listing *five types*: face, content, construct, predictive, and concurrent, and Harris (1969) urged test writers to establish characteristics of a good test by examining them in terms of content, empirical (predictive and concurrent), and face validity. The *Standards* were reworked during this time (1966 version) and the interrelatedness of the *three different aspects of validity* (content, criterion related, and construct validities) was recognized in the 1974 version. This trinitarian doctrine of content and criterion-related concurrent and predictive validity of the 1954 version. Along with construct validity continued to dominate the field. In 1985, the *Standards* were reworked and titled "Standards for Educational and Psychological Testing" (instead of "Standards for Tests"). This new version included Messick's (1989) unified and expanded conceptual framework of validity that included facets of validity of test-score interpretation in terms of values and social consequences of tests and testing. Bachman (1990) and McNamara (1998, 2006), presented and discussed Messick's unified and expanded view of validity and empirical research; Cumming (1995) and Kunnan (1998) also documented the popularity of this approach.

But within the field of educational measurement and assessment, fairness as a concept in test development, use, and analysis only emerged in the late 1980s. The *Code of Fair Testing Practices in Education* in 1988 (*Code* for short) from the Joint Committee on Testing Practices in Washington, DC, was the first to articulate ideas on fairness. Much later, the AERA, APA, and the NCME's *Standards* in 1999 and 2014 expanded the concept of validity and included the concept of fairness in its revised *Standards*.

The Code of Fair Testing Practices in Education

The *Code* (1988) presented standards for educational test developers and users in four areas: developing and selecting tests, interpreting scores, striving for fairness, and informing test takers. The standards for implementation and acceptability for the qualities were then discussed here. To illustrate the assessment developer-score user dichotomy, here is an excerpt from Section C, *Striving for Fairness*:

> **Test developers** should strive to make tests that are as fair as possible for test takers of different races, gender, ethnic backgrounds, or handicapping conditions... (and) **Test users** should select tests that have been developed in ways that attempt to make them as fair as possible for test takers of different races, gender, ethnic backgrounds, or handicapping conditions.
>
> *(Code, 1988, pp. 4–5)*

In 2004, the Joint Committee on Testing Practices developed the *Code of Fair Testing Practices in Education* (revising and replacing the 1988 *Code*). The new *Code* was intended to be consistent with the relevant parts of the *Standards* (AERA, APA, & NCME, 1999). All relevant assessment agencies such as schools and individuals were encouraged to commit themselves to fairness in testing and testing practices. Its preface states:

> *The Code of Fair Testing Practices in Education (Code)* is a guide for professionals in fulfilling their obligation to provide and use tests that are fair to all test takers regardless of age, gender, disability, race, ethnicity, national origin, religion, sexual orientation, linguistic background, or other personal characteristics. Fairness is a primary consideration in all aspects of testing. Careful standardization of tests and administration conditions helps to ensure that all test takers are given a comparable opportunity to demonstrate what they know and how they can perform in the area being tested. Fairness implies that every test taker has the opportunity to prepare for the test and is informed about the general nature and content of the test, as appropriate to the purpose of the test. Fairness also extends to the accurate reporting

of individual and group test results. Fairness is not an isolated concept, but must be considered in all aspects of the testing process.

(p. 2)

The scope of the *Code* was broad and it was relevant to large-scale as well as teacher-prepared assessments.[6]

The AERA, APA, and NCME Standards (1999, 2014)

The 4th revision of the *Standards* in 1999 differed from its previous versions significantly. Drawing on Messick's (1989) influential treatise on validity, this version of the *Standards* restructured our way of thinking about validation. Messick presented validity as a unitary concept with two facets of validity (test interpretation and test use) and two types of evidence (evidential and consequential) instead of the traditional conceptualization of validation with the trinitarian types of validity. He argued that validation is a process of inquiry in which evidence is marshaled and arguments are put forward for or against in terms of the uses of assessment scores.

Related to Messick's (1989) inclusion of consequential evidence as part of the validation evidence, the 1999 *Standards* included a chapter titled, "Fairness in Testing and Test Use" for the first time. The authors stated by way of background that the

> concern for fairness in testing is pervasive, and the treatment accorded the topic here cannot do justice to the complex issues involved. A full consideration of fairness would explore the many functions of testing in relation to its many goals, including the broad goal of achieving equality of opportunity in our society.
>
> *(p. 73)*

The document acknowledged the difficulty in defining fairness: "[T]he term *fairness* is used in many different ways and has no single meaning. It is possible that two individuals may endorse fairness in testing as a desirable social goal, yet reach quite different conclusions" (p. 74). With this caveat, the authors outlined four principal ways in which the term is used[7] (emphasis added):

> The first two characterizations. . . relate fairness to *absence of bias* and to *equitable treatment of all examinees* in the testing process. There is broad consensus that tests should be free from bias. . . and that all examinees should be treated fairly in the testing process itself (e.g., afforded the same or comparable procedures in testing, test scoring, and use of scores). The third characterization of test fairness addresses the *equality of testing outcomes* for examinee subgroups defined by race, ethnicity, gender, disability, or other characteristics. The idea that fairness requires equality in overall passing rates for

different groups has been almost entirely repudiated in the professional test-ing literature. A more widely accepted view would hold that examinees of equal standing with respect to the construct the test is intended to measure should on average earn the same test score, irrespective of group member-ship. . . The fourth definition of fairness relates to *equity in opportunity to learn* the material covered in an achievement test. There would be general agreement that adequate opportunity to learn is clearly relevant to some uses and interpretations of achievement tests and clearly irrelevant to oth-ers, although disagreement might arise as to the relevance of opportunity to learn to test fairness in some specific situations.

(Standards, 1999, p. 74; emphasis added)

The document discussed two other main points: bias associated with test con-tent and response processes and fairness in selection and prediction. Based on these discussions, the document formulated 12 *Standards for Fairness*. Extract 2.2 lists key *Standards* relevant to fairness.

In the 2014 *Standards*, the 5th revision, the chapter on "Fairness in Testing" was placed as a foundational chapter along with chapters on "Validity" and

---

EXTRACT 2.2   1999 APA, AERA, AND NCME STANDARDS: KEY STANDARDS RELEVANT TO FAIRNESS

Standard 7.4: Test developers should strive to identify and eliminate lan-guage, symbols, words, phrases, and content that are offensive by members of racial, ethnic, gender, or other groups, except when judged to be neces-sary for adequate representation of the domain.

Standard 7.6: When empirical studies of differential prediction of a criterion for members of different subgroups are conducted, regression equations (or appropriate equivalent) should be computed separately for each group.

Standard 7.9: When tests or assessments are proposed for use as instruments of social, educational, or public policy, the test developers or users proposing the test should fully and accurately inform policymakers of the characteris-tics of the tests as well as any relevant and credible information that may be available concerning the likely consequences of test use.

Standard 7.12: The testing or assessment process should be carried out so that test takers receive comparable and equitable treatment during all phases of the testing or assessment process.

"Reliability/Precision and Errors in Measurement." The authors stated that "fairness is a fundamental validity issue and requires attention throughout all stages of test development and use" (p. 49).

The authors further articulated four general views of fairness: (1) fairness in treatment during the testing process, (2) fairness as lack of measurement bias, (3) fairness in access to the construct as measured, and (4) fairness as validity of individual test score interpretations for the intended use. They also identified threats to fair and valid interpretations of test scores: test content, test context, test response, opportunity-to-learn, and test accommodations (adaptations, modifications, and score reporting from accommodated and modified tests).

The authors outlined 20 standards with annotated commentaries in the 2014 document in four clusters:

> (1) Test design, development, administration, and scoring procedures that minimize barriers to valid score interpretations for the widest possible range of individuals and relevant score groups; (2) Validity of test score interpretations for intended uses for the intended examinee population; (3) Accommodations to remove construct-irrelevant barriers and support valid interpretations of scores for their intended uses; and (4) Safeguards against inappropriate score interpretations for intended uses,
>
> *(p. 63)*

Extract 2.3 lists key *Standards* relevant to fairness.

In summary, the current AERA, APA, and NCME *Standards* have come a long way from the earliest *Standards* in including and highlighting the importance of fairness in assessment and assessment practice.

Other Standards Documents

Educational Testing Service's Standards for Quality and Fairness

Following this general trend of the *Standards* documents, Educational Testing Service (ETS) in Princeton, New Jersey, USA, developed its own set of standards. In the 2002 document, there were 13 chapters devoted to various aspects of test design, development, and research. Chapter 4 was titled "Fairness" and it has eight specific standards related to "fairness in the design, development, administration;" "empirical evaluation of fairness for studied groups;" "impartial access;" "group differences;" "appropriate, reasonable, and comparable accommodations;" "language differences;" and "research studies on separate studied groups."

A few years later, ETS developed its *International Principles for Fairness Review of Assessments: A Manual for Developing Locally Appropriate Fairness Review Guidelines*

EXTRACT 2.3   2014 APA, AERA, AND NCME STANDARDS: KEY STANDARDS RELEVANT TO FAIRNESS

Standard 3.2: Test developers are responsible for developing tests that measure the intended construct and for minimizing the potential for tests' being affected by construct-irrelevant characteristics, such as linguistic, communicative, cognitive, cultural, physical, or other characteristics.

Standard 3.4: Test takers should receive comparable treatment during the test administration and scoring process.

Standard 3.6: Where credible evidence indicates that test scores may differ in meaning for relevant subgroups in the intended examinee population, test developers and/or users are responsible for examining the evidence for validity of score interpretations for intended uses for individuals from those subgroups. What constitutes a significant difference in subgroup score and what actions are taken in response to such differences may be defined by applicable laws.

Standard 3.8: When tests require the scoring of constructed responses, test developers and/or users should collect and report evidence of the validity of score interpretations for relevant subgroups in the intended population of test takers for the intended uses of test scores.

Standard 3.9: Test developers and/or test users are responsible for developing and providing test accommodations, where appropriate and feasible, to remove construct-irrelevant barriers that otherwise would interfere with examinees' ability to demonstrate their standing on the target constructs.

Standard 3.13: A test should be administered in the language that is most relevant and appropriate to the test purpose.

Standard 3.19: In settings where the same authority is responsible for both provision of curriculum and high stakes decisions based on testing of examinees' curriculum mastery, examinees should not suffer permanent negative consequences if evidence indicates that they have not had the Opportunity-to-learn the test content.

in Various Countries (ETS, 2009). Its main purpose was "to help the people who design, develop, and review items and tests to:

- better understand fairness in assessment
- avoid the inclusion of unfair content or images in tests as they are developed
- find and eliminate any unfair content or images in tests as they are reviewed, and
- reduce subjective differences in decisions about fairness" (p. 3).

The document also provides principles for fairness review of assessments:

- Avoid cognitive sources of construct-irrelevant variance (such as background knowledge in a reading assessment)
- Avoid affective sources of construct-irrelevant variance (such as offensive content, strong emotions, controversial prompts or materials)
- Avoid physical sources of construct-irrelevant variance (such as small font and colors)

The document then outlined areas of special interest: skills tests and content-tests (subject-matter tests) and groups of test takers (of special interest in the U.S.) in terms of age, disability, ethnicity, gender, national or regional origin, native language, race, religion, sexual orientation, and socioeconomic status.

In 2013, ETS issued a third set of guidelines for test development practices to ensure both validity and fairness for international language proficiency assessments. The key chapters focused on planning and developing an assessment, using selected-response and constructed-response items, statistical analyses of test results in terms of validity, and providing guidance to stakeholders and giving a voice to stakeholders in the testing process. Although the last two topics (on the role of stakeholders) were new ideas articulated for the first time, there was nothing new in terms of validity that had not been stated in previous documents, including the *Standards* and previous ETS ones. In terms of fairness, there was no new position; in fact the two previous documents from the ETS (ETS, 2002, 2009)[8] provided more guidance regarding the concept of fairness and how to research fairness.

ILTA's Guidelines for Practice

The International Language Testing Association (ILTA) issued its *Guidelines for Practice* (2010) as presented in Extract 2.4. The *Guidelines* are in two parts, with the first focusing on test developers' responsibilities and obligations, and the second focusing on the rights and responsibilities of test takers.

Soon, many other test development agencies such as the Association of Language Testers in Europe (ALTE), the European Association for Language Testing

---

EXTRACT 2.4   THE INTERNATIONAL LANGUAGE TESTING ASSOCIATION *GUIDELINES FOR PRACTICE* (2010)

Part 1

A.   Basic considerations for good testing practice in all situations
B.   Responsibilities of test designers and test writers
C.   Obligations of institutions preparing or administering high stakes examinations
D.   Obligations of those preparing and administering publicly available tests
E.   Responsibilities of users of test results
F.   Special considerations

Part 2

G.   Rights and responsibilities of test takers

---

and Assessment (EALTA), the Cambridge English Language Assessment (CELA), and the Pearson Test of English (PTE) developed their own guidelines for test development and practice.

Application to Language Assessment

Test Usefulness (Bachman and Palmer, 1996)

One of the most well-known applications of the *Standards* approach was promoted by Bachman and Palmer (1996). Translating Messick's (1989) conceptual framework, they articulated their ideas regarding test evaluation qualities in what they called *test usefulness*: "the most important consideration in designing and developing a language test is the use for which it is intended, so that the most important quality of a test is its usefulness" (p. 17). They expressed their notion thus: "Usefulness = Reliability + Construct Validity + Authenticity + Interactiveness + Impact + Practicality" (p. 18). This representation of test usefulness, they asserted, "can be described as a function of several different qualities, all of which contribute in unique but interrelated ways to the overall usefulness of a given test" (p. 18). Although not directly focusing on fairness, this approach included the notion of impact, which operationalizes the idea of consequential validity as proposed by Messick (1989). This approach was initially received as an operational version of Messick's (1989) unified theory of validity (construct validity, reliability, and impact) along with some language (authenticity and interactiveness) and practical considerations (practicality). But as questions regarding the concepts of authenticity and interactiveness emerged (Lewkowitz, 2000), Bachman signaled the end of test usefulness when he championed the case for building a justification for test use (Bachman, 2005) and subsequently for the Assessment Use Argument (Bachman and Palmer, 2010).

Illustrative Assessment Evaluations

A few examples of reviews of assessments from books and journals are provided in order to illustrate the range and scope of typical reviews.

Reviews of English Language Proficiency Tests (Alderson, Krahnke, & Stansfield, 1987)

This collection of reviews was the first published set of formal reviews of English language assessments, primarily from the U.S., the U.K., and Australia. Forty-seven tests were reviewed by 47 reviewers (i.e., each test was reviewed by one reviewer), but each review was also read by another reviewer and commented on by the test authors or publishers. The authors claimed this process resulted in more balanced and more accurate reviews. However, just as in the case of the *Mental Measurement Yearbook*, no assessment performance data were provided by the authors or developers to the reviewers for analysis.

The tests reviewed included some well-known ones such as the *Australian Second Language Proficiency Ratings, Bilingual Syntax Measure I and II, Cambridge First Certificate in English, Cambridge Certificate of Proficiency in English, Cambridge Preliminary English Test, General Test of English Language Proficiency, the Ilyin Oral Interview, the John/Fred Test, the Michigan Test of English Language Proficiency, the Oxford Examinations in English as a Foreign Language, the Oxford Placement Test, the Test of English as a Foreign Language, the Test of Spoken English,* and *the Test of Written English.* The structure of the reviews was as follows: Synopsis (test information details), Authors/Developers' Test References, Review, and Reviewers' References. The main part of the review was the section in which the reviewer provided a description and the format of the test, some comments on validity (mainly content and criterion validity), reliability, scoring, and limitations, but unfortunately, not all reviews contained comments on these aspects.

ESOL Tests and Testing Reviews (Stoynoff & Chapelle, 2005)

This edited collection of reviews was a follow-up to the Alderson et al. (1987) volume. In addition to reviewing 20 tests, it provided a useful introductory chapter titled "Understanding Language Tests and Testing Practices" to help readers understand how to read and understand the reviews. After the 20 reviews, the authors also provided three additional chapters titled "Using the Test Manual to Learn More about the Test," "Evaluating the Usefulness of Tests," and "Deciding to Develop a Test." These chapters do not directly relate to the reviews themselves. In fact, they are a rich resource as the authors discuss test specifications, administration, scoring, and different types of evidence to be collected for validity, reliability, and reviewing test manuals. They also have a chapter devoted to Bachman and Palmer's (1996) *Qualities of Test Usefulness,* where the authors offer a sample test usefulness analysis. In the last chapter, there are a few comments on fairness, test consequences, and codes and critical perspectives. But the 20 test reviews were not structured according to the *Qualities of Test Usefulness* and did not provide comments on test fairness and critical perspectives. Instead, the reviews had the following structure: Test Information, Test Purpose, Test Methods, and Justifying Test Use. The main part of the review was "Justifying Test Use" in which reviewers provided comments on validation and other technical features (such as reliability and correlations). As in the case of the Alderson et al. (1987) volume, no assessment performances were examined or reanalyzed.

Mental Measurements Yearbook Reviews

The MMY has been influential in the academic community, although it is hard to say whether its recommendations were as closely followed as *Consumer Reports* or *Car Magazine* or *Auto Car.* One main reason is that it is not as frequently produced; it has had 20 editions in the last 80 years. In each edition, tests in education, psychology, and languages are reviewed in a pre-specified format that includes information on the test and its review. Each test is generally reviewed by two professionals. In the 9th edition (1985), 265 tests were reviewed, of which 30 tests were directly related to language. They included *Bilingual Syntax Measure, Cloze Reading Tests 1–3, Diagnostic Screening Test: Language, Reading, Spelling (3rd edition), Edinburgh Reading Tests, Language Assessment Battery, London Reading Test, Michigan Prescriptive Program in English,* and *Nelson Reading Skills Test.* The tests reviewed were primarily for first-language users of English; there were no second-language tests of English or any other language.

In the 19th edition (2014), 283 tests were reviewed of which 25 tests were directly related to language. They included *BEST Literacy, CASAS Life and Work Listening and Work Reading Assessments, Early Language & Literacy Classroom Observation Tool (K-3 and Pre-K), Examination for the Certificate of Competency in English, Examination for the Certificate of Proficiency in English, Computerized Oral Proficiency Instrument, Oral and Written Language Scales (Second Edition): Listening Comprehension and Oral Expression, and Reading Comprehension and Written Expression, Michigan English Test, Preschool Language Scales—Screening Test, Spanish,* and *Spanish Screening Test, 5th edition.* In the editions in between the 9th and 19th, there have been a few reviews of tests of Chinese, Spanish, and Arabic as a second language.

The process of the MMY review is as follows: the reviewer (once commissioned) receives documents such as an actual copy of a retired form (or live form) of the test materials (including print and audio or video), test manuals, and/or reports that the testing agency is willing to share with the MMY editors and test reviewers. No data in the form of test performances are provided, nor are the scored data provided. Thus, reanalyses for any of the purposes that are critical for establishing the usefulness of the assessment are not possible. The early structure provided by the MMY editors was as follows: Purpose, Features, Test Development, Reliability, Validity, Summary, References. A useful collection of test details (including purpose, edition number, year of publication, target population, number of forms, price data, duration of test, and names of author and publisher) is provided at the top of the review that is copied from the manual or test booklet information. In more recent years, the structure of the review has been modified slightly: *Description, Development, Technical, Commentary, Summary, References.*

At the request of the MMY editors, I reviewed the *Chinese Proficiency Test* (Kunnan, 1995c) whose purpose was to evaluate the level of proficiency in (Mandarin) Chinese attained by American and other English-speaking learners of Chinese. I also reviewed the *Arabic Proficiency Test* (Kunnan, 2005) whose purpose was to evaluate applicants for admission, placement, or exemption to/from an Arabic study program, application for a scholarship or an appointment, competency testing upon exit from an Arabic program, certification of Arabic language proficiency for occupational purposes, and evaluation of an Arabic instructional program. The structure of the reviews followed the structure provided that did not allow for examinations of bias or unfairness of the assessments. Even if the MMY permitted this type of evaluation, it was not easy to do as no test performance data were available for the reviews.

In 2014, when I was asked to review two new assessments, the *Examination for the Certificate of Competency in English* and *the Computerized Oral Proficiency Instrument,* a section on fairness was included in each review because of my interest in this matter. Here are extracts fairness part from the review that I wrote with Wagner:

The Examination for the Certificate of Competency in English (Kunnan & Wagner, 2014)

> *Fairness.* An additional area of investigation that complements reliability and validity is fairness: whether the ECCE is fair to test takers from different groups such as gender, age, and disability. DIF analyses were conducted, and about 14% of the items were flagged for DIF, with roughly half of these items favoring males and half favoring females. However, because test takers from different age groups take this test, it would be necessary to know whether the test tasks are of comparable difficulty for the different age groups of test takers. Finally, as more test takers with disabilities are taking such tests, it would be necessary to know what accommodations are provided to test takers with various disabilities and whether any studies have been conducted to ensure the accommodations provided are not biased in favor of or against test takers with disabilities. These studies would enhance the value of the ECCE.
>
> *(pp. 287–288)*

Language Testing Reviews

In 1999, the journal *Language Testing* started a new regular feature titled *Test Reviews.* I was appointed test reviews editor by the then editors of the journal, Charles Alderson and Lyle Bachman. The Test Reviews feature was intended to provide readers with information about published tests that would assist them in either selecting a test that might be suitable for a particular use or for better understanding and interpreting results obtained from such tests. In the guidelines that were developed for test reviewers, fairness and impact or consequences were included for the first time, although they were previously ignored despite *Standards* (1999) discussing fairness and Messick's (1989) exhortation regarding consequential validity. But the reviews remained conceptual as no empirical data from test performance were examined for the reviews. This difficulty has not been overcome in recent reviews in journals. It is like writing a *Car Magazine* review by examining all the written material from the manufacturer but without any opportunity to test drive the car!

The first test reviewed in the journal was the *Michigan English Language Assessment Battery* (MELAB) by Weigle (2000). The structure of the review was as follows: *Test Information, Introduction, Description, Strengths and Weaknesses, Fairness, Documentation, Summary,* and *References*. Reviews were around 3000 words long, and authors commented on traditional areas such as validity and reliability but also on fairness. Many reviews used this structure: Luoma's (2001) review of the *Test of Spoken English* and Banerjee's (2003) review of the *TOEFL Computer-Based Test*. Bailey's (2005) review of the *Cambridge Young Learners English* tests had a more detailed structure. With detailed comments on fairness and impact, the reviews showed that the new model for test reviews was developing. The Wang, Choi, Schmidgall, and Bachman (2012) review of Pearson's *Test of English Academic* used the Bachman and Palmer (2010) AUA approach. Here is an extract from the Weigle review:

Michigan English Language Battery (Weigle, 2000)

> *Fairness.* A growing concern in language assessment is the issue of equity, or fairness, to examinees in terms of such issues as content familiarity, bias in favour of particular groups of examinees, and access. On this score the MELAB generally fares well. While the MELAB technical manual does not explicitly address the issue of test bias or differential item functioning, it does present comparative statistics for examinees grouped by reason for testing, sex, age and native-language groups. In terms of test content, the test writers have attempted to include content on a wide variety of subjects that would appeal to many different kinds of examinees, thus minimizing the risk that some examinees would be advantaged or disadvantaged by unequal content knowledge. Finally, the MELAB is considerably less expensive than the TOEFL, putting the test within reach of a broader spectrum of potential examinees.
>
> *(p. 453)*

Language Assessment Quarterly (LAQ) Reviews

After the launch of LAQ in 2004, test reviews were commissioned with less structure so that reviewers could write about tests and testing practices in a review format that resembled the *Consumer Report* or *Car Magazine* style. The first two reviews that appeared structured themselves: Gorman and Ernst's (2004) review of *The Comprehensive Adult Student Assessment System Life Skills Reading Tests* and Callet's (2005) review of the *California High School Exit Exam*: General Description, Test Descriptions, Test Fairness (Validity, Reliability, Absence of Bias, Access, Administration), Personal Observations, Summary, References. Chun's (2002) review of the *PhonePass*, Lee's (2007) review of the *Multimedia Assisted Test of English Speaking*, Shih's (2008) review of the *General English Proficiency Test*, Zhang and Elder's (2009) review of the *College English Test—Spoken English Test*, and Wagner and Kunnan's (2015) review of the *Duolingo English Test* addressed fairness from various aspects. Here are two extracts from the Callet review and the Wagner and Kunnan review.

The Comprehensive Adult Student Assessment System Life Skills Reading Tests (Callet, 2005)

> Kunnan (2004), in defining absence of bias, includes several kinds of evidence: (a) offensive content or language, which consists of stereotypical language or racial slurs; (b) unfair penalization based on a test taker's background; and (c) disparate impact and standard setting, which refers to differential performance on the test by the subgroups. The test developers of the CAHSEE have taken particular care to avoid biased and stereotypical language as evidenced by the released test items. The test appears to be fair in terms of language and topics. Informational and literary passages are somewhat familiar to students, and the questions that follow could be answered by perhaps any demographic. Informational topics are broad and neutral, meaning that the topics do not necessarily favor any one demographic—males over females or Whites over African Americans, for example—and the topics can be categorized as general knowledge. Students might read a passage on any one of the following topics: California, electric cars, vitamins, animals, and so on.
>
> *(pp. 297–299)*

The Duolingo English Test (Wagner & Kunnan, 2015)

> *Absence of Bias.* There is no published research that has investigated the issue of bias with the DET. . . . An important consideration for future research is how the performance of test takers with little or no familiarity or expertise in computer use might be affected by the need to use computers or smart phones when taking the test. In addition, it would be necessary to examine the content of the tasks (topics) and test performance for possible bias against types of test takers (by gender, race and ethnicity, socioeconomic status, and international status). . . .
>
> *Access.* The DET's low-cost barriers and ease of accessibility due to not having to travel to a test center is the test's most positive quality. However,

for potential test takers who do not have access to computers or smart phones, or to the Internet, taking the test is not possible... The issue of access also applies to test takers with disabilities. To date, no research has been conducted regarding how test takers with disabilities might perform on the test, nor have there been any studies examining possible accommodations for test takers with disabilities.

(pp. 328–329)

In summary, researchers used standard practices or standards stipulated by books and journals or the APA, AERA, and NCME *Standards* (1999) in their evaluations of language assessments. Whichever approach was used, the concepts that were commonly used were validity, reliability, and an occasional interest in fairness. But, unfortunately, no revires conducted by independent researchers were based on assessment performance data.

The Argument-Based Approach

The argument-based approach to evaluation of assessments has been discussed in the field of language assessment for the last two decades. Primarily, it has taken the form of finding an argument-based or jurisprudential approach to validation. Although this approach is gaining popularity today, it should be acknowledged that Cronbach and Meehl (1955) articulated this view many decades ago:

Construct validation takes place when an investigator believes that his instrument reflects a particular construct, to which are attached certain meanings. The proposed interpretation generates specific testable hypotheses, which are a means of confirming or disconfirming the claim.

(p. 290)

More recently, Cronbach (1988) argued for validation as a persuasive argument:

Validation of test or test use is evaluation (Guion, 1980; Messick, 1980), so, I propose here to extend to all testing the lessons from program evaluation. What House (1977) has called 'the logic of evaluation argument' applies, and I invite you to think of 'validity argument' rather than 'validity research'. . . Validation speaks to a diverse and potentially critical audience; therefore, *the argument must link concepts, evidence, social consequences, and values* . . . questions about tests originate in five perspectives: the functional, the political, the operationist, the economic, and the explanatory. Validators should take seriously questions of all these types.

(pp. 4–5; emphasis in original)

The main argumentation model that has been used in validation is Toulmin's (1958) pioneering model. A brief review of his model is presented next followed by an illustration of how such a model has been used in language assessment.

Toulmin's Argumentation Model

Toulmin, in *The Uses of Argument* (1958/2003), presented his argumentation model as an alternative to the standard argument structure that was based on inductive and deductive logic and an analysis of premises and conclusion called *syllogisms*. He believed that for an argument to succeed, it needs justification for its conclusion or claim. In order to achieve this, he proposed a layout containing six interrelated components for analyzing arguments; the first three are considered essential, and the remaining three may be needed in some arguments.

(1) *Claim or conclusion:* A claim or conclusion is a merit that must be established like a thesis. For example, if a person tries to convince a reader that an assessment is consistent or reliable, the claim would be "Assessment A is consistent or reliable."

(2) *Grounds or fact:* Grounds are the foundation or principles for a claim. For example, if the claim is that an assessment is consistent or reliable, then the grounds can be supported by the principle that "All assessments ought to be consistent or reliable."

(3) *Warrant:* A statement that authorizes movement from the grounds or principle to the claim. For example, in order to move from the grounds or principle in (2), "All assessments ought to be consistent or reliable," to the claim in (1), "Assessment A is consistent or reliable," there needs to be a warrant to bridge the gap between (1) and (2) with the statement "Assessment A's consistency or reliability can be inferred from research consistency or reliability research using test taker performance data."

(4) *Backing:* Backing is the research evidence that must be introduced to support the warrant (3). For example, if the warrant (3) is not credible enough, then the backing should include the following: "Based on research studies of consistency or reliability of Assessment A, we have support that Assessment A is consistent or reliable."

(5) *Rebuttal:* A statement that negates the claim. For example, "Assessment A is not consistent or reliable." Appropriate backing will be necessary for a rebuttal of the claim.

(6) *Qualifier:* Words expressing the degree of certainty concerning the claim. For example, "Assessment A is probably or partially or somewhat consistent or reliable."

A summary of the key features is presented in Extract 2.5.

EXTRACT 2.5 TOULMIN'S *THE USES OF ARGUMENT'S SIX COMPONENTS* (1958)

Claim: Conclusion or thesis (1)
Ground: Foundation or principles (2)
Warrant: Inference from data or ground to claim (3)
Backing: Support for warrant (4)
Rebuttal: Counter-claims (5)
Qualifier: Degree of certainty (6)

Application to Language Assessment

Kane (2001); Chapelle, Enright, and Jamieson (2008); and Bachman and Palmer (2010) have applied Toulmin's (1958/2003) argumentation model to language assessment.

Kane (2001, 2012)

Kane (2001) promoted the concept of *validity as argument* following Cronbach's (1988) "five perspectives on validity argument." Kane's (2001) approach to validation includes the following steps:

(1) State an interpretive argument laying out the network of inferences that go from test scores to conclusions to be drawn and decisions to be based on these conclusions
(2) State the validity argument assembling all available evidence relevant to the inferences and assumptions in the interpretive argument
(3) Evaluate the problematic assumptions of the argument in detail
(4) Reformulate the interpretive and validity arguments, if necessary, and repeat step three until all inferences in the interpretive argument are considered plausible, or the interpretive argument is rejected.

(p. 330)

Kane (2012) further argued that the validation of a proposed interpretive argument can be separated into two stages: the development stage (i.e., the test development stage) and the appraisal stage (i.e., the evaluation stage):

> *Stage 1: The Development Stage*: Creating the test and the interpretive argument. This stage of developing an assessment could be organized in three steps: "First an interpretive argument is outlined and a test plan is developed. . . Second, the test would be developed. . . Third, the inferences and assumptions in the interpretive argument would be evaluated to the extent possible

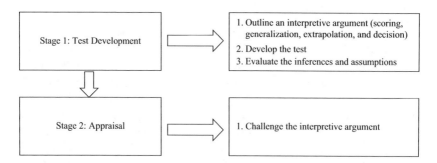

FIGURE 2.1 Kane's (2012) suggested process for a validation argument

during test development. Any weaknesses unveiled by these analyses may indicate the need to modify the interpretive argument or the test."

Stage 2: Appraisal Stage: Challenging the interpretive argument. During the appraisal stage, the test is taken as a finished product and the overall plausibility of the interpretive argument is examined.

(pp. 25–26)

Figure 2.1 represents Kane's suggested process for the validation of a proposed interpretive argument. Specifically, in Stage 1, Kane (2012) expects test developers to have detailed interpretive arguments for four major inferences: scoring, generalization, extrapolation, and decision. In Stage 2, these inferences are to be appraised.

There are two concerns regarding Kane's (2012) approach. First, the chain of inferences begins with scoring and goes all the way to decision-making, but much in test development takes place before the scoring stage, such as specifying the test purpose, surveying tasks in the target language use domain, selecting source material and content, and the writing of tasks development, and finally beyond decision-making, into consequences of an assessment. These processes need to be part of the interpretive argument as the data from these processes need to be part of the appraisal stage so that a comprehensive evaluation of an assessment can be undertaken.

Second, as the interpretive argument is articulated by test developers during the time of test development, there is a likely problem of conflict of interest that needs to be resolved. The interpretive argument will naturally include appropriate arguments for the inferences that the test developer may value, but may ignore or downgrade ones that they do not choose to include but which may be critical to an assessment. For example, test developers may choose not to include arguments related to ensure fairness in test content, test score interpretation, or decision-making, and therefore, in the appraisal stage, the test will be evaluated without these matters related to fairness of the assessment. Thus, an appraisal of an assessment conducted only in terms of the interpretive argument developed by a test developer is too internal and can potentially lead to a conflict of interest and a biased evaluation of an assessment.

Chapelle, Enright, and Jamieson (2008)

Chapelle, Enright, and Jamieson (2008) applied the validity argument approach by expanding on the Kane, Cohen, and Crooks' (1999) three-bridge validity argument (evaluation, generalization, and extrapolation) to include domain description, explanation, and utilization as well in their evaluation of the TOEFL. They then mapped their research findings using the Toulmin-influenced Bachman and Palmer's AUA framework. However, like Kane, Chappelle, Enright, and Jamieson's (2008) application of the inferences in the TOEFL validity argument, as presented in Table 9.5, pp. 347–348, did not explicitly address any aspect of fairness, although the Educational Testing Service, who developed the TOEFL, has its own *International Principles for Fairness Review of Assessments* (ETS, 2009) in place.

Bachman and Palmer (2010)

Bachman and Palmer (2010)[9] argued that the Assessment Use Argument (AUA) is a process of assessment justification that serves two essential purposes:

(1) It guides the development and use of a given language assessment and provides the basis for quality control throughout the entire process of assessment development.
(2) It provides the basis for test developers and decision makers to be held accountable to those who will be affected by the use of the assessment and the decisions that are made (p. 95).

Using the Toulmin model of argumentation, Bachman and Palmer (2010) put forward *a priori* four claims and associated warrants that need to be included in the AUA (see Figure 2.2):

Claim 1: Consequences are beneficial.
Claim 2: Decisions made are value sensitive and equitable.
Claim 3: Interpretations are meaningful, impartial, generalizable, relevant, and sufficient.
Claim 4: Assessment records are consistent (p. 104).

In contrast to Kane (2012), Bachman and Palmer's (2010) AUA is wider in scope, ranging from consequences to assessment scores, which is in consonance with Messick, as he, too, advocated including consequences of assessment in the validation argument. However, Bachman and Palmer do not include test content, a major part of test development that takes place before scores become relevant. This missing element is critical, as test content could influence much that comes after. For example, if test content is biased against a certain group of test takers, the validation argument could be invalid weakening the whole evaluation.

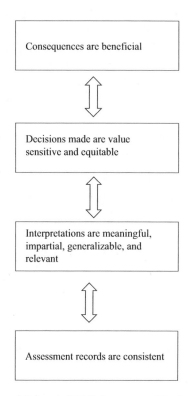

FIGURE 2.2 Bachman and Palmer's (2010) Assessment Use Argument

Illustrative Assessment Evaluations

Two recent assessment reviews that used the AUA approach are Llosa (2008) and Wang et al. (2012).

Validity Argument for a Standards-Based Classroom Assessment (Llosa, 2008)

Llosa (2008) argued that many of the studies of classroom–based assessment based on teacher judgments rely on one type of analysis—mainly correlation between teacher judgments and an external criterion, or qualitative investigations. This, she argued, provided only limited information. As Kane (2006) pointed out, "individual studies in a validity argument may focus on statistical analyses, content analyses, or relationships to criteria, but the validity argument as a whole requires the integration of different kinds of evidence from different sources" (p. 23).

Llosa (2008) "first articulated the claims, warrants, rebuttals, and backing needed to justify the link between teachers' scores on the ELD Classroom Assessment and the interpretations made about students' language ability" (p. 33). "A secondary purpose. . . was to illustrate the usefulness of an argument-based approach for identifying and organizing the collection of relevant supporting evidence" (p. 40). She concluded that the AUA provided "a coherent framework that allows for a comprehensive examination of all warrants and potential rebuttals in order to justify interpretations and decisions to stakeholders" (p. 40). However, no evidence was collected regarding fairness of the ELD classroom assessment.

Pearson Test of English Academic (Wang, Choi, Schmidgall, & Bachman, 2012)

Wang et al. (2012) reviewed the new Pearson *Test of English Academic* using Bachman and Palmer's (2010) AUA as their framework. They outlined their procedures as follows:

> it follows an approach to test development and use that Bachman and Palmer (2010) call(ed) the process of 'assessment justification.' This process focuses on investigating the extent to which the intended uses of a particular test can be justified to stakeholders.
>
> *(p. 603)*

Wang et al. outlined the two interrelated activities required: articulating an AUA (Bachman, 2003, 2005; Bachman & Palmer, 2010) that links test takers' performance with the consequences of test use and collecting evidence to support the claims articulated in the AUA.

The AUA used in this review contained three elements: (1) claims and warrants desired for the intended test use, (2) supporting evidence and rebuttal data from documents provided by the test developer, and (3) potential rebuttals. The claims and warrants were based on documents provided by the test publisher—Pearson. The evidence for impartiality and equitability are presented here based on these documents.

Claim 1: Impartiality

> *Warrant B1:* The test tasks do not include response formats or content that may either favor or disfavor some test takers.
>
> *Evidence:* Materials are available on the test website to help test takers familiarize themselves with the task format before taking the test. Item bias reviews are designed to effectively prevent content that may introduce bias. Items that showed differential item functioning (DIF) were also identified. Concerns about construct-irrelevant factors such as time management and unfamiliarity with test format that test takers raised in feedback collected from a field trial helped identify potential bias in task formats and content.

These concerns were addressed by test revisions (Zheng & De Jong, 2011, p. 21; research conducted by *researchers working at Pearson;* emphasis added).

Potential rebuttal(s): No empirical evidence is available to demonstrate the extent to which the identified issues have been resolved in the operational tests (emphasis added).

Warrant B2: The test tasks do not include content that may be offensive (topically, culturally, or linguistically inappropriate) to some test takers.

Evidence: Bias and item sensitivity reviews were implemented. Items that were regarded as inappropriate, offensive, or emotionally charged for certain groups of test takers were removed. (pp. 610–611)

Claim 2: Equitability

Warrant B1: The same cut scores and decision rules are used to classify all students who have applied for the same program, and no other considerations are used.

Evidence: None is available in the documents that were reviewed (emphasis added).

Potential rebuttal(s): There is no direct evidence that stakeholders who use PTEA scores use them in a manner that supports this warrant.

Warrant B2: Test takers and other affected stakeholders are fully informed about how decisions will be made and whether decisions are actually made in the way described to them.

Evidence: Stakeholders who make admission decisions based on PTEA scores typically specify minimally acceptable scores on their websites, promotional materials, or applications. Pearson facilitates distribution of this information through its website and promotional material.

Potential rebuttal(s): There is no direct evidence to demonstrate that the admission decisions are actually made as described.

(p. 614; emphasis added)

Lessons from Evaluations

The standards-based approach has a history of over 60 years. Assessment institutions have used them to guide their own internal evaluations of their assessments, and researchers have used them to plan their research agendas. However, as there are many standards emphasizing different aspects of assessment and assessment practice, some standards seem to be more equal than others. Valid score interpretations and consistency in scoring have emerged as the main foci. But fairness and access of assessments, and consequences of assessment practice, are generally not considered critical and thus are not routinely examined. This view needs to be corrected.

In the words of Plake and Wise (2014), the *Standards*

> promote the sound and ethical use of tests and to provide a basis for evaluating the quality of testing practices. The *Standards* . . . provide criteria for evaluating tests, testing practices, and the effects of test use. The *Standards* also provide information to test developers, publishers, and users about key elements in a testing program that should inform the development, selection, and use of tests.
>
> *(p. 4)*

However, justifying an assessment in terms of "industry standards" seems more of a legalistic way of responding to an evaluation, which may be appropriate for a licensing arrangement but much less appropriate as a means of convincing test takers, users, and policy makers that an assessment and assessment practice are ethical.

On the other hand, the argument-based approach has offered a new structure to evaluate assessments, but it has remained somewhat technical, especially the articulation of claims and warrants. But the segmentation of an evaluation into an examination of an assessment's claims and warrants, the backing for the warrants, and possible rebuttals could have a practical appeal instead of the overarching Messickian validation research process. However, as Kane argued, the claims and warrants that have been articulated have their bases in the *Standards* published by various organizations and agencies. Thus, the approach is circular; there needs to be an independent way of articulating claims from principles.

Assessment reviews (in the *MMY*, *Language Testing*, and *Language Assessment Quarterly*) have served in lieu of formal evaluations of assessments and sometimes of assessment practices. This genre has contributed to the field as they have informed the public of whether an assessment has the features that its authors or publishers advertised (form, length, cost, score reporting practice), whether it has met certain minimum qualities (such as validity and reliability), and whether it has been generally beneficial to the public. But the reviews have also failed in some critical ways. Here are the most important:

(1) *Not concerned with fairness issues*: Generally, frameworks like those used in the MMY reviews do not follow the *Standards* (1999 or 2014) approach toward fairness, although they follow the *Standards* in other aspects. This is unfortunate, as many publications that follow the MMY framework reflect the MMY structure and do not mention fairness. Only the Wang et al. (2012) review, following Bachman and Palmer (2010), of the Pearson Test of English addressed fairness issues.

(2) *Unclear intellectual basis*: Although the standards-based and the argument-based approaches have increasingly included the concept of fairness in the last decade, they seem to have been included without much of an intellectual basis for the concept despite Messick's articulation of the philosophical basis for his approach to validation (1989; see Messick's discussion of an inquiring

system; p. 33). The argument-based approach does not seem to have a clear philosophical approach except in terms of using Toulmin's argumentation model, which is used as a link to reasoning as a critical transaction. Perhaps this is why many researchers have not embraced it wholeheartedly and still continue to use the standards-based approach (see recent reviews in both *Language Testing* and *Language Assessment Quarterly*).

(3) *No access to performance data*: Assessment reviews continue to be conducted without access to test taker performance data. This has been the bane of reviews in the *MMY*, *Language Testing*, *Language Assessment Quarterly*, and other publications where reviews are published. In some cases, test publishers make available only retired forms of the assessment. This would be like writing an automobile review without even seeing the real car but just from photographs!

(4) *Institutional justice*: Assessment reviews almost always focus only the assessment, leaving aside institutional practices that need to be commented on as well. Practices that need to be commented on include assessment policies that mandate an assessment, cut-off standards for pass-fail or grades, access and accommodations (for test takers with disabilities and test takers who are English language learners required to take subject-matter assessments in English), and the consequences of an assessment. All of these matters lead to the question of whether the assessment is beneficial to the community and whether the institution agency is a just assessment institution in the way it administers, scores, reports, and makes decisions.

(5) *Insiders' research findings*: As test performance data are not available to independent researchers for the most part, research findings that are reported in the assessment reviews are findings from sponsored research or institutional staff members' research. In almost all cases, no independent research studies are commissioned, conducted, and reported. This is mainly because there are no independent regulatory bodies to monitor or oversee language assessment agencies and their assessments and systems.

(6) *Static vs. dynamic*: Although the standards-based approach is popular with test reviewers even today, the reviews can be characterized as static, as the standards are fixed by an external agency or body (as in the case of the APA, AERA, and NCME *Standards*), and the reviewers evaluate the assessments against these standards. On the other hand, the argument-based approach, although less popular as it is newer and less familiar, has the potential of being dynamic, as the claims can be articulated by assessment agencies or external organizations based on their own contexts and ethical principles.

(7) *Brief and sound bite–like*: Almost all reviews are brief and do not have the status of regular full-length articles in journals. Thus, they tend to be squeezed for space, and authors are forced to write succinctly and on the most salient features, which most of the time involves primarily descriptions with very little or no critical analyses. These reviews tend to be similar to publishers' blurbs.

(8) *Narrow in scope*: Reviews tend to be narrow in scope in that they focus on the test materials. Issues left unexamined include Opportunity-to-learn; biased content, reliability, and validity; familiarity of procedures or equipment; access and accommodations; and intended and unintended consequences, as well as assessment policy.

Conclusion

The current chapter presented two approaches to assessment evaluations—standards based and argument based—and extracts of language assessments reviews that included the concept of fairness. As pointed out after the illustrations, there are many deficiencies in the way evaluations are done: there is little intellectual foundation for the evaluations, fairness is included as one aspect of the evaluation sometimes, test performance data are rarely available, no independent research findings are available, and evaluations are brief and not comprehensive. The key questions then are as follows: How can we change this? What ought to be done? If the public needs to be informed of assessments from many points of view, including fairness and justice, what kind of framework should we have in place? The next chapter will offer an ethics-based approach to fairness and justice.

Notes

1 From website: www.consumerreports.org
2 From website: www.carmagazine.co.uk
3 From website: www.autocar.co.uk
4 Buros, O. (1938). Foreword. In O. Buros (Ed.), *Mental measurement yearbook* (pp. xiii–xiv). Lincoln, NE: University of Nebraska. Retrieved on December 30, 2015 from: www.buros.org
5 Retrieved on December 30, 2015, from: www.buros.org
6 Here is the relevant excerpt:

> The *Code* applies broadly to testing in education (admissions, educational assessment, educational, diagnosis, and student placement) regardless of the mode of presentation, so it is relevant to conventional paper-and-pencil tests, computer-based tests, and performance tests. It is not designed to cover employment testing, licensure or certification testing, or other types of testing outside the field of education. The *Code* is directed primarily at professionally developed tests used in formally administered testing programs. Although the *Code* is not intended to cover tests prepared by teachers for use in their own classrooms, teachers are encouraged to use the guidelines to help improve their testing practices. The *Code* addresses the roles of test developers and test users separately.
>
> *(p. 2)*

7 The authors of this document also acknowledge that many additional interpretations of the term "fairness" may be found in the technical testing and popular literature.
8 Updated in 2014: *Standards for Quality and Fairness*. (2014). Educational Testing Service. Princeton, NJ: Author.
9 Bachman and Palmer (2010) is the most widely cited work related to the AUA, although Bachman (2005) provided the groundwork for the later work.

References

Alderson, J. C., Krahnke, K., & Stansfield, C. (Eds.). (1987). *Reviews of English language proficiency tests.* Washington, DC: TESOL.

American Educational Research Association, American Psychological Association, & National Council on Measurement on Education. (1954). *Technical recommendations for psychological tests and diagnostic techniques.* Washington, DC: Author.

American Educational Research Association, American Psychological Association, & National Council on Measurement in Education. (1966). *Standards for educational and psychological tests and manuals.* Washington, DC: Author.

American Educational Research Association, American Psychological Association, & National Council on Measurement in Education. (1974). *Standards for educational and psychological tests.* Washington, DC: APA.

American Educational Research Association, American Psychological Association, & National Council on Measurement in Education. (1985). *Standards for educational and psychological testing.* Washington, DC: APA.

American Educational Research Association, American Psychological Association, & National Council on Measurement in Education. (1999). *Standards for educational and psychological testing.* Washington, DC: AERA.

American Educational Research Association, American Psychological Association, & National Council on Measurement in Education. (2014). *Standards for educational and psychological testing.* Washington, DC: AERA.

Bachman, L. F. (1990). *Fundamental considerations in language testing.* Oxford, UK: Oxford University Press.

Bachman, L. F. (2005). Building and supporting a case for test use. *Language Assessment Quarterly, 2,* 1–34.

Bachman, L. F., & Palmer, A. S. (1996). *Language testing in practice.* Oxford, UK: Oxford University Press.

Bachman, L. F., & Palmer, A. S. (2010). *Language assessment in practice.* Oxford, UK: Oxford University Press.

Bailey, A. L. (2005). Review of the Cambridge Young Learners English test. *Language Testing, 22,* 242–252.

Banerjee, J. (2003). The TOEFL CBT (computer-based test). *Language testing, 20,* 111–123.

Callet, J. V. (2005). High-stakes testing: Does the California High School Exit Exam measure up? *Language Assessment Quarterly, 2,* 289–307.

Chapelle, C. A., Enright, M. E., & Jamieson, J. (Eds.). (2008). *Building a validity argument for the Test of English as a Foreign Language.* London: Routledge.

Chun, C. W. (2002). An analysis of a language test for employment: The authenticity of the PhonePass test. *Language Assessment Quarterly, 3,* 295–306.

Cronbach, L. J. (1988). Five perspectives on validity argument. In W. Howard & H. I. Braun (Eds.), *Test validity* (pp. 1–14). Hillsdale, NJ: Lawrence Erlbaum.

Cronbach, L. J., & Meehl, P. E. (1955). Construct validity in psychological tests. *Psychological Bulletin, 52,* 281–302.

Cumming, J. D. (1995). The Internet and the English language. *English Today, 11,* 3–8.

Davies, A. (Ed.). (1968). *Language testing symposium: A psycholinguistic approach.* Oxford, UK: Oxford University Press.

ETS International Principles for Fairness Review of Assessments. (2009). *A manual for developing locally appropriate fairness review guidelines in various countries.* Princeton, NJ: Author.

Gorman, D., & Ernst, L. M. (2004). The CASAS life skills reading tests. *Language Assessment Quarterly, 1,* 73–84.

Guion, R. M. (1980). On Trinitarian doctrines of validity. *Professional Psychology, 11,* 385–398.

Harris, D. P. (1969). *Testing English as a second language.* New York: McGraw-Hill.

International Language Testing Association. (2010). *International Language Testing Association Guidelines for Practice.* Author.

Joint Committee on Testing Practices. (1988). *The code of fair testing practices in education.* AERA, APA & NCME. Washington, DC: Author.

Joint Committee on Testing Practices. (2004). *The code of fair testing practices in education.* AERA, APA & NCME. Washington, DC: Author.

Kane, M. (2001). Current concerns in validity theory. *Journal of Educational Measurement, 38,* 319–342.

Kane, M. (2006). Validation. In R. Brennan (Ed.), *Educational measurement,* 4th Edn. (pp. 17–64), Westport, CT: American Council on Education and Praeger.

Kane, M. (2012). *Validating score interpretations and uses.* Princeton, NJ: Educational Testing Service.

Kane, M., Cohen, A. S., & Crooks, J. T. (1999). A generalized examinee–centered method for setting standards on achievement tests. *Applied Measurement in Education, 12,* 343–366.

Kunnan, A. J. (1995a). *Test taker characteristics and test performance: A structural equation modeling approach.* Cambridge, UK: Cambridge University Press.

Kunnan, A. J. (1995b). Review of the Chinese speaking test. In J. C. Coloney & J. Kramer (Eds.), *The 13th Mental Measurements Yearbook* (pp. 250–251). Lincoln, NE: Buros Institute of Mental Measurements.

Kunnan, A. J. (1995c). Review of the Chinese proficiency test. In J. C. Coloney & J. Kramer (Eds.), *The 13th Mental Measurements Yearbook* (pp. 247–248). Lincoln, NE: Buros Institute of Mental Measurements.

Kunnan, A. J. (1998). Approaches to validation. In A. J. Kunnan (Ed.), *Validation in language assessment* (pp. 1–14). Mahwah, NJ: Lawrence Erlbaum Associates.

Kunnan, A.J. (2004). Test fairness. In M. Milanovic & C. Weir (Eds.), *European language testing in a global context* (pp. 27-48). Cambridge, UK: Cambridge University Press.

Kunnan, A. J. (2005). Review of the Arabic proficiency test. In J. C. Impara & B. S. Plake (Eds.), *The 16th Mental Measurement Yearbook* (pp. 57–59). Lincoln, NE: Buros Institute of Mental Measurements.

Kunnan, A. J., & Wagner, E. (2014). Review of the Examination for the Certificate of Competency in English. In J. Carlson, K. Geisinger & J. Jonson (Eds.), *The 19th Mental Measurements Yearbook* (pp. 286–288). Lincoln, NE: Buros Institute of Mental Measurements.

Lado, R. (1961). *Language testing.* London, UK: Longman.

Lewkowicz, J. (2000). Authenticity in language testing: Some outstanding questions. *Language Testing, 17,* 43–64.

Llosa, L. (2008). Building and supporting a validity argument for a standards-based classroom assessment of English proficiency based on teacher judgments. *Educational Measurement, 27,* 32–40.

Luoma, S. (2001). The Test of Spoken English. *Language Testing, 18,* 463–481.

McNamara, T. (1998). Policy and social considerations in language assessment. *Annual Review of Applied Linguistics, 18,* 304–319.

McNamara, T. (2006). Validity in language testing: The challenge of Sam Messick's legacy. *Language Assessment Quarterly, 3,* 31–51.

Messick, S. (1980). Test validity and the ethics of assessment. *American Psychologist, 35,* 1012–1027.

Messick, S. (1989).Validity. In R. Linn (Ed.), *Educational measurement* (3rd Edn.) (pp. 13–103). London, UK: Macmillan.

Plake, B. S., & Wise, L. L. (2014).What is the role and importance of the revised AERA, APA, NCME Standards for Educational and Psychological Testing? *Educational Measurement, 33*, 4–12.

Shih, C. M. (2008).The General English Proficiency Test. *Language Assessment Quarterly, 5*, 63–76.

Stoynoff, S., & Chapelle, C. A. (Eds.). (2005). *ESOL tests and testing: A resource for teachers and administrators.* Alexandria,VA: TESOL.

Toulmin, S. (1958/2003). *The uses of argument* (2nd Edn.). Cambridge, UK: Cambridge University Press.

Wagner, E., & Kunnan, A. J. (2014). Review of the Computerized Oral Proficiency Instrument (Arabic and Spanish). In J. Carlson, K. Geisinger & J. Jonson (Eds.), *The 19th Mental Measurements Yearbook* (pp. 189–191). Lincoln, NE: Buros Institute of Mental Measurements.

Wagner, E., & Kunnan, A. J. (2015). Review of the Duolingo English Test. *Language Assessment Quarterly, 12*, 320–331.

Wang, H., Choi, I., Schmidgall, J., & Bachman, L. (2012). Review of Pearson test of English academic: Building an assessment use argument. *Language Testing, 29*, 603–619.

Weigle, S. C. (2000). Review of the Michigan English Language Assessment Battery. *Language Testing, 17*, 49–455.

Zhang,Y., & Elder, C. (2009). Measuring the speaking proficiency of advanced EFL learners in China:The CET-SET solution. *Language Assessment Quarterly, 6*, 298–314.

Zheng,Y., & de Jong, J. (2011). *Establishing construct and concurrent validity of Pearson Test of English Academic: Research note.* Retrieved from: http://pearsonpte.com/wp-content/uploads/2014/07/RN_EstablishingConstructAndConcurrentValidityOfPTEAcademic_2011.pdf

Websites

Consumer Reports—non-profit organization that publishes expert independent product reviews in the U.S. (2015, December 20). Retrieved from: www.consumerreports.org

Car Magazine—expert car review. (2015, December 20). Retrieved from: www.car magazine.co.uk

Auto Car—expert car review. (2015, December 20). Retrieved from: www.autocar.co.uk

3

ETHICS-BASED APPROACH TO ASSESSMENT EVALUATION

Introduction

In the previous chapter, two approaches to assessment evaluation—the standards-based and the argument-based approach—were discussed. The standards-based approach brought concepts from good practices and from the APA, AERA, and NCME experts. These concepts first included validity and reliability, and these became standards (for example, see the early APA, AERA, and NCME's *Standards*, 1985). Following Messick's (1989) validation approach, consequential evidence and fairness were introduced into the mix of components (see APA, AERA, and NCME's *Standards*, 1999). Proponents of the argument-based approach (Bachman, 2005; Bachman and Palmer, 2010; Kane, 1992, among others) applied Toulmin's (1958) argumentation model. Although Kane provided guidance toward building a validation argument in two steps, Bachman and Palmer (2010) added impartiality and equitability to the earlier concepts. But as mentioned in the previous chapter, what is clearly missing is the lack of a clear philosophical basis behind the approaches.

The perspective from the world of moral philosophy is one in which an ethic or ethical knowledge can develop and be used to morally justify behaviors and institutions. This is not different from how an assessment and an assessment practice can be morally justified. An ethics-based approach can also be seen as the wellspring of ideas on how to develop an assessment evaluation system, a place from where we can ask fundamental questions. General questions that could be asked include: Where do our deeply held beliefs about right and wrong come from? Is our moral judgment based on our personal upbringing or professional training? Or, are our thoughts merely in consonance with societal or religious approval? Or, are they beliefs expressing what we care about? And, applied to language assessment, we could ask two main questions: What ought to be the qualities of a fair assessment? How can an assessment be beneficial to society?

This chapter introduces an ethical perspective that can be used in the development of an assessment ethic and assessment principles. As a first step, a discussion of concepts that are both central and obligatory cornerstones of an ethics–approach is presented.

An Ethics-Based Approach

An ethics-based approach to professions can offer ways to think about general abstract questions such as "How ought I to practice my profession?" Applied ethics connects ethical theories to modern professions such as medicine, science, engineering, the environment, or education and to specific pressing concerns such as the right to abortion and euthanasia and the question of the death penalty, to name a few. In language assessment, we could ask equally important questions: What rights does a test taker have? What responsibilities does a test developer or test score user have? What ought I to do when I encounter an unfair assessment or unfair practice?

Traditional virtues from religion-based ethics have existed for centuries. These … include: virtues of consciousness, benevolence, and self-restraint (from Buddhist ethics); neighborly love; natural morality (from Judeo-Christian ethics); social and individual duties (from classic Hindu ethics); obligatory acts such as charity, kindness, and prayer (from Islamic ethics); humanity and goodness; rightness and duty; consideration and reciprocity; and loyalty and commitment (from Chinese ethics). The first writings on ethics came from ancient religious thinkers like Lao Tzu (6th or 7th century BCE), Confucius (551–479 BCE), Gautama Buddha (563–483 BCE), Mencius (371–289 BCE), St. Augustine (354–430 CE), and St. Thomas Aquinas (1225–1274 CE) and religious writings in the *Bhagavad Gita*, the *Bible*, the *Guru Granth Sahib*, the *Dhammapada*, the *Torah*, the *Qur'an*, and so on.

The common themes that were addressed in these works through their poems, sayings, sermons, parables, and scriptures include prescriptive statements about moral values (for example, the righteous path), normative ethics (human conduct and moral principles and standards), and sacred and political obligations (duties toward God and the monarchy). These views make up the Divine Command Theory, the view that morality is dependent upon God and that moral obligations consist of obedience to God's commands. But as we are interested in institutions such as assessments and assessment agencies that are secular, an appeal to traditional virtues from religion-based ethics would be insufficient and may even be inappropriate. The discussion that follows focuses on secular and applied ethics.

Secular philosophers from the early period included the trio from Greece: Socrates (470–399 BCE), Plato (428–348 BCE), and Aristotle (384–322 BCE). Whereas Socrates and Plato searched for the meaning of justice, Aristotle promoted the notions of moral and intellectual virtues. The main proponents who addressed these questions later were secular Enlightenment philosophers who were utilitarians— for example, Locke (1632–1704), Hume (1711–1776), Bentham (1748–1832), Mill (1806–1873), and Sidgwick (1838–1900). Because the predominant perspective for centuries was utilitarianism, an overview of utilitarianism follows.

Utilitarianism

The philosophical doctrine termed *utilitarianism* (utility based) was advanced by Bentham and Mill. It is a general moral theory that holds that the rightness or wrongness of an action is determined by the balance of good over evil that is produced by that action. Thus, rightness of actions (both by the individual and institutional) should be judged by their consequences (caused by actions). This important aspect of utilitarianism is termed *consequentialist* thinking in which outcomes of an event could be used as tools to evaluate an institution. Another doctrine is the Greatest Happiness Principle; it promotes the notion that the highest principle of morality is the greatest happiness for the greatest number of people; to maximize utility and to balance pleasure over pain. As a result, the utility principle would trump individual rights.

Implementing utilitarianism in the assessment context could mean that decisions about an assessment may be made solely on the basis of utility and consequences. For example, if an assessment brought in a great deal of revenue as a result of large numbers of test takers taking an assessment, the assessment could be considered successful and its practice justified. Or, if the consequences of an test was positive for a large majority, then the assessment could be considered beneficial to the community. But maximizing happiness or minimizing unhappiness can result in sacrificing fairness and justice. For example, suppose an assessment was biased against a particular group of test takers and to improve the current version or to develop a new assessment would entail a great deal of expenditure. This expense, if carried out, then would result in everyone paying more for the assessment and causing harm to all. An option that could be considered would be that the assessment be continued the way it is without any improvement. Strict utilitarians, in this case, would argue that these are bad choices and the lesser harmful of the two options would need to be chosen. Such utilitarians would hold that even if the assessment is biased against a particular group and fairness and justice have been sacrificed, we will have to just live with the assessment without any improvement, as it is the better of the two options. It still would maximize happiness and minimize unhappiness.[1]

Deontology

Another way of thinking of ethics emerged with *deontological* (duty-based) ethics pioneered by the work of Kant (1724–1804). He argued that to act in the morally right way, people must act from duty, and unlike utilitarianism, it was not the consequences of actions that made them right or wrong but the motives of the person who carried out the action. He also maintained that in order to find the basis for morality, we need to examine how people *ought* to behave rather than how they behave. Deontology is also known to have a moral absolutism approach, the belief that some actions are wrong no matter what consequences follow, even if the consequences are partially beneficial. In contrast, moral relativists argue that consequences of an action need to be considered. For example, if lying is never permitted according to the absolutist, what if lying was going to protect a person from being harmed? Moral relativists would approve of lying in this case, as it would be right thing to do, but Kant's principles would not. Kant also introduced the notion of the Categorical Imperative, which is a universal, absolute, and unconditional requirement that exerts its authority in all contexts and circumstances.

A more relaxed version of deontology was proposed by Ross (1877–1971) who offered seven *prima facie* duties that need to be taken into consideration when deciding which duty should be acted upon: duty of beneficence (to help other people to increase their pleasure, improve their character, etc.), duty of non-maleficence (to avoid harming other people), duty of justice (to ensure people get what they deserve), duty of self-improvement (to improve ourselves), duty of reparation (to recompense someone if you have acted wrongly toward them), duty of gratitude (to benefit people who have benefited us), and duty of promise-keeping (to act according to explicit and implicit promises, including the implicit promise to tell the truth).

But, as Ross lists many duties, there could be conflicts and therefore priorities need to be set. For example, Ross would argue that his duty to tell the truth may conflict with his duty not to cause harm to another person. Such dilemmas need to be resolved through an intuitive faculty and reasoning process. In fact, Ross stated that moral decisions or actions are fraught with at least some element of conflict. Applying Ross's duties in the field of language assessment would need a similar setting up of priorities. Some of the obligatory duties could be the duty of beneficence, the duty of non-maleficence toward test takers, the duty toward justice and reparations, and the duty of promise-keeping.

In the next section, a discussion of the main concepts and principles from Rawls and Sen, two contemporary thinkers following in the footsteps of Kant and Ross, will be presented. This will be followed by a discussion of how their concepts can be applied to language assessment so that there is a moral basis for the concepts of fairness and justice.

Rawls's A Theory of Justice

Rawls (1921–2002) was a contemporary theorist who took the works of Kant and Ross forward with more depth and clarity. In his 1971 treatise "A Theory of

---

EXTRACT 3.1   RAWLS'S (1971, 2001) *KEY TENETS*

Thought experiment of the "original position and the veil of ignorance"

Public justification

Reflective equilibrium

Justice" about justice and fairness, he formulated a theory and principles of fairness and justice in which he argued that *fairness is prior to justice*, but is foundational and central to justice.

To quote from Sen's (2009) summary of Rawls's work: In the Rawlsian theory of "justice as fairness," *the idea of fairness relates to persons (how to be fair between them)*, whereas the Rawlsian principles of *justice are applied to the choice of institutions (how to identify "just institutions")* (p. 72, emphasis added). Rawls's intention was that, for his theory to work, society had to be well ordered—in other words, democratic—with a representative government and, as Sen puts it, with a "government by discussion" and not just with elections and balloting. The case for justice as fairness for Rawls was for a "well-ordered society" that had a "fair system of social cooperation" and had "citizens who are free and equal persons" (p. 72).

Further, he presented a procedural plan for how a just institution could provide social arrangements that promote justice. He introduced three inter-related concepts: (1) the hypothetical thought experiment, which he called "the original position and the veil of ignorance;" (2) "public justification;" and (3) "reflective equilibrium."

The Original Position (OP)

In Rawls's thought experiments of the Original Position (Extract 3.2) and the veil of ignorance, members of a society were not allowed to know their social position in society, their backgrounds (race, ethnicity, or gender), or their endowments (capabilities, talents) when considering principles of justice. Therefore, as members do not know anything about themselves, they would not be able to gamble to become beneficiaries of any benefits. This setup, Rawls argued, would give members a way to derive principles of justice without any biases or prejudices as they know any decisions they make could affect them. The principles of justice, Rawls argued, that would emerge from such a procedure would have unanimous agreement. He later amended this idea to allow for "overlapping consensus," as he recognized the limits of agreement on justice in pluralistic democracies where conflicting religious, philosophical, and moral doctrines may make unanimity unlikely.

In assessment institutions, the OP and the veil of ignorance could be used in assessment development: imagine an assessment developer with a team of designers,

---

EXTRACT 3.2   RAWLS'S (1971, 2001) *TWO PRINCIPLES OF JUSTICE*

1. Each person has the same indefeasible claim to a fully adequate scheme of equal basic rights and liberties, and this scheme is compatible with the same scheme for all.

2a. *The equal opportunity principle* in general provides fair equality of opportunity.

2b. *The difference principle,* in which the least advantaged members of society are better off when primary goods are unequally distributed (between least advantaged and more advantaged members) than when primary goods are equally distributed between the two groups.

---

writers, and others who do not know about each other's backgrounds (gender, age, nationality, ethnicity, qualifications, experience, etc.). Such a team, therefore, would be able to develop an assessment that is fair in terms of the entire design, including language/dialect, content/topics, response format, scoring guidelines, reporting procedures, decision-making rules, and so on with favors for any group. Although this thought experiment might be difficult to replicate (as most often we know team members' backgrounds), the idea of developing an assessment without enabling a particular test taker group to do better or discriminating against a test taker group could theoretically result in an assessment that is fair.

Public Justification and Reflective Equilibrium

Rawls contended that for fairness to work, public justification was a necessary part of the process. He argued that it was necessary to justify political decisions to fellow citizens so that public consensus could be reached. He also suggested the use of the methodology of "reflective equilibrium" to help in the public justification process. In this methodology, initial ideas, beliefs, or theories are subjected to reason, reflection, and revision until the ideas, beliefs, or theories reach a state of equilibrium in public justification.

Using the concept of reflective equilibrium, Rawls offered two principles of justice as a guide in the design of just institutions. The *first principle of justice* stated: Each person has the same indefeasible claim to a fully adequate scheme of equal basic rights and liberties (2001, p. 42) This principle includes five sets of basic liberties: liberty of conscience and freedom of thought, freedom of association, equal political liberties, the rights and liberties that protect the rights and liberties of the person, and rights and liberties covered by the law.

The *second principle of justice* had two parts: The first part, the *equal opportunity principle*, is familiar, as assessments in general provide fair equality of opportunity. For example, the establishment of assessment institutions to assess abilities opened up fair opportunities that would have otherwise been decided in terms of heredity, nobility, and social position by birth. The second part, *the difference principle*, referred to economic opportunities in which the least advantaged members of society were better off when primary goods were unequally distributed (between least advantaged and more advantaged members) than when primary goods were equally distributed between the two groups.

In summary, in Rawls's theory of justice as fairness, the focus was on developing *ideal just institutions* by identifying what just institutions would look like. This, Rawls proposed, could be achieved in a well-ordered society with free and equal citizens interested in social cooperation to bring about justice as fairness. Thus, by using the OP and the veil of ignorance, principles of justice can be publicly justified through the process of reflective equilibrium. When this is done, Rawls argued, principles of justice would guide the building of a just institution.

Schematic Diagram

Figure 3.1 shows Rawls's schematic diagram of how fairness and justice are framed in terms of practical reasoning. Following from the concept of right and the path from individuals to requirements to obligations, we see the path to *fairness* and fidelity, and from individuals to permissions, we see the path to *beneficence*, courage, and mercy. And from the concept of right to social systems and institutions, we see the path to *justice* and efficiency.

Sen's The Idea of Justice

Sen (2009), a philosopher and economist, advanced Rawls's thinking significantly with three major ideas: (1) a realization-focused concept of justice instead of Rawls's arrangement-focused concept of justice, (2) the thought experiment of the impartial spectator, and (3) a non-parochial, global perspective.

Realization-Focused Approach

Sen contended that Rawls's theory of justice as fairness was primarily aimed at the ideal of establishing just institutions (which Sen terms "transcendental institutionalism") and that it did not have any mechanism to evaluate human transgressions that bring about unjust societies through public reasoning. More specifically, Sen contended that Rawls's approach was *arrangement focused* (justice conceptualized in terms of organizational arrangements like institutions, regulations, and behavioral rules, and the active presence of these would indicate that justice is being done). This is in contrast to Sen's view of justice as a *realization-focused* understanding

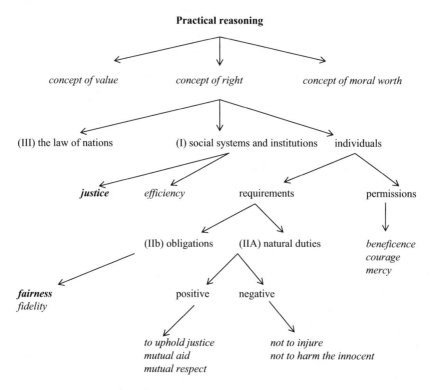

Practical reasoning

concept of value concept of right concept of moral worth

(III) the law of nations (I) social systems and institutions individuals

justice *efficiency* requirements permissions

(IIb) obligations (IIA) natural duties *beneficence*
courage
mercy

fairness
fidelity positive negative

to uphold justice not to injure
mutual aid not to harm the innocent
mutual respect

FIGURE 3.1 Schematic diagram of fairness and justice

Adapted from Rawls, 1971, p. 108

of justice (examining what emerges in society, the kinds of lives people can lead, given the institutions and rules, but also actual behavior that would inescapably affect human lives). Applying this concept to assessment institutions, Sen would argue that Rawls was interested in developing ideal institutions, whereas Sen would examine institutions for any injustice and work with them to improve their institutions become just.

The Impartial Spectator

Sen (2009) invoked Adam Smith's thought experiment of the "impartial spectator."[2] This device, Sen argued, could be used "when judging one's own conduct, 'to examine it as we imagine an impartial spectator would examine it'" (p. 124). He argued that this approach of the impartial spectator has a major advantage over Rawls's original position with a veil of ignorance in arriving at principles of justice. Although both approaches attempted to remove vested interests and goals of individuals, in this approach, spectators or disinterested people from other societies can participate in deliberations, whereas outsiders were restricted in the Rawlsian approach. Sen argued that Smith's open impartiality—including the voice of the people who do not belong to the focal group—is superior to Rawls's closed impartiality which restricted the voice of the people to focal group members—as it provided the opportunity for cross-societal and cross-border deliberations.

In assessment institutions, the impartial spectator could be used in assessment development as an outside voice that would provide an impartial perspective on assessment development matters.

The Non-parochial, Global Perspective

The non-parochial, global perspective view is a central part of Sen's thesis. He was concerned with the parochial nature that some nations espoused when it came to the service of justice for two reasons: First, what happens in a particular country in terms of how its institutions operate can have huge consequences on the rest of the world, and, second, each country or society may have parochial practices that need to come under examination and scrutiny from others with distant judgments who are impartial spectators. Recall Martin Luther King's warning: "Injustice anywhere is a threat to justice everywhere."

Further, he argued, the global reach of justice was necessary in a world where globalization was taking place: in trade, commerce, business, travel, technology, and so on. Similarly, Sen also criticized the view of Asian government leaders for promoting "(East) Asian values." Their leaders have argued that the denial of political and personal freedoms and suppression of media freedoms in exchange for economic growth were part of "Asian values," different from those of the West. This is defective reasoning, Sen argued, as Asian countries have a tradition of democratic values and principles as well. Third, Sen argued that public reasoning is a critical component in advancing justice. His requirements were similar to those of Rawls: a well-ordered society—in other words, a democratic state (in the

---

EXTRACT 3.3   SEN'S (2009) KEY TENETS

Realization-focused understanding of justice versus Rawls's *arrangement-focused view of justice*

Thought experiment of the "impartial spectator"

Public reasoning

Non-parochial, global perspective on justice

sense of "government by discussion" with political and personal freedoms) —with free and equal persons (who are capable of challenging injustice)—that would be able to safeguard principles of fairness through public justification and reasoning. Such states would have in place transparent mechanisms for the fair selection and use of assessments, public reasoning of the assessment in use (in public forums), and regulations and laws that have adequate provisions for appeals and redress. An authoritarian regime, on the other hand, with few or no political and personal freedoms, would be less compelled to need or allow public justification and reasoning of principles of fairness. The lack of such reasoning, along with inadequate accompanying regulations and laws for appeals and redress, would make it difficult for such institutions to be just.

In summary, Sen argued that the focus of justice must be on the advancement of the cause of justice through the methodology of public reasoning. His methodology for doing this was through the distant judgment of the impartial spectator in his open partiality mode with outsiders and the world examining and scrutinizing the practices of institutions. He also indicated the need for a global reach of justice. Applying Sen's ideas to assessment, the plan would be to improve existing institutions to be just by using an impartial spectator in assessment development for an independent view and by promoting non-parochial, global norms of justice.

Applying Ethics to Language Assessment

Applying ethics to language assessment that leads to the development of a principles-based framework for evaluation based on the thinking presented by Rawls and Sen will require the resolution of a few fundamental issues that are discussed next.

Fundamental Issues

Universal or Contextual?

An important issue is whether any principles should be universal and applied universally or whether they should be contextual and therefore have limited or no applicability across contexts. Universalists would like to argue that we should be able to write fundamental principles of fairness that can govern all our actions in all circumstances and that such basic principles should be invariant across contexts. On the other hand, contextualists would like to argue that principles should be context specific, as principles connect to contexts in unique ways, and therefore principles should be written for local contexts.

In other words, should fairness and justice have boundaries? Sen (2009) makes his plea:

> [E]very person anywhere in the world, irrespective of citizenship, residence, race, class, cast or community, has some basic rights which others should

respect. . . from resisting torture, arbitrary incarceration and racial discrimination to demanding an end to hunger and starvation, and to medical neglect across the globe.

(p. 355)

Translating this idea to language assessment, the following questions are relevant: Should principles of fairness be written by expert scholars (like the experts who write the AERA, APA, and NCME *Standards*) for all contexts across the world with no consideration of context? Further, should principles and standards for educational assessment proposed by AERA, APA, and NCME's *Standards* (1999, 2014) and *Code of Ethics* proposed by ILTA (2000) be applicable to all contexts across the world? Alternatively, should each context, community, country, or institutional agency propose their own principles and standards, keeping in mind their own strengths and constraints and ignoring a global perspective?

Of course, there will always be exceptions to the strong positions in these approaches, and weaker options may be more suitable. Thus, it may be a practical necessity to craft a mixed system in which there are universal principles (which are guiding principles) and specific principles that are locally developed for different contexts. Examples of such mixed approaches in language assessment could include the following: a principle that allows for different levels of language proficiency required by different countries for immigration and/or citizenship (such as A2 to B2 on the CEFR scale); or a principle that requires reliable ratings of essays but allows for either single or double ratings (as most school contexts will not have double ratings); or a principle that allows for human ratings or automated computer-generated ratings (as most contexts will not have automated computer-generated ratings); or a principle that requires an opportunity to write an essay either by typing essays on a computer or writing by hand; or a principle that allows a single topic for writing or speaking assessment (although the topic may be biased against different test taker groups); or a principle that allows different types of interlocutors in a group oral test (where male and female, introverts and extroverts, higher proficiency and lower proficiency interlocutors are all mixed in). Would some of these arrangements compromise the principle of fairness, or will they serve fairness well? These questions are pertinent for assessment agencies and assessment users to discuss and debate before considering and writing principles of fairness.

Fact Independent or Fact Dependent?

Another important issue is whether principles of fairness and justice should be formulated without interest in the facts on the ground; that is, should they be fact independent? If this approach is followed, the argument would be that principles would be free from facts and would be pure and not suffer any distortion or contamination. On the other hand, the opposing view would be that principles should be fact dependent. This line of argument would mean that basic principles are necessarily based on facts, as we are already filled with facts and cannot claim to formulate pure principles without any reference to contextual facts. But if this approach is followed, would there be the danger that facts could distort principles, especially when different facts exist in different situations? This approach could then lead principles to be ideological, not philosophical.

To illustrate, should principles in a school assessment context be based on pure ideas (such as principles of fairness) without using prior knowledge or dependence on facts that may exist? For example, if girls who have blonde hair or boys with extra weight are generally discriminated against, should school authorities ignore this information and devise principles of fairness even though they know these two groups of students are being discriminated against? Or would the available information blinker school authorities from writing principles of fairness in such a way that others who may be discriminated against in different ways or in the future may not be covered or ignored? These questions are pertinent for school teachers and administrators to discuss and debate before considering and writing principles of fairness.

Fundamental Aspects

In addition, four fundamental aspects are central and obligatory to the concepts of fairness and justice in assessments. They are *transparency, equity, impartiality*, and *uniformity*.[3]

Transparency is the first fundamental requirement of fairness. In the assessment context, all test takers (and other stakeholders) ought to know what the content, procedures, and processes of an assessment are about; how the scoring is going to be done; and how score reports and decisions are going to be made. Absent such information, test takers would be vulnerable to assessors who could "move the goal posts" whenever they wanted to for whatever reason. Such a situation would be ripe for discrimination against test takers and would undermine the very purpose of assessment. If, on the other hand, the assessment content, procedures, and processes are all transparent to all test takers, there would be less likelihood of unfairness.

Equity is the second fundamental requirement of fairness. In the assessment context, equity could be described as receiving credit or an equal share of appropriate benefits. For example, test takers with identical abilities (based on scores) should receive identical or equitable treatment in decision-making (receiving high credit, pass or fail grades) irrespective of family background, gender, the color of their skin, the region they come from, or any other test taker characteristic. If equity is achieved, then there would be less likelihood of unfairness.

Impartiality is the third fundamental requirement of fairness. An example during the Chinese Civil Service Examination of impartiality was the process of anonymizing test taker responses to questions. This was done by examination officials who recopied test takers' answers before they were rated by examiners so that the examiners would not be able to identify test takers (Miyazaki, 1976). In modern times, similar anonymity has been achieved through the use of examination registration numbers so that examiners are unable to identify test takers. Other examples include the use of topics in test materials that are familiar to all test takers, checks regarding whether test takers have had the opportunity to acquire the knowledge or skills prior to the assessment, the use of appropriate and transparent and defensible standard setting for decision-making. Thus, in assessments today, when an assessment is impartial, we could say it does not favor any test takers.

Uniformity in assessment is the fourth fundamental requirement of fairness. This factor ensures that all test takers have the same opportunity to demonstrate their abilities. This means that in terms of tasks, administrative procedures, scoring, reporting, and decision-making, there is no difference in how test takers are treated. Without uniformity, assessments cannot be fair to test takers. For example, if an assessment in reading is administered with 30 items, all test takers should be given the 30 items; giving more or fewer items to some test takers would mean the assessment is not uniform (unless the test is a computer-adaptive test and administering fewer or more items is supported by research). Or if a grammar and spell check program is permitted in a computer-based writing task, it should be available and enabled for all test takers; or, the rubrics or standards used to judge an essay or a speech should be the same for all test takers; or, decision-making cut-off scores for pass–fail or high–low grade should be used in the same way for all test takers. Or, if immigration law requires a particular level of language ability for a pass, this law should be uniformly enforced. Thus, when an assessment practice or policy is uniform, we could say that it does not favor any test takers.

Fundamental Questions

Based on the fundamental issues and aspects that are central to the concepts of fairness and justice in assessments discussed above, Kunnan (2014) raised a few fundamental questions:

(1) Does every test taker have the right to a fair assessment? Is this rule inviolable? Are rights of test takers to a fair assessment universal or only applicable in states or countries that provide equal rights?

(2) Is it adequate that most test takers are assessed fairly whereas a few are not? Would it be appropriate to use a cost–benefit analysis to evaluate whether assessments should be improved or not? And if harm is done to test takers, does such harm need to be compensated?

(3) Would the rights of test takers to a fair assessment be supported in authoritarian states that do not provide for equal rights? Would institutions in such states feel less compelled to provide a fair assessment?

(4) Should assessment developers and users be required to offer public justification or reasoning? Should they present their justifications for assessments
backed by research findings in appropriate forums?

(5) Should assessment institutions be just in their approach?

(6) Should an assessment be beneficial to the society in which it is used?

Previous Applications of Ethical Theories

An ethics-based approach to assessment evaluation and assessment practice has
been slow to develop. Spolsky (1995) argued that it was not evident in the 1960s
and 1970s, although ethical theories of different persuasions had been in exist-
ence for several centuries. He pointed out convincingly that from the 1910s to
the 1960s, social, economic, and political concerns among key language testing
professionals in the U.S. (mainly at the Ford Foundation, the College Board, and
Educational Testing Service) and the U.K. (mainly at the University of Cambridge
Local Examinations Syndicate) dominated boardroom meetings and decisions,
not ethical concerns or ethics-based principles. Many decades later, a few different approaches were advocated by individual researchers and institutions; these
are discussed next.

Davies's "Test Virtues" Approach

Davies (1977) made an early argument for "test virtues," reflecting Aristotelian
virtue ethics. This paper could be considered the first suggestion of ethical concerns in language assessment. In essence, Davies argued that test developers or
agencies ought to act as moral individuals or agents who have ethical principles
and therefore ought to do the right thing for the right reasons. Davies later guest-
edited two special issues of journals—*Language Testing* (1997) and *Language Assessment Quarterly* (2004)—in which he articulated the first views of how to apply
ethics to language assessment.

Kunnan's (1997) Fairness Agenda

Kunnan (1997) proposed a fairness agenda after reviewing 100 validation studies that
were conducted by well-known language assessment researchers. He argued that

> a social postmodernist view, in contrast, would value validation research
> that is attentive to social and cultural difference, not just by merely learning
> about difference among test takers or indulging in an easy relativism which
> in practice might result in not taking difference seriously, but by engaging
> in a research program that would incorporate social and cultural difference
> within the validation process. In other words, what I am arguing for is to
> delimit the validation process and centralize the concept of research on

social and cultural difference. This process would help start a research program that brings into clear focus fairness in language assessment and make it part of the validation process.

(p. 93)

Willingham and Cole's (1997) Approach

Willingham and Cole (1997), in their study of gender and fair assessment, argued that

> test fairness is an important aspect of validity. . . anything that reduces fairness also reduces validity. . . test fairness is best conceived as comparability in assessment; more specifically, comparable validity for all individuals and groups.
>
> *(pp. 6–7)*

Using the notion of comparable validity as the central principle, Willingham and Cole (1997) suggested three criteria for evaluating the fairness of a test: "comparability of opportunity for examinees to demonstrate relevant proficiency, comparable assessment exercises (tasks) and scores, and comparable treatment of examinees in test interpretation and use" (p. 11). Based on these ideas, four characteristics of fairness that are the most critical to fair assessment practices emerge:

(1) Comparable or equitable treatment in the testing process
(2) Comparability or equality in outcomes of learning and Opportunity-to-learn
(3) Absence of bias in test content, language, and response patterns
(4) Comparability in selection

FairTest's Approach

FairTest, a non-profit organization at The National Center for Fair and Open Testing in Boston,[4] has devoted its entire work to the cause of fair assessments. Its mission is to advance

> quality education and equal opportunity by promoting fair, open, valid and educationally beneficial evaluations of students, teachers and schools. *FairTest* also works to end the misuses and flaws of testing practices that impede those goals. We place special emphasis on eliminating the racial, class, gender, and cultural barriers to equal opportunity posed by standardized tests, and preventing their damage to the quality of education.[5]

Although the organization is called FairTest, its focus is primarily on exposing unfairness in assessment and does less on presenting models of fair assessments. It issues numerous reports regularly regarding U.S.-based assessments that promote the use of unfair assessments and/or have unfair policies in place.

ILTA Code of Ethics

In the late 20th century, the International Language Testing Association (ILTA) embarked on an ambitious program to develop a *Code of Ethics*. This was the culmination of efforts in this direction by many individuals and groups. For example, Stansfield (1993) urged language testers to develop ethics and standards in the profession; Davies (1997) cautioned us about the limits of ethics; and a conference colloquia was devoted to the topic at LTRC in 1996 in Finland, and an ethics seminar sponsored by the TOEFL program in Pasadena, California, (that I organized), addressed ethical applications to language assessment.

The ILTA *Code of Ethics* (2000), chaired by Davies, articulated nine principles; they are expected to be used by assessment agencies affiliated with ILTA:

Principle 1: Language testers shall have respect for the humanity and dignity of each of their test takers. They shall provide them with the best possible professional consideration and shall respect all persons' needs, values and cultures in the provision of their language testing service.

Principle 2: Language testers shall hold all information obtained in their professional capacity about their test takers in confidence and they shall use professional judgement in sharing such information.

Principle 3: Language testers should adhere to all relevant ethical principles embodied in national and international guidelines when undertaking any trial, experiment, treatment or other research activity.

Principle 4: Language testers shall not allow the misuse of their professional knowledge or skills, in so far as they are able.

Principle 5: Language testers shall continue to develop their professional knowledge, sharing this knowledge with colleagues and other language professionals.

Principle 6: Language testers shall share the responsibility of upholding the integrity of the language testing profession.

Principle 7: Language testers in their societal roles shall strive to improve the quality of language testing, assessment and teaching services, promote the just allocation of those services and contribute to the education of society regarding language learning and language proficiency.

Principle 8: Language testers shall be mindful of their obligations to the society within which they work, while recognising that those obligations may on occasion conflict with their responsibilities to their test takers and to other stakeholders.

Principle 9: Language testers shall regularly consider the potential effects, both short and long term on all stakeholders of their projects, reserving the right to withhold their professional services on the grounds of conscience.

To conclude, whatever the methodological persuasion (utilitarianism, Kantian and deontological systems, and virtue-based ethics), language-testing professionals need an ethic to support a framework of applied ethical principles that could guide professional practice. Corson (1997), broadly addressing applied linguists, made a case for the development of a framework of ethical principles by considering three principles: the principle of equal treatment, the principle of respect for persons, and the principle of benefit maximization.

Additional questions that could be asked in terms of language assessment could include: What qualities should a language assessment have to be considered an ethically fair assessment? What qualities should a language assessment practice have to be considered just? What qualities should a code of ethics or a code of practice include so that its professionals follow ethical practice?

Toward Principles of Fairness and Justice

Drawing on insights from moral philosophy—Rawls's and Sen's conceptual understanding of fairness and justice—we can now consider how their ideas and arguments can be used to develop principles of fairness and justice. First, individual rights and inequalities in test takers' life prospects have to be the central focus of the principles. Second, consequences of an assessment should be centrally connected to and factored into validation arguments of an assessment. Third, Rawls's idea of public justification and Sen's similar notion of public reasoning have to be part of this application.

Based on these ideas, two general principles of fairness and justice and subprinciples are proposed.

Principle 1: The Principle of Fairness

An assessment *ought* to be fair to all test takers; that is, there is a presumption of treating every test taker with equal respect.

> *Sub-principle 1:* An assessment *ought* to provide adequate opportunity to acquire the knowledge, abilities, or skills to be assessed for all test takers.
> *Sub-principle 2:* An assessment *ought* to be consistent and meaningful in terms of its test score interpretation for all test takers.
> *Sub-principle 3:* An assessment *ought* to be free of bias against all test takers, in particular by avoiding the assessment of construct-irrelevant matters.
> *Sub-principle 4:* An assessment *ought* to use appropriate access, administration, and standard-setting procedures so that decision-making is equitable for all test takers.

Principle 2: The Principle of Justice

An assessment institution *ought* to be just, bring about benefits in society, promote positive values, and advance justice through public reasoning.

> *Sub-principle 1:* An assessment institution *ought* to foster beneficial consequences to the test-taking community.

Sub-principle 2: An assessment institution *ought* to promote positive values and advance justice through public reasoning of their assessment.

To begin with, the first principle, the principle of fairness, has to exist before the second, the principle of justice, because if the first principle is not satisfied, then the second principle cannot be satisfied. In other words, if the presumption that treating every test taker with equal respect in an assessment is not satisfied, then the assessment will not succeed in being beneficial to the community and bringing justice to the community.

Second, in terms of the relationship between the general principles and the sub-principles, the respective sub-principles provide the framing for the two general principles, and therefore, the sub-principles have to be individually satisfied in order for the general principle to be satisfied.

Third, the principles and sub-principles are written as obligations (obligatory actions signaled with the use of *ought*) and not as categorical or unconditional imperatives, but the assumption is that there will be near-universal application. As argued earlier, justice should be non-parochial and impartial beyond one's community, as everyone should be treated in the same manner. This is particularly true of current globalized assessment institutions that operate in numerous countries. It does not seem defensible to propose otherwise despite the objection of being imperialist as to how there could be different approaches to fairness and justice. The very few exceptions allowed would be to overcome economic difficulties so that assessments can still function in a fair and just manner even if they are not developed in the best manner possible.

Bases for Principles

Principle 1 states that an assessment ought to be fair to all test takers, which includes a presumption of treating every test taker with equal respect. This emphasis on the test taker rather than an assessment or its scores should be sufficient to reject the argument that validity of an assessment (or valid score interpretations or validity arguments) guarantees that all test takers will be treated with equal respect. The focus of validity concerns has either been on the assessment itself or, at most, on various aspects of assessment practice; the focus has never been on the individual test taker. Second, the sub-principles provide guidance for detailed investigations of assessments to build arguments regarding the general principle of fairness. The sub-principles of Principle 1 focus on the test takers' Opportunity-to-learn, consistency of the assessment and meaningfulness of the assessment, and whether the assessment is free of bias and that standard setting has been conducted in an equitable manner. These matters are relevant to the individual test taker and affect the test taker positively or adversely depending on the qualities of the assessment. Thus, they are essential components of Principle 1.

Principle 2 follows the first principle, but it is a necessary component. The principle states that an assessment ought to bring about benefits to society and that assessment institutions ought to promote justice. Assessment institutions are not any different from other social or economic institutions; they certainly have a higher responsibility in a community than the Department for Beautiful Gardens, as they are responsible for awarding benefits to test takers. Therefore, just institutions are the backbone of assessment practice. If assessment institutions are just institutions, then the principle of justice is satisfied.

Flow from Ethics to Fairness and Justice

In this approach, the flow of ideas therefore would be from ethics to principles of fairness and justice (Figure 3.2). Ideas from ethics (from utilitarian or deontology or virtue based) influence the framing of the principles of fairness and justice so that claims articulated by assessment agencies can be based on ethical considerations rather than purely economic or political considerations. Such principles are likely to be sound and firmly grounded so that evaluations of assessments can be based on fairness and justice and ensure assessments that are beneficial to society.

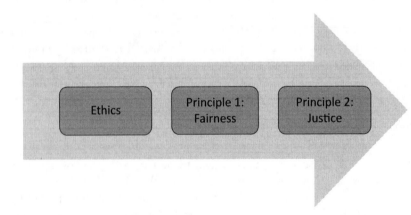

FIGURE 3.2 The flow from ethics to fairness to justice

Conclusion

This chapter has provided a principled basis for fairness and justice in language assessment by drawing on theoretical work from moral philosophers Rawls and Sen. Applying arguments from Rawls and Sen to language assessment provided the background that led to the proposed principles of fairness and justice as instruments being used to evaluate assessments and assessment institutions.

The methodology of principles of fairness and justice may be based on philosophical preference. Rawls and Sen offer ways in which this can be done through the original position/veil of ignorance and the impartial spectator, respectively. Both these thought experiments are methods that may not work in their purest form. Therefore, appropriate variants need to be devised and put in place in order to enable the development of fair assessments and just institutions. As Sen argued, it is not sufficient to use principles to design and establish just institutions, but efforts should be made to remove manifest injustice that exists in the world today. He also argued that a non-parochial, global justice view would be best suited to review unjust institutions. This is critical to globalized assessment institutions; they need to be evaluated by enforcing *ought-to* general principles.

The chapter also put forth the idea that there should be public reasoning of assessments. This would mean that whether an assessment is fair or not and whether an institution is just or not should be a matter of public discourse for which public reasoning is necessary. This is a critical part of justifying or defending assessments and institutions.

Finally, the main point of this chapter is to present a case for ethics-based principles for fairness and justice in language assessment. It is not to debate whether the putative principles of fairness and justice proposed in this chapter are appropriate or workable for all contexts across the world, but to find principles that can guide us to the right action when we encounter examples of unfair assessments and unjust institutions. The next chapter presents discussions on how to build a framework for fairness and justice based on the principles proposed in this chapter.

Notes

1 H. J. McCloskey (1957) provides a sharp criticism of utilitarianism with this example:

> Suppose that a sheriff were faced with the choice either of framing a Negro for a rape that had aroused hostility to the Negroes (a particular Negro generally being believed to be guilty but whom the sheriff knows not to be guilty)—and thus preventing serious anti-Negro riots which would probably lead to some loss of life and increased hatred of each other by whites and Negroes—or of hunting for the guilty person and thereby allowing the anti-Negro riots to occur, while doing the best he can to combat them. In such a case the sheriff, if he were an extreme utilitarian, would appear to be committed to framing the Negro.
>
> McCloskey (1963, p. 505) also argued: Surely the utilitarian must admit that whatever the facts of the matter may be, it is logically possible that an 'unjust' system of punishment—e.g. a system involving collective punishments, retroactive laws and punishments, or punishments of parents and relations of the offender—may be more useful than a 'just' system of punishment?

2 This is not exactly similar to Adam Smith's notion of the impartial spectator in *The Theory of Moral Sentiments* (1759), although Roderick Firth (1952) argues that Smith's concept is that of an ideal observer. For a full treatment of Smith's view, see Raphael's (2007) *The Impartial Spectator*.

3 I am borrowing, expanding, and applying factors of fairness discussed by Rescher (2002) regarding the theory and practice of distributive justice.

4 From website: www.fairtest.org

5 Retrieved on June 15, 2013, from www.fairtest.org

References

American Educational Research Association, American Psychological Association, the National Council on Measurement in Education. (1985). *Standards for educational and psychological testing.* Washington, DC: Author.

American Educational Research Association, American Psychological Association, the National Council on Measurement in Education. (1999). *Standards for educational and psychological testing.* Washington, DC: Author.

American Educational Research Association, American Psychological Association, the National Council on Measurement in Education. (2014). *Standards for educational and psychological testing.* Washington, DC: Author.

Bachman, L. F. (2005). Building and supporting a case for test use. *Language Assessment Quarterly, 2,* 1–34.

Bachman, L. F., & Palmer, A. S. (2010). *Language assessment in practice.* Oxford, UK: Oxford University Press.

Corson, D. (1997). Critical realism: An emancipatory philosophy for applied linguistics? *Applied Linguistics, 18,* 166–188.

Davies, A. (Ed.). (1977). *The Edinburgh course in applied linguistics: Testing and experimental methods (Vol. 4).* London, UK: Oxford University Press.

Davies, A. (1997). Introduction: The limits of ethics in language testing. *Language Testing, 14,* 235–241.

Davies, A. (2004). Introduction: Language testing and the golden rule. *Language Assessment Quarterly, 1,* 97–107.

Firth, R. (1952). Ethical absolutism and the ideal observer. *Philosophy and Phenemological Research, 12,* 317–345.

International Language Testing Association. (2000). *ILTA code of ethics.* Washington, DC: Author. Retrieved from: www.iltaonline.org on March 11, 2015.

Kane, M. (1992). An argument-based approach to validity. *Psychological Bulletin, 112,* 527–535.

Kunnan, A. J. (1997). Connecting fairness and validation. In A. Huhta, V. Kohonen, L. Kurti-Suomo & S. Luoma (Eds.), *Current developments and alternatives in language assessment* (pp. 85–105). Jyvaskyla, Finland: University of Jyvaskyla.

Kunnan, A. J. (2014) (Ed.), *The companion to language assessment.* Malden, MA: Wiley.

McCloskey, H. J. (1957). An examination of restricted utilitarianism. *The Philosophical Review, 66,* 466–485.

McCloskey, H. J. (1963). A note on utilitarian punishment. *Mind, 72,* 599.

Messick, S. (1989). Validity. In R. Linn (Ed.), *Educational measurement* (pp. 13–103). London, UK: Macmillan.

Miyazaki, I. (1976). *China's examination hell: The Civil Service Examinations of imperial China.* (Translated by C. Schirokauer). New Haven, CT: Yale University Press.

Raphael, D. D. (2007). *The impartial spectator: Adam Smith's moral philosophy.* Oxford, UK: Oxford University Press.

Rawls, J. (1971). *A theory of justice.* Boston, MA: Harvard University Press.

Rawls, J. (2001). *Justice as fairness: A restatement.* Boston, MA: Harvard University Press.

Rescher, N. (2002). *Fairness: Theory and practice of distributive justice.* New Brunswick, NJ and London, UK: Transaction Publishers.

Sen, A. (2009). *The idea of justice.* Boston, MA: Harvard University Press.

Smith, A. (1759). *The theory of moral sentiments.* London, UK: A. Millar.

Spolsky, B. (1995). *Measured words.* Oxford, UK: Oxford University Press.

Stansfield, C. (1993). Ethics, standards, and professionalism in language testing. *Issues in Applied Linguistics*, *4*, 189–206.

Toulmin, S. (1958). *The uses of argument*. Cambridge, UK: Cambridge University Press.

Willingham, W. W., & Cole, N. (1997). *Gender and fair assessment*. Mahwah, NJ: Lawrence Erlbaum.

Website

FairTest, a non-profit organization at The National Center for Fair and Open Testing in Boston, USA. (2015, June 15). Retrieved from: www.fairtest.org

4

BUILDING THE FAIRNESS AND JUSTICE ARGUMENT

Introduction

The previous chapter presented an ethical basis for the principles of fairness and justice, and this chapter takes the idea forward by demonstrating how to build an argument for fairness and justice. Chapter 2 discussed how the *Standards* were used to evaluate assessments and how proponents of the argument-based approach used the Toulmin approach for developing arguments. In this chapter, the *Standards* and the Toulmin approach are both put to work with the principles of fairness and justice. The chapter presents an introduction to Toulmin's concept of argument and argumentation, which is followed by a worked example of how to build an argument for fairness and justice principles and sub-principles. Finally, the chapter discusses how to evaluate arguments and concludes with issues related to the application of the fairness and justice argument approach to language assessment.

Argument and Argumentation

In the Toulmin (1958) approach, an argument is an assertion or claim followed by supporting facts or evidence presented in order to convince the listener or reader of the assertion. As van Eemeren pointed out, "arguments by definition seek to establish something. That means there is a gap between some claim and acceptance of that claim. The claim is in doubt and an argument seeks to remove the doubt, thus closing the gap" (cited in Freeman (2011, p. 42). To illustrate, a language instructor can put forth a claim that a certain commercially produced language assessment is the best instrument to assess the English language ability of air traffic controllers. This is a specific claim, but if her claim is not obvious or convincing to her colleagues, it needs backing or reasons. She has to therefore provide facts or evidence that can help her make an argument. As Freeman (2011) succinctly put it, an "argument is the attempt to convince a sceptical but rational judge of the rightness of the rational acceptability of a claim" (p. 42).

In its simplest form, an argument must contain a conclusion and a premise. Here is an illustration:

(1) My essay was graded consistently because (2) two raters in my school gave me the exact score.

Here, (1) is the *conclusion* regarding the consistency of the assessment and (2) is the *premise* that supports the conclusion. This argument can be made in monologic fashion when there is no challenger. But in arguments in forums such as court hearings, arguments involve two parties and thus two roles: a person putting forward a conclusion and another person who is the questioner who challenges the answerer's conclusion (by asking something like "What evidence have you got to go on?" or "On what basis can you say that?"). This dialectical situation is the best way to understand the idea of argument and argumentation. Consider:

A. (1) My debate performance last week was excellent.
B. On what basis do you say that?
A. Because (2) my *debate coach* rated my debate performance as excellent.
B. How did the *speech coach* rate it?
A. (3) The speech coach rated the same debate performance as poor.

Here, (1) is the *conclusion* regarding the quality of the debate and (2) and (3) are two *premises* that are divergent.[1] The argument is therefore unsuccessful; for successful argumentation, there should be a convergence of premises to support a conclusion.

Toulmin's Approach

Unlike the simple two-part analysis of an argument presented earlier, Toulmin (1958) in *The Uses of Argument* deconstructed arguments into *six argument roles or elements* as described in Chapter 2. We will follow a more recent exposition of Toulmin's argumentation model—the approach used by Toulmin, Rieke, and Janik (1984) in their book *An Introduction to Reasoning*. Toulmin et al.'s (1984) model of argumentation included four main elements and how they are connected in terms of the soundness of arguments: *claims, grounds, warrants*, and *backing*. According to this approach, *claims* are assertions that could be a destination or a conclusion in an argument, *grounds* are the foundation or principles on which claims can be accepted rest, *warrants* are inference rules or elaborations of claims that bridge grounds with claims, and *backing* is considered the underlying basis for a warrant. Collectively, these elements form the structure for a sound argument. Two other elements in terms of the strength of arguments, termed *qualifiers* and *rebuttals*, were also introduced. For Toulmin et al. (1984), the individual elements of argumentation constitute the microstructure, whereas the whole structure of argumentation (with all the elements) embodies the macrostructure of an argument.[2]

Uses of Argumentation

There can be many uses of argumentation in the evaluation of language assessment. First, argumentation can be used in support of a claim. For example, an assessment agency may be interested in public reasoning of their assessment. Public reasoning either in oral form (through a conference talk) or in written form (in an assessment review for a journal or book) would be an appropriate venue for an assessment agency to present an argument in support of a claim. If the argument is presented in a talk or in a written argument, it may be followed by an invited response. The invited response may or may not challenge the argument; if it does, based on logical or substantive points and/or test performance analysis, this could lead to a dialectic process where there is discussion of claims and counter-claims. The expectation would be that the assessment agency and the challenger could reach a consensus on the agreeable and disagreeable points of the argument. This is like in a court of law, where the assessment agency and the challenger may take adversarial positions, with the resolution being a ruling by a judge or jury in favor of one or the other party, or a compromise or an agreeable settlement.

Second, an argument can be used to challenge a claim, particularly if an assessment seems to be detrimental to the community and the assessment institution is alleged to be unjust. This may be done as a professional benefit to all stakeholders, including test takers and test score users. In this case, the argument made by a member of the community could be a new argument or a rebuttal or counter-claim of the argument made by the assessment agency. This situation could lead to an adversarial position and may need to be adjudicated in public or in a court of law with appropriate backing.

Third, argumentation can be used to prosecute an assessment agency. For example, a complaint, grievance, or appeal could be filed by a test taker in contexts where appropriate redress procedures are available. If the procedures allow this, then the test taker could request data and warrants that support the assessment claims and build a rebuttal to challenge the assessment agency's argument. This type of challenge has been successful in the U.S. where test takers with disabilities have challenged an assessment agency's lack of accommodations as a rebuttal against the assessment agency's arguments for a valid, reliable, and fair assessment.

Fourth, argumentation can be used to defend an assessment's claims. For example, if an assessment agency is challenged in a court of law where there is provision to challenge an assessment, then an argument model can help in the challenge, although legal reasoning is generally based on questions of fact, questions of law, and the demands of justice. For example, if an assessment agency (the defendant) is challenged in terms of gender bias in an assessment, it will no doubt need to make available to the court its grounds, warrants, and claims (in the form of test development and research documents and research reports) that support their claim that the assessment is not biased in terms of gender. The assessment agency may hire an expert in the field to provide expert testimony in court to support their claim that the assessment is not biased in terms of gender. The plaintiff, who may be an individual or an organization representing a single individual or a class, may contest the data, warrants, and claims (and produce their own documents and reports and an expert witness) to challenge the assessment agency's claim. In this situation, the resolution of the case would be a judgment in favor of one or the other depending on facts and case law or a settlement out of court or under the court's orders. Typically, if the ruling is in favor of the plaintiff, there could be a ban of the particular assessment, suspension of the assessment, or suspension and restitution to the plaintiff if punitive damages are considered and awarded. If the ruling is in favor of the defendant, the challenge will be dismissed.

Thus, there are many considerations to keep in mind when using argumentation. The scope and detail of the argumentation will depend on the context, such as whether it is meant for a private board meeting, a public forum, or a court of law.

Application to Language Assessment

Applying the Toulmin Argumentation Model

Practically, when applying the Toulmin argumentation model, first, the principles of fairness and justice can be used to help generate the claims and sub-claims. Specifically, assessment developers, agencies, and policy makers as well as independent researchers could articulate claims and sub-claims based on the principles of fairness and justice specific to their assessment context (school, college, university, employment, immigration, citizenship, etc.) and standards that may be based on best practices or written by experts (like the APA, AERA, and NCME *Standards*).

Second, as stated earlier, the principle of fairness is necessary before the principle of justice. This means that the principle of fairness has to be adhered to prior to the principle of justice. If the principle of fairness cannot be adhered to, then the principle of justice cannot be adhered to either. The downward arrow from Principle 1, Fairness, to Principle 2, Justice, indicates this relationship (Figure 4.1).

Linking Principles to Standards

Once the principles of fairness and justice are articulated, standard operating procedures (or *Standards* for short), either written by experts in the field of assessment or local standards based on best practices in the field, can be used to operationalize

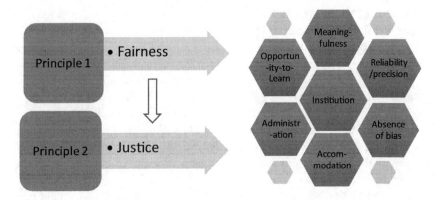

FIGURE 4.1 Linking principles to standards

principles. Figure 4.1 indicates how principles can be linked to standards from experts or standards based on best practices. The various components, from meaningfulness to reliability/precision, to absence of bias, to opportunity-to-learn, to accommodation and administration, are all connected with each other and depend on guidance from principles.

In the APA, AERA, and NCME *Standards* (2014), experts from the fields of psychology, education, and measurement provided a rationale for the *Standards for Educational and Psychological Testing*. They articulated standards in the areas of validity, reliability/precision, and fairness as foundations; test design and development, scores, scales, norms, scale linking, and cut scores; test administration, scoring, reporting, and interpretation; documentation for tests; and rights and responsibilities of test takers and test users.

Here are a few main APA, AERA, and NCME *Standards* (2014) that can be used to link principles to standards and the standards to claims (which would be articulated by assessment agencies or by researchers).

Validity: Standard 1.0

Clear articulation of each intended test score interpretation for a specified use should be set forth, and appropriate validity evidence in support of each intended interpretation should be provided.

(p. 23)

Reliability/Precision: Standard 2.0

Appropriate evidence of reliability/precision should be provided for the interpretation for each intended score.

(p. 42)

Fairness: Standard 3.0

All steps in the testing process, including test design, validation, development, administration, and scoring procedures, should be designed in such a manner as to minimize construct-irrelevant variance and to promote valid score interpretations for the intended uses for all examinees in the intended population.

(p. 63)

Program Evaluation, Policy Studies, and Accountability: Standard 13.4

Evidence of validity, reliability, and fairness for each purpose for which a test is used in a program evaluation, policy study, or accountability system should be collected and made available.

(p. 210)

Articulating Claims and Building an Argument Structure

General Ideas

Before beginning to articulate claims (based on standards by experts or local standards), it would be useful to consider these questions: Where does a claim come from? Who is making the claim? Is it from the assessment agency or from a test score user? Is it an explicitly stated claim or an implicitly stated claim? Is it clearly documented? Is the claim limited to the purpose and context of the assessment? Is it based on the assessment agency's philosophical and/or theoretical position? Other questions regarding claims could include the following: Can a claim be post hoc, after the assessment is designed and decisions are made? Can a claim be made by independent researchers (not by the assessment agency)? Or can a claim be made by reviewers or evaluators instead of by the assessment agency? Further, we might ask questions like: What may *not* count as a claim? What do we make of ambiguous or unclear claims or claims that cannot be backed up?

Specifically, a claim is an assertion (an unsupported claim) made by an assessment agency or developer (university or non-profit or commercial agency or an examination or even a teacher) that informs the public as to what ability is being assessed (English language, health care communication, or aviation English, for example) and for what purpose (selection to a program, placement into a program, or employment, for example). Such a claim may be made explicitly in a document or on the agency website or implicitly through documents or reports. A claim ought to be made specifically for a particular purpose and context; if an assessment is used for varied purposes, separate claims ought to be made for each.

Claims should be based on ethical principles espoused by the assessment development agency (that is utility or outcomes based, duty based, or of a mixed nature) so that the claims have a strong foundation. This is the approach taken in this book: where ethical knowledge from theorists such as Rawls and Sen are used to provide a strong basis for the two ethics-based principles that are derived. Based on the two principles and the APA, AERA, and NCME *Standards* (2014), claims and sub-claims are articulated. These claims and sub-claims can then be examined with warrants and backing. If there is evidence from research findings feeding into the backing, the claims and sub-claims are supported; if there is insufficient evidence, claims and sub-claims are not supported.

Illustrated Example

Relating Principles to Claims and Sub-Claims

Bringing it together, Principle 1 of fairness with four sub-principles has one general claim and four sub-claims, and Principle 2 of justice with two sub-principles has one general claim and two sub-claims. As an illustrated example of how to build an argument, the claims and sub-claims are written for a language assessment for naturalization purposes in the U.S. (U.S. Naturalization Test, or USNT, for short). The statute that authorized the assessment of the English language of applicants for naturalization and a description of the USNT are provided in Chapter 1.

> *Principle 1—The Principle of Fairness:* The USNT *ought* to be fair to all test takers; that is, there is a presumption of providing every test taker with equal opportunities to demonstrate their abilities.
> *General Claim:* The U.S. Naturalization test is fair to all test takers.
> Figure 4.2 represents the general principles and claims for Principle 1, Fairness.

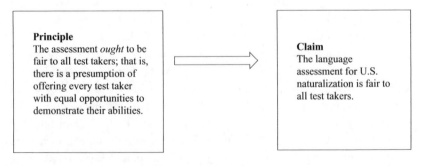

FIGURE 4.2 Principle 1, Fairness—Principle directs the Claim

Sub-principle 1: The USNT *ought* to provide adequate opportunity to acquire the knowledge, abilities, or skills to be assessed for all test takers.

Sub-claim 1 (based on sub-principle 1): Prior to taking the USNT, adequate opportunity, time, practice with technology, and experience are provided.

Sub-principle 2: The USNT *ought* to be meaningful and consistent in terms of its test score interpretation for all test takers.

Sub-claim 2 (based on sub-principle 2): The USNT is both meaningful and consistent.

Sub-principle 3: The USNT *ought* to be free of bias against all test takers, in particular by avoiding the assessment of construct-irrelevant variation.

Sub-claim 3 (based on sub-principle 3): The USNT is free of bias.

Sub-principle 4: The USNT *ought* to use appropriate access, administration, and standard-setting procedures so that decision-making is equitable for all test takers.

Sub-claim 4 (based on sub-principle 4): The USNT uses appropriate access, administration, and standard-setting procedures.

Figures 4.3 is a representation of the relationship between the principle of fairness and sub-principles and the general claim and sub-claims for the USNT.

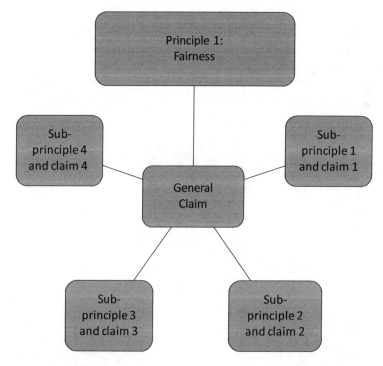

FIGURE 4.3 Principle 1, Fairness—Claims and sub-claims of the USNT

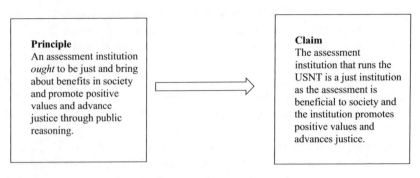

Principle
An assessment institution *ought* to be just and bring about benefits in society and promote positive values and advance justice through public reasoning.

Claim
The assessment institution that runs the USNT is a just institution as the assessment is beneficial to society and the institution promotes positive values and advances justice.

FIGURE 4.4 Principle 2, Justice—Principle directs the Claim

> *Principle 2—The Principle of Justice:* The institution that runs the USNT (currently the USCIS)[3] *ought* to be just and bring about benefits in society, promote positive values, and advance justice through public reasoning.
>
> *General Claim:* The institution that runs the USNT *is a just institution* as the assessment is beneficial to society and the institution promotes positive values and advances justice.
>
> Figure 4.4 represents the general principles and claims for Principle 2, Justice.
>
> *Sub-principle 5:* The institution that runs the USNT *ought* to bring benefits to society by making a positive social impact.
>
> Sub-claim 5 (based on sub-principle 1): The institution that runs the USNT is beneficial to society.
>
> *Sub-principle 6:* The institution that runs the USNT *ought* to promote positive values and advance justice through public reasoning of their assessment.
>
> Sub-claim 6 (based on sub-principle 2): The institution that runs the USNT promotes positive values and advances justice.

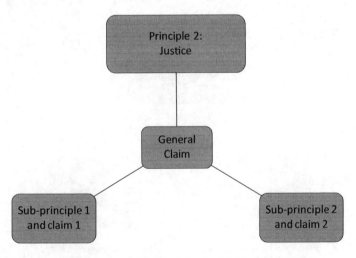

FIGURE 4.5 Principle 2, Justice—Claims and sub-claims of the USNT

Figure 4.5 is a representation of the relationship between the principle of justice and sub-principles and the general claim and sub-claims for the USNT.

Providing Warrants

A warrant is an inference rule or an elaboration or statement of what the claim or sub-claim specifically states. A warrant is helpful in justifying a claim with relevance and clarity. Therefore, it is necessary to articulate a warrant in as much detail as needed. Figure 4.6 is a representation of the flow from claims to principles supported by warrants in support of a claim or sub-claim. The main sub-claim (sub-claim 1) is presented first broken down into parts (sub-claims 1a to 1c). Warrants and backing are written to correspond to the sub-claims (warrants 1a to 1c).

Here are the claims, sub-claims, and warrants for both principles.

Principle 1: The Principle of Fairness

General Claim: The USNT is fair to all test takers.

Sub-claims 1a to 1d

Sub-claim 1: Prior to taking the USNT, adequate opportunity, time, practice with technology, and experience are provided.

Sub-claim 1a: Prior to taking the USNT, adequate Opportunity-to-learn is provided.

Sub-claim 1b: Prior to taking the USNT, adequate time preparation is provided.

Sub-claim 1c: Prior to taking the USNT, adequate practice with new technology is provided.

Sub-claim 1d: Prior to taking the USNT, adequate semiotic embodied experience in the domain of the assessment is provided.

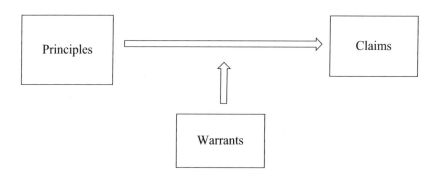

FIGURE 4.6 The flow from principle to claim backed by warrants

Warrants for Sub-claims 1a to 1d

1a. Research on the USNT will show that adequate opportunity (in terms of curriculum and materials) to learn knowledge, abilities, or skills to be assessed is available prior to taking the assessment.

1b. Research on the USNT will show that adequate time for preparation to learn knowledge, abilities, or skills to be assessed is available prior to taking the assessment.

1c. Research on the USNT will show that adequate practice with new technology to perform tasks to demonstrate knowledge, abilities, or skills to be assessed is available prior to taking the assessment.

1d. Research on the USNT will show that adequate semiotic embodied experience in the domain of the assessment is available.

Sub-claims 2a to 2g

Sub-claim 2: The USNT is both meaningful and consistent.

Sub-claim 2a: The USNT is meaningful in terms of the blueprint and specifications or curriculum objectives.

Sub-claim 2b: The USNT is meaningful in terms of the constructs of the language ability in the assessment.

Sub-claim 2c: The USNT is meaningful in terms of the language, content, and topics of the assessment.

Sub-claim 2d: The USNT is meaningful in that it is able to predict performance in terms of external criteria.

Sub-claim 2e: The USNT is consistent within sets of items/tasks in terms of different constructs.

Sub-claim 2f: The USNT is consistent across multiple assessment tasks, forms, and/or occasions of assessments (in different regions, offices, and rooms).

Sub-claim 2g: The USNT is consistent across multiple examiners/immigration officers involved in the assessment.

Warrants for Sub-claims 2a to 2g

2a. Research on the USNT blueprint and specifications or curriculum objectives will show that these aspects are meaningful.

2b. Research on the USNT constructs to be assessed will show that the constructs are meaningful.

2c. Research on the USNT language, content, and topics will show that these aspects are meaningful.

2d. Research on the USNT will show that the assessment is able to predict performance in terms of external criteria.

2e. Research on consistency of the USNT will show that the assessment is consistent within sets of items/tasks in terms of different constructs.

2f. Research on consistency of the USNT assessment across multiple assessment tasks, forms, and/or occasions of assessments (in different regions, offices, and rooms) will show that the assessment is consistent.

2g. Research on consistency across multiple USNT examiners/immigration officers involved in the assessment will show that the scoring is consistent.

Sub-claims 3a to 3b The USNT is free of bias

Sub-claim 3a: The USNT is free of bias in terms of dialect, content, or topic across test taker groups.

Sub-claim 3b: The USNT is free of differential performance by different test taker groups of similar ability (in terms of gender, age, race/ethnicity, and native language).

Warrants for Sub-claims 3a to 3b

3a: Research on the USNT in terms of dialect, content, or topic across test taker groups will show that the assessment is free of bias.

3b: Research on the USNT in terms of differential performance by different test taker groups of similar ability (in terms of gender, age, race/ethnicity, and native language) will show that the assessment is free of bias.

Sub-claims 4a to 4h

Sub-claim 4: The USNT uses appropriate access, administration, and standard-setting procedures.

Sub-claim 4a: The USNT is affordable to test takers.

Sub-claim 4b: The USNT is administered at locations that are accessible to test takers.

Sub-claim 4c: The USNT is accessible to test takers with disabilities, with appropriate accommodations.

Sub-claim 4d: The USNT is accessible to test takers whose first language is not English (including in the history and civics part of the USNT).

Sub-claim 4e: The USNT is administered uniformly to test takers.

Sub-claim 4f: The USNT is administered without any fraud or breach of security.

Sub-claim 4g: The USNT score interpretation is based on defensible standard-setting procedures.

Sub-claim 4h: The USNT decision-making is based on defensible grounds, including legal and ethical.

Warrants for Sub-claims 4a to 4h

Warrant 4a: Research on the USNT costs will show that the assessment is affordable.

Warrant 4b: Research on the USNT administrations locations will show that it is accessible.

Warrant 4c: Research on the USNT in terms of accommodations for test takers with disabilities will show that it provides appropriate accommodations.

Warrant 4d: Research on the USNT in terms of access to test takers whose first language is not English (including in the history and civics part of the USNT) will show that appropriate access is provided.

Warrant 4e: Research on USNT administration will show that the assessment is uniformly administered.

Warrant 4f: Research on the USNT will show that it is administered without any fraud or breach of security.

Warrant 4g: Research on the USNT score interpretation will show that the score interpretations are based on defensible standard-setting procedures.

Warrant 4h: Research on the USNT decision-making will show that the decision-making is based on defensible grounds, including legal and ethical.

Principle 2: The Principle of Justice

General claim: *The assessment institution that runs the* USNT is a just institution, as the assessment is beneficial to society and the institution promotes positive values and advances justice.

Sub-claims 5a to 5d

Sub-claim 5 (based on sub-principle 2): The USNT-based decision-making is beneficial to the immediate community and larger society.[4]

Sub-claim 5a: The USNT decision-making is beneficial to immediate stakeholders (e.g., test takers, instructors in citizenship courses in community colleges, and college administrators).

Sub-claim 5b: The USNT decision-making is beneficial to test takers (in terms of gender, age, race/ethnicity, urban/rural).

Sub-claim 5c: The USNT decision-making is beneficial to the instructional program (e.g., teaching-learning and the learning environment, also known as "washback").

Sub-claim 5d: The USNT decision-making is beneficial to the wider stakeholders (e.g., school district, community, province/state, country).

Warrants for Sub-claims 5a to 5d

Warrant 5a: Research on the USNT decision-making will show that the assessment is beneficial to immediate stakeholders (e.g., test takers, instructors in citizenship courses in community colleges, and college administrators).

Warrant 5b: Research on the USNT decision-making will show that the assessment is beneficial to test takers (in terms of gender, age, race/ethnicity, urban/rural).

Sub-claim 2 (based on sub-principle 2):The USNT decision-making promotes positive values and advances justice.

Warrant 5c: Research on the USNT decision-making will show that the assessment is beneficial to the instructional program (e.g., teaching-learning and the learning environment, also known as "washback").

Warrant 5d: Research on the USNT decision-making will show that the assessment is beneficial to the wider stakeholders (e.g., school district, community, province/state, country).

Sub-claims 6a to 6d

Sub-claim 6 (based on sub-principle 2):The USNT decision-making promotes positive values and advances justice.

Sub-claim 6a: The USNT has a provision for administrative remedies to challenge decisions such as rescoring or re-evaluation.

Sub-claim 6b: The USNT has a provision for legal challenges related to decision-making.

Sub-claim 6c: The USNT decision-making is not detrimental to test-taking groups and corrects existing injustice (if any) to test-taking groups.

Sub-claim 6d: The USNT institution promotes positive values and advances justice.

Warrants for Sub-claims 6a to 6d

Warrant 6a: Research on the USNT will show that it has a provision for administrative remedies to challenge decisions such as rescoring or re-evaluation.

Warrant 6b: Research on the USNT will show that it has a provision for legal challenges related to decision-making.

Warrant 6c: Research on the USNT decision-making will show that it is not detrimental to test-taking groups and corrects existing injustice (if any) to test-taking groups.

Warrant 6d: Research on the USNT institution will show that it promotes positive values and advances justice.

Supplying the Backing

Once warrants have been provided for sub-claims, then the warrants need to be turned into research questions or hypotheses. Thus, for any sub-claim there may be many warrants, and therefore backing or research will need to be conducted with multiple research questions or hypotheses. Backing can take many forms: historical documents (such as the Immigration and Nationality Act of 1952), assessment manuals, regulations, statutes and laws, court rulings, test performance, prior research findings, or current research findings.

Figure 4.7 represents how the backing provides the evidence to the warrants, which in turn support the claim.

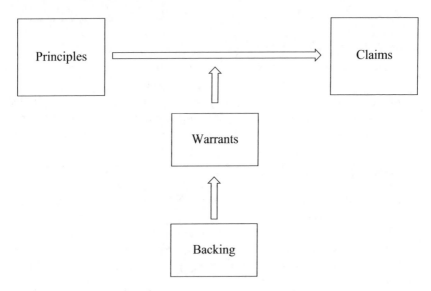

FIGURE 4.7 Principles direct the Claims backed by warrants

Introducing Qualifiers

Once all the elements are in place for a sound argument in support of a claim, then there is the question of the degree of the strength of the argument. This question could be asked thus: How strong is the support for the claim? Is it unconditional or is it conditional? Adverbs and adverb phrases are often used in general arguments, and they apply here as well: words like "certainly," "in all probability," "very likely," "plausibly," "apparently," "presumably," and so on. Such qualifiers will have to be placed between the grounds and claim after considering the warrants and the backing.

Introducing Counter-claims and Rebuttals

Counter-claims and rebuttals can be articulated in the same way as claims. A counter-claim could be a retaliatory claim challenging the original claim with the intent to reduce the effect of the original claim. To illustrate, imagine the original claim that, prior to taking the USNT, adequate practice with new technology was available as 20 hours of practice time was provided. The counter-claim is a retaliatory claim that challenges the original claim by providing evidence that only 10 hours of practice time was provided. In contrast, a rebuttal could be a refutation of the original claim that 20 hours of practice time was provided.[5] Figure 4.8 presents the position of the qualifier and counter-claim or rebuttal in relation to the other elements of the argument.

In summary, the argument structure that is being proposed comprises ethics-based principles leading to general claims for fairness and justice, which then can

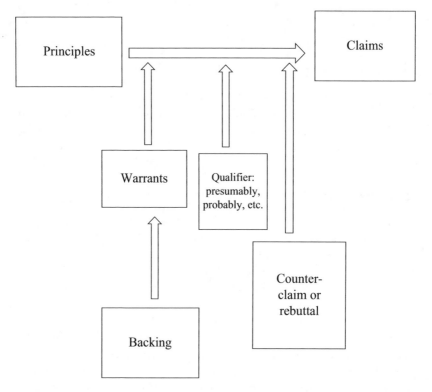

FIGURE 4.8 Position of the qualifier and counter-claim or rebuttal in relation to the other elements

---

EXTRACT 4.1   ARGUMENT STRUCTURE

First level: Principle(s)

Second level: General claims based on principle(s); can be positive or negative (as in most counter-claims)

Third level: Claims narrowed to **sub-claims** that more specifically clarify claims

Fourth level: Sub-claims narrowed to **warrants** that outline what evidence is needed to support each sub-claim

Fifth level: Backing, or the actual evidence to support each warrant

be narrowed into sub-claims, and then to the warrants, which indicate the evidence that needs to be collected, and to the backing, which is the actual evidence. This structure is represented in Extract 4.1.[6]

Evaluating an Argument

After arguments for fairness and justice are built, there needs to be a way to evaluate the quality of those arguments. Just building the argument does not guarantee the soundness or the strength of the argument. The scope and detail of the backing have to be considered depending on the context. Further, in evaluating arguments, we need to judge whether they are fully or partially accepted or rejected or deferred.

Scope and Detail

The scope and detail of the argumentation will depend on the goals discussed earlier in the chapter and the context of the argumentation. In a journal article, conference talk, or seminar, as space or time may be limited, and therefore the scope and detail may also need to be limited. But in a court of law or a public deposition, everything pertaining to the lawsuit will be necessary. These may include the principles, claims, warrants, and backing; all assessment development documents; bias reviews; arrangements for accommodations; procedures for administration, scoring, reporting, and decision-making; public documents such as technical manuals; and internal and public research reports.

The level of detail will also depend on what the lawsuit is about: Is it claiming the assessment has poor design or not assessing what it needs to assess? Is it about race, ethnicity, or gender bias and discrimination, or is it about lack of accommodations for test takers with disabilities, or lack of due process regarding the launching of an assessment in a community, or something else? Each of these matters will need special documentation regarding issues that surround the topic. And during the process of discovery (at least in the U.S. legal system), both sides will have the materials that are submitted to the court to contest each other's claims, warrants, and backing. Expert witnesses or testifiers also will need to be specialized if a specific aspect of an assessment has to be defended or challenged.

Specifically, if a lawsuit alleges gender bias, then all matters related to gender bias of the assessment in question needs to be available. This would also include principles, claims, warrants, and backing, particularly test review forms, review panel decisions, and research reports that discuss gender-related differential item/test functioning studies using appropriate classical test theory or item response theory methods. Expert testimony from specialists in gender bias analysis who may be able to identify the source of the bias or lack of it may be necessary to defend or support the challenge.

Arguments that Fail

Despite all the earlier arrangements regarding the elements of an argument, some arguments can be unsound. Such unsound arguments are called fallacies by logicians and rhetoricians. According to Toulmin et al. (1984), there are five fallacies that result from missing grounds, irrelevant grounds, defective grounds, unwarranted assumptions, and ambiguities in argument. These are relevant in assessment contexts as well.

Missing grounds include the familiar fallacy of "begging the question," which is making a claim and then arguing in support of the claim by advancing the claim in similar words. It is a failure of not providing or advancing evidence in support of a claim. For example, here is a set of hypothetical statements presented in support of an assessment:

(1) A.   The USNT is an admirable naturalization assessment.
     B.   Yes. The USNT is one of the best assessment agencies in the world.

(2) A.   The USNT is a fair assessment.
     B.   Why do you say that?
     A.   Because the institution that runs the USNT would not produce an unfair assessment.

In example (1), B's statement is a restatement of A's statement with no additional grounds. Similarly, in example (2), A's second statement is a sort of restatement of her first statement with an appeal to the name of the institution that runs the assessment but with no facts or evidence to support the first statement. Thus, the failure in these arguments is that the speakers do not offer any backing in support of the first statement or claim.

Irrelevant grounds happen when irrelevant material is presented to advance arguments in support of a claim. This can happen by evading the issue, appealing to authority, arguing against the person, appealing to people, and appealing to compassion, among others. For example, here is an exchange between A (assessment reviewer) and B (assessment agency representative):

(3) A.   Is the USNT a fair assessment?
     B.   Fairness is an important consideration for all stakeholders. I have raised this issue many times in conferences and meetings. I really deplore assessments that are not fair.

(4) A.   The USNT must be a really good assessment as it is so popular.
     B.   Yes, it has increased its test takers from one million to two million in the last five years.

In example (3), B does not answer the question or provide any grounds in support of an argument for the claim that the USNT is fair. In example (4), A makes an appeal to the USNT's popularity as a way to support its quality and B supports this view. Both arguments fail on the basis of irrelevant grounds.

Evading the question can also include *red herring* and *straw man* (or Aunt Sally) arguments. A red herring argument is a way to misdirect the argument by bringing up another argument that is only tangentially related to the argument on hand. Here is an illustration with two speakers, A (teacher) and B (student):

(5) A. So, why did you cheat on the test today?
     B. I know I should not have cheated. I know it is a mistake, but if I get a low score my parents will be very unhappy with me and they will take away my phone.

In example (5), the student is misdirecting or distracting the teacher from the real issue of his cheating.

Similarly, a straw man argument is another diversionary type of argument in which the original argument is misrepresented or selectively applied. Here is an example between two assessment experts:

(6) A. I don't think USNT is a fair assessment.
     B. No test is fair because if tests were fair then we would not have politicians who are corrupt.

There are also other ways of presenting fallacious arguments. Here are a few pairs of statements made by two persons:

(7) A. The USNT is not a fair assessment.
     B. But the agency that develops and administers the USNT is doing very well on the stock market.

(8) A. I took the USNT yesterday and I did not think it was a fair test.
     B. Why do you say that? The USNT has been in use for the last 25 years, so it must be fair.

(9) A. The USNT is not a fair assessment.
     B. I agree; one of the developers working in the agency that produces the USNT is racist.

In examples (7) to (9), B's response is irrelevant to A's claim; thus appeals to the stock market, its popularity, and the racist nature of one worker are all fallacious arguments.

Defective grounds include the fallacy of hasty generalization in which a general conclusion is drawn from too few specific or untypical examples. For example, consider these statements from a test taker:

(10) The USNT scores are reliable because my student's scores did not change much, although she took the assessment twice.
(11) In the college where I study, students are allowed to take open book exams occasionally, so the USNT should be an open book exam.

(12) The USNT is unfair because my computer in the testing center did not work properly and I could not do well on the listening and speaking tasks.

(13) The USNT's reading section materials were all from science and engineering; it was so unfair to me.

Example (10) shows a clear case of hasty generalization as the assessment's score reliability cannot be estimated or judged from one test taker's scores from two test performances. Example (11) asking for an open book USNT based on another open book assessment is another example of hasty generalization. Example (12) is a case of an untypical situation where the computer in one test center did not work, but this cannot be the basis of evaluating the assessment. In example (13), once again, the assessment's reading section cannot be evaluated from one form of the assessment, which may have had many science and engineering reading passages.

Unwarranted assumption fallacies occur when complex questions are not separated into questions that can be answered. The classic example of this fallacy is the question "Have you stopped beating your wife?" Whichever way this question is answered, yes, or no, the assumption will incriminate the answerer. Here are a few examples from the assessment context:

(14) Has the USNT stopped being biased toward immigrants?

(15) Is the USNT going to lower the quality of its assessments by providing accommodations to test takers with disabilities?

In examples (14) and (15), two distinct issues are raised but combined into one. Thus, any answer would incriminate the assessment agency.

Ambiguities in argument arise when words, phrases, or entire propositions are ambiguous because of confusion with meanings generally under the concept of equivocation or basing an argument on an inference that something must be true as a whole because it is true of all its parts, or vice versa. Here are a few examples from the assessment context:

(16) A. The USNT is a very reliable test according to a technical report on the website.

B. Yes, I agree the assessment is offered every Friday at 8 AM and 1 PM without fail.

(17) Newspaper headline: FAIR TEST! This headline was used covering an article about how an assessment was making attempts to rid its test of gender bias.

(18) In quickly going over the USNT, it looks like a fair assessment, so it must be fair in all respects.

In example (16), the word *reliable* means different things to A and B and hence it is a fallacious argument. In (17), the newspaper's cryptic headline may create a false argument when one or two more words could disambiguate the intended meaning. In (18), more is being inferred than warranted from an initial reading.

Thus, avoiding fallacies is critical to the soundness and strength of arguments. When fallacious arguments are discovered, this should be pointed out so that the arguer can rebuild the argument more soundly. The reformulation of principles, claims, rearticulation of warrants, and use of qualifiers (which typically weaken claims) could help repair fallacious arguments. More specifically, in terms of language, the use of clearer definitions; changing abstract statements to more concrete ones; and using more precise language can help develop clearer, sounder, and stronger argumentation.

How to Accept or Reject Arguments

Although Toulmin (1958) and Toulmin et al. (1984) have elaborate discussions regarding building arguments, they did not discuss how arguments are to be evaluated. In other words, how are we to determine acceptable or unacceptable arguments? Based on the many points made in this chapter, a few key components are necessary in an acceptable argument that supports a claim based on the fairness and justice principles:

(1) Principles and claims have to be *clear and unambiguous.*
(2) Warrants and backing should be *relevant* to the claim being supported.
(3) Backing should be based on *sufficient* size in terms of test taker samples, assessment materials, conditions, administration and scoring, reporting, and decision-making procedures.
(4) Backing should provide *positive* evidence (not negative evidence, as the absence of something does not mean that something is present).
(5) Backing should lead to *convergent* findings (not divergent), especially in the case of multiple warrants; divergent findings could lead to delayed judgments.[7]
(6) Backing should be based on *primary analysis of test performance data* and not based on test manuals and technical reports.
(7) In rebuttals, backing should *defeat or undercut* the claim.

Once arguments are made in support of a claim, reviewers or evaluators have to make a judgment as to the soundness and strength of the arguments. If the claims are clear and the evidence is strong, then there is a strong argument in support of the claims; if the claims are clear and the evidence is weak, there is only a weak argument in support of the claims. If the claims are unclear, then the argument cannot be examined properly. In summary, when decisions have to be made, a few options are available:

(1) *Reasoned full acceptance* of the claim when there is relevant, sufficient, positive, and convergent evidence to support the claim.
(2) *Reasoned partial acceptance* of the claim when there is only partially relevant, sufficient, positive, and/or convergent evidence to support the claim. In this

situation, some of the assessment's claims may be accepted and others are rejected or deferred.

(3) *Reasoned rejection* of the claim when there is not enough relevant, sufficient, positive, and/or convergent evidence (or there are divergent findings) to support the claim. In this situation, there could be rebuttals or counter-claims to the original claims.

(4) *Deferred judgment* of the claim when there is not enough or clear relevant, sufficient, positive, and convergent evidence (or there are divergent findings) to support or reject the claim. In this situation, more evidence is necessary to make a judgment on this claim.

In the event of negative or deferred decisions, there should be a dialectic process in the evaluation of assessments where there is discussion, and deliberations and rejections of claims could result in rebuttals or counter-claims and support for them.

In addition, it is possible that not all assessments may be ready for a full evaluation of all their claims, which include fairness and justice matters. This may be the case with teacher-made assessments or low-stakes assessments. In these situations, a shorter evaluation of claims for a brief period of certification may be appropriate, provided it is based on test performance data from piloted data. Certification is currently not part of most assessment contexts, but it is advisable that assessments be certified so that the assessment is known to adhere to fairness and justice principles and thus be beneficial to the community.

However, for large-scale assessments, a full evaluation of all their claims, which include fairness and justice matters, is essential for certification before the assessment is launched. This evaluation needs to be conducted with all materials available to reviewers—explicitly or implicitly stated claims, stated warrants, and backing from research from test performance data. A full evaluation then can be completed; if the assessment is then certified for a particular use, any minor deficiencies that have been identified can be corrected in a set period. If an assessment is not certified before its launch date, the assessment institution should notify its users about this or indicate that certification is pending with a statutory board or by independent reviewers. This type of compliance to quality and safety is no different from quality management systems like ISO 9000 that help ensure the quality of products and services.

Conclusion

In this chapter, a worked example of building an argument about the USNT based on the principles and sub-principles of fairness and justice using a modified Toulmin model of argumentation is provided. Warrants for each sub-claim were articulated. The chapter then discusses how to evaluate arguments and concludes with issues related to the application of argument in the field of language assessment.

Chapters 5 to 7 will examine the three claims from Principle 1, Fairness (opportunity-to-Learn, meaningfulness, and absence of bias), and Chapter 8 will examine the claims from Principle 2, Justice (beneficial consequences). Findings from illustrative studies will be used to examine whether the claims of the assessments can be supported or not.

Notes

1 Freeman (2011) offers a beautiful example of *divergent* structure:

> (1) There is a perennial classical question that asks which part of the motorcycle, which grain of sand in which pile, is the Buddha. Obviously, (2) to ask that question is to look in the *wrong direction*, for (3) *the Buddha is everywhere*. But just as obviously (4) to ask that question is to look in the *right direction* for (3) the Buddha is everywhere.
>
> *[from R. Persig, Zen and the Art of Motorcycle Maintenance]*

The figure for the divergent structure would be:

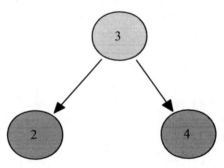

2 Freeman (2011), though, makes a slight distinction between the argument microstructure and argument macrostructure. He states "by the *microstructure* of an argument, we mean its logical form as studied in deductive or inductive logic. Specifically, in formal deductive logic, microstructural analysis reveals [. . .] the constituent statements of functional connectives, quantifiers, and in some cases other operators such as modifiers and modal or propositional attitude connectives... By contrast, the *macrostructure* of an argument in which its component statements (together with other elements) fit together as wholes to allegedly lend support to some claim or claims" (p. 1). Either way, the microstructure and macrostructure of argumentation provide the mechanism for a sounder and stronger argumentation.

3 According to the United States Citizenship and Immigration Service (USCIS), the Office of Citizenship is within the USCIS and is responsible for the USNT and naturalization.

4 For convenience, the sub-claims and warrants for Principle 2 (5 and 6) are numbered consecutively after Principle 1 (1 to 4).

5 Freeman (2011) citing Pollock's (1995) work in epistemology distinguishes between two types of rebuttals: *a rebutting defeater* that offers negative evidence (such as an alibi in a criminal case) and *an undercutting defeater* (such as the reliability of a witness in a criminal case).

6 I want to credit Matthew Wallace for suggesting this summary provided in Extract 4.1.

7 Freeman (2011) provides a clear example of *convergent* structure where individual premises separately support a conclusion:

> (1) He is a morally good man because (2) his disposition evinces an underlying kindness and (3) his character displays real integrity.

The figure for the convergent structure would be:

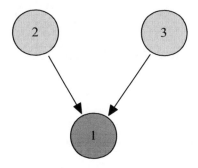

References

American Educational Research Association, American Psychological Association, the National Council on Measurement in Education. (2014). *Standards for educational and psychological testing.* Washington, DC: Author.

Freeman, J. B. (2011). *Argument structure: Representations and theory (Vol. 18).* New York: Springer Science and Business Media.

Immigration and Nationality Act. (1952, June 27). *An act to revise the laws relating to immigration, naturalization, and nationality; and for other purposes.* H.R. 13342; Pub.L. 414; 182 Stat. 66. 82nd United States Congress.

Pollock, J. L. (1995). *Cognitive carpentry.* Cambridge, MA: The MIT Press.

Toulmin, S. (1958). *The uses of argument.* Cambridge: Cambridge University Press.

Toulmin, S., Rieke, R. D., & Janik, A. (1984). *An introduction to reasoning.* London, UK: Macmillan.

5

OPPORTUNITY-TO-LEARN

Introduction

It is obvious to individuals involved in education that adequate educational opportunities are critical to student success in schools, colleges, or universities. Specifically, these opportunities could include physical facilities (buildings, classrooms, desks, chairs, playgrounds, etc.), intellectual resources (textbooks, libraries, etc.), personnel (teachers, administrators, coaches, etc.), financial resources (tuition, fees, etc.), and learning opportunities (from teachers, peers, texts, online materials, etc.). It is the last type—learning opportunities—that we will focus on in this chapter. This is of high importance in school contexts for students who are economically disadvantaged; have physical and mental disabilities; and are different in terms of first language, race and ethnicity, nationality, and sexual orientation. These students are likely to have less access to learning opportunities outside the classroom.

In terms of assessment, Opportunity-to-Learn refers to learning resources that test takers have access to, to learn the content and skills that they are going to be assessed on before they take an assessment. This opportunity is seen as critical in terms of fairness of the assessment to test takers. The chapter discusses the sub-claim of Opportunity-to-Learn (OTL) under Principle 1, Fairness, using the Toulmin model of argumentation. The sub-claim is also illustrated with warrants and backing and with brief descriptions of findings from relevant empirical studies.

Defining OTL

Opportunity-to-Learn can be defined as opportunities that are made available directly in the classroom for learning content and skills with the help of teachers and textbooks and related activities. The UCLA Institute for Democracy, Education and Access (2003) defines OTL as follows:

> OTL is a way of measuring and reporting whether students and teachers have access to the different ingredients that make up quality schools. The more OTL ingredients that are present in an individual school, school district, or even in schools across the state, the more opportunities students have to benefit from a high quality education. OTL standards provide a benchmark against which the opportunities that a school provides can be measured. Using OTL standards as a guide, students can measure whether they have a realistic shot at learning the subjects the state requires and whether they will have a fair chance to compete for college. OTL standards can also help students, parents, communities and school officials to discover and correct problems in schools. By measuring and reporting the presence or absence of learning opportunities against a set of standards, OTL can bring to light examples of unfair conditions—both within a school or across the state school system—that limit students' equal access to a high quality education.
>
> *(UCLA Institute for Democracy, Education and Access, 2003)*

They provided an example list of OTL: (1) qualified teachers, (2) clean and safe facilities, (3) up-to-date books and quality learning materials, (4) high-quality coursework, and (5) school conditions that provide students a fair and equal Opportunity-to-Learn and achieve knowledge and skills.

The UCLA/IDEA document acknowledged that OTL standards across California schools show that

> some schools provide students with great opportunities to learn while other schools offer very few opportunities. . . . For example, research shows that schools with the highest numbers of Latino/a and African American students enrolled have the biggest shortages of textbooks and the lowest numbers of qualified teachers.
>
> *(p. 4)*

Although these questions deal directly with teaching and learning and some assessments in the classroom, OTL is also critical in the all-important assessments that are administered in many schools, particularly annual school exams as well as school exit exams generally administered at the end of schooling (at Grade 12 or equivalent). Adequate OTL for an assessment is a critical factor in taking an assessment because it would mean that all test takers have a fair chance of equal success through learning the materials and skills prior to taking the assessment.

OTL is also important for other stakeholders in the school context: the teacher, school administrators, and state or national policy makers in understanding whether the curricula goals are appropriate for the grade level and whether instructional strategies and resources are available to all students. Adequate time for preparation and adequate practice with technology are also critical. Lack of these opportunities can lead an assessment to be unfair to some or all test takers and, therefore, scores obtained from such assessments and the decisions made based on the scores are likely to be invalid, unfair, and unjust.

Of course, no discussion of OTL can minimize the effects of contextual factors such as out-of-school factors, for example, socioeconomic levels of school students. These socioeconomic factors include parents'/household income, number of household members, number of siblings, parental education/skill level, home nutrition levels, etc. Such factors have a bearing on the learning ethos of the home, which include number of books at home, number of hours spent on homework per day and week, socialization of children into schooling and the value of school learning, etc.

Effects of OTL on Achievement

The Schott Foundation for Public Education in Cambridge, Massachusetts, in a document titled *Lost Opportunity 50 State Report*[1] (2009) examined OTL across the U.S. They produced a set of inter-state comparison maps of quality of instruction and achievement by income and by minorities compared to White and non-White students. The report stated that

> In the United States, every student should have the equal right to a high-quality education. But as our most recent data demonstrates, for far too many students, quality and equity are aspirations, not realities. Few states are providing public school educations that result in academic proficiency for students. And even fewer states are providing access to a high-quality education to all students, particularly those from historically disadvantaged groups. As we look at school system improvement in the United States, what resources do our systems need to improve? What are the benefits of further investment in our education systems?
>
> *(Schott Foundation, 2009)*

The report concluded:

> We cannot have equity without quality. And we cannot have true quality without real equity. All children, regardless of skin color, ethnicity or socioeconomic status, deserve access to high-quality education and a fair and

substantive Opportunity-to-Learn. They deserve access to: 1) high-quality early education; 2) highly qualified and skilled teachers and instructors in grades K-12; 3) college preparatory curricula that will prepare them for college, work and community; and 4) equitable instructional resources. And yet today, disadvantaged students—Black, Latino, Native American and low-income—have half the Opportunity-to-Learn as their White, non-Latino fellow students.

(from www.otlstatereport.org/)

Banicky (2000) from the University of Delaware Education Research and Development Center issued an education policy brief in which she asserted that OTL directly affects achievement:

> Previous research has narrowly defined OTL as the amount of overlap between what is taught and what is tested. In these studies, information on the amount and the quality of exposure to new knowledge has been gathered through teachers' self-reports, direct observation of classroom instruction, or by examining the curriculum materials used. Many of these studies have found positive relationships between the amount of content covered and performance in that content area, but many researchers argue that content coverage is just one facet of OTL. Beyond content coverage, several studies of programs in disadvantaged urban and rural schools suggest that OTL is also influenced by school factors.
>
> *(from www.rdc.udel.edu/ p. 2)*

Further, using a sociocultural approach Moss, Pullin, Gee, Haertel, and Young (2008) in their study "Assessment, Equity and Opportunity-to-Learn" focused on literacy, social practices, sociocultural practices, cultural modeling, and situated learning building from conventional notions of OTL. They argued that access to content tested, access to resources, and access to instructional processes are critical. Thus, it is obvious that OTL is a multifaceted construct requiring much more attention, particularly with regard to how it could affect student achievement in high-stakes testing.

What OTL Can Tell Us About Achievement

Porter (1993) argued that OTL standards can be used to "(a) to serve as a basis for school-by-school accountability; (b) to provide an indicator system; and (c) to present a clearer vision of challenging curriculum and pedagogy" (p. 1). Schwartz (1995) suggested that OTL strategies can be implemented in terms of access to courses, curriculum, and teacher competence. In general, the consensus is that understanding OTL would provide insight into differential student achievement, if it exists. Herman, Klein, and Abedi (2000) argued that OTL information can be used to verify if students from all diverse backgrounds have had the same opportunity to meet expected standards of achievement.

OTL Standards, NCTE (1994)

It is with this background in mind that the *Opportunity-to-Learn Standards* developed by the National Council of Teachers of English (NCTE) in 1994 should be understood. It attempted to list all components so that all students have equitable access to high-quality education. The *Standards* were:

- Enable all students to achieve high content standards and learn to their full potential
- Be directly tied to students' learning and performance in content standards
- Consider the diverse, multiple ways students learn
- Enable all teachers to teach all students
- Be supported by the best classroom practice and research
- Be based on research on how effective schools use resources
- Address necessary conditions and resources for successful learning in our schools as well as effective use of resources, including safe, secure environments free of prejudice and violence; attractive, comfortable environments that invite learning, risk taking, and problem solving; updated library media centers and technologies
- Consider opportunities for preschool and beyond school learning.

(National Council of Teachers of English, 1994)

Although the *Standards* cover many academic and non-academic matters, the NCTE states in summary that OTL standards should provide "time for students to learn and reflect; time for teachers to plan, teach, and reflect; appropriate learning resources; and resources from the community" (National Council of Teachers of English, 1994, p. 1).

OTL Standards, APA, AERA, and NCME (2014)

The most recent APA, AERA, and NCME *Standards of Educational and Psychological Testing* (2014) considered OTL as a fairness issue as well as a threat to fair and valid interpretations of test scores. They offered a definition and two specific standards:

> Opportunity-to-Learn—the extent to which individuals have had exposure to instruction or knowledge that affords them the opportunity [to] learn the content and skills targeted by the test—has several implications

for the fair and valid interpretation of test scores for their intended uses. . . Opportunity-to-Learn is a fairness issue when an authority provides differential access to Opportunity-to-Learn for some individuals who have not been provided that opportunity accountable for their test performance.

(pp. 56–57)

Standard 3.19

In settings where the same authority is responsible for both provision of curriculum and high-stakes decisions based on testing of [the] examinee's curriculum mastery, examinees should not suffer permanent negative consequences if evidence indicates that they have not had the Opportunity-to-Learn the test content.

(p. 72)

Standard 12.8

When test results contribute substantially to decisions about student promotion or graduation, evidence should be provided that students have had an Opportunity-to-Learn the content and skills measured by the test.

(p. 197)

This brief review of how OTL is defined, its effect on achievement, and articulated standards show how critical OTL is for student success in general learning, as well as for assessments. The *Standards* listed help in clarifying what exactly developers, user scorers, test takers, and stakeholders need to do in terms of providing test takers OTL prior to taking an assessment. We now proceed to build a fairness argument based on OTL.

Building a Fairness Argument for OTL

Principles

Keeping in mind this background to OTL and limiting its focus to OTL's impact on assessment, the general principle of fairness is articulated as follows with specific claims.

Principle 1: Fairness

An assessment *ought* to be fair to all test takers; that is, there is a presumption of providing equal opportunities to all so that they can demonstrate their content knowledge or skills.

Claims

Although a general claim can be investigated directly, a preferred method would be to deconstruct the general claim into specific sub-claims so that the general claim can be supported through warrants and backing from the sub-claims. Following this procedure, the general claim is based on many sub-claims. Figure 5.1 shows the relationship between the principles and general claim. Extract 5.1 shows how all of these are related.

EXTRACT 5.1   FAIRNESS ARGUMENT FOR OTL

Principle 1: Fairness

An assessment *ought* to be fair to all test takers; that is, there is a presumption of providing equal opportunities to all so that they can demonstrate their content knowledge or skills.

General Claim 1: Prior to taking the CST, adequate opportunity, time, and practice with technology and experience are provided.

Sub-claim 1a: Prior to the CST, adequate Opportunity-to-Learn and to prepare for the assessment is provided.
Warrant 1a: Research on the CST will show that adequate Opportunity-to-Learn for the assessment is provided prior to taking the CST.

Sub-claim 1b: Prior to taking the CST, adequate time for preparation is available.
Warrant 1b: Research on the CST will show that adequate time for preparation for the assessment is available prior to taking the test.

Sub-claim 1c: Prior to taking the CST, adequate practice with new technology is available (example from TOEFL).
Warrant 1c: Research on the CST will show that adequate practice with new technology is available prior to taking the test (example from TOEFL).

Sub-claim 1d: Prior to taking the CST, adequate opportunity is available in the semiotic domain and relevant social practices and embodied experiences.
Warrant 1d: Research on the CST will show that adequate opportunity is available in the semiotic domain and relevant social practices and embodied experiences prior to taking the test.

Also: see *Standards 3.19, 12.8* from AERA, APA, NCME (2014)

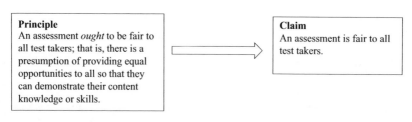

Principle
An assessment *ought* to be fair to all test takers; that is, there is a presumption of providing equal opportunities to all so that they can demonstrate their content knowledge or skills.

Claim
An assessment is fair to all test takers.

FIGURE 5.1   Principle 1, Fairness; generic structure

Sub-claims, Warrants, and Backing

A general claim can be operationalized into many sub-claims.[2] The examples used in this chapter all relate to school assessments. However, the hypothetical claims listed next are related to the California Standards Test (CST) administered to students in English and mathematics (from Grades 3 to 8). The sub-claims and warrants follow. Warrants need to mirror the sub-claims. They should be written to show what research findings would help support the sub-claims. The relationships between these claims and the various warrants are shown in Figure 5.2.

> *Sub-claim 1a:* Prior to taking the CST, adequate opportunity (in terms of curriculum, materials, feedback) to acquire knowledge, abilities, or skills to be assessed is provided.
> *Warrant 1a:* Research on the CST's curriculum, materials, and feedback will show that adequate opportunity to acquire knowledge, abilities, or skills to be assessed is provided.

It is obvious that opportunity to learn the content and skills that are to be assessed should be available to all test takers. Although this assumption may be obvious, it is not always easy to ensure. There are many contexts where this basic requirement may not be met. For example, in the educational context, this provision of adequate content or skill coverage is possible to ensure when the assessment involves a single classroom teacher and her students. But it is difficult to ensure when the assessment involves a statewide or national assessment, which involves multiple teachers in multiple schools in multiple districts or states.

This problem was observed in the *California Standards Test* that is administered to all students from Grade 3 to 8 in English and mathematics. It was routinely observed that not all teachers were able to complete the chapters/units in the curriculum before the assessments were administered, resulting in lower scores for the students in those classrooms. When teachers were surveyed regarding the problem, they reported that it was not possible in their classrooms to complete pre-set goals in the curriculum due to extra time needed to proceed through earlier chapters/units based on student general ability and English language ability (Kunnan, 2000). Thus, in such large-scale, high-stakes assessments in the school context,

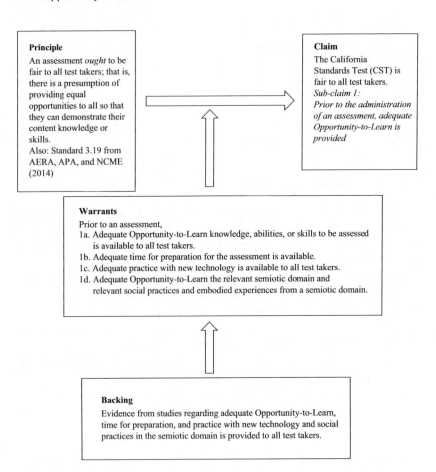

FIGURE 5.2   Generic structure for the principle, claim and sub–claim, warrants, and backing for Principle 1, Fairness—OTL

differential opportunities to learn will result in unequal advancement of students and quite obviously an unfair testing and practice. Inadequate OTL can also be a major factor among low-performing and disadvantaged and ELL students when compared to White, non-Latino students, and non-ELLs.

In terms of curricular validity, there have been disagreements as to how educational agencies can demonstrate what students have been taught. Some argue that the formal written school curriculum can be used to match knowledge and skills measured in the assessment. Others argue that it is not the formal written curriculum that should be used to check curricular validity, but the instructional curriculum of the classroom. Assessment researchers have also made the same argument that they prefer to examine whether test takers have had the OTL the knowledge and skills in the classroom rather than merely matching test knowledge and skills with a formal written curriculum.

Such examples of inadequate OTL in a high-stakes test can often result in lawsuits in the U.S. under the Equal Protection and Due Process clauses of the 14th Amendment of the U.S. Constitution. A well-cited case in this regard is *Debra P. v. Turlington* (1981). The grounds for a legal challenge (known as substantive due process) was inadequate Opportunity-to-Learn, as the curriculum for the assessment was not made known to African American test takers who took a minimum competency test but had approximately 10 times the failure rate as White test takers. The Court found for the plaintiff (the African American test takers) stating that "if the test covers material not taught to the students, it is unfair and violates the Equal Protection and Due Process clauses of the 14th Amendment of the U.S. Constitution" (Debra P., at 402). Therefore, based on this ruling an assessment has been considered a property right subject to due process protection by U.S. courts.

> *Sub-claim 1b:* Prior to taking the CST, adequate time for preparation for the assessment is available.
>
> *Warrant 1b:* Research on the CST's time for preparation will show that adequate time for the assessment is available.

Adequate time for preparation is also an obvious consideration before an assessment is launched in a community. Although normally an assessment cannot be launched before adequate time is provided, there are times when this requirement is violated. For example, in the U.S., students in a school (and their parents) have the right to due process (known as procedural due process). This means that the students and parents must receive adequate notice regarding the launch of a test; for example, for a high school graduation or exit exam, there should be adequate time for students (parents, teachers, schools, etc.) to prepare for the test.

In U.S. courts, inadequate time for preparation can be challenged in a court under the provision of the 14th Amendment of the U.S. Constitution. The grounds for this challenge are based on the provision that test takers did not receive adequate advance notice or that test takers did not receive instruction on the test content/knowledge and skills (this is also known in legal circles as curricula validity). Courts have interpreted this requirement to mean anywhere between two and four years of advance notice before an assessment becomes effective.

> *Sub-claim 1c:* Prior to taking the CST, adequate practice with new technology is available.
>
> *Warrant 1c:* Research on the CST's practice with new technology will show that adequate practice is available.

With the use of new technology with assessments, it is once again obvious that test takers should have the familiarity and skill in using the appropriate technology in such a way that the technology does not pose any difficulty for test takers. If the technology does pose a problem, then the scores are likely to be confounded with the familiarity and skill of using the technology. For example, assessment agencies should conduct survey studies in familiarity and skill in technology use such as computers, videos, tablets, smartphones, etc., before using such technology in an assessment. In addition, the skill level of test takers using the keyboard and mouse with functions such as cutting and pasting, scrolling up and down, typing in essays, formatting texts, etc., needs to be surveyed.

To give an example from the computer-based TOEFL, Kirsch, Jamieson, Taylor, and Eignor (1998) conducted a study of computer familiarity prior to the launch of the test. They concluded from the sample studied that test takers who are likely to take the TOEFL would have the necessary computer skills (in terms of typing in answers and using the screen and the mouse) to take the test and that their scores would not be compromised by the use of new technology. Although this study provided adequate evidence that the sample test takers were able to take the TOEFL on a computer, it did not necessarily follow that students used computers on a regular basis (and therefore were fluent) prior to the study (see more on this in the about the Opportunity-for-Success section).

This matter could also be a subject that can be challenged under the due process clause of the 14th Amendment of the U.S. Constitution as materials, equipment, and technology should be familiar to test takers (substantive due process). Phillips (1995) clarified that whereas

> procedural due process focuses on the administration of an assessment and sets an expectation that the procedures and processes implemented will be fair and equitable, substantive due process focuses on the assessment instrument itself and sets an expectation that it will follow professional standards, be valid and reliable, and be fair to all test takers. Substantive due process can be violated when the knowledge and skills being assessed are judged to be arbitrary, capricious, or unfair.
>
> *(p. 381)*

In both cases, assessment agencies are expected to uphold the general notion of adequate Opportunity-to-Learn.

Sub-claim 1d: Prior to taking the CST, adequate opportunity is available in the relevant semiotic domain and relevant social practices and embodied experiences.

Warrant 1d: Research on the CST's opportunity in the relevant semiotic domain and relevant social practices and embodied experiences from a semiotic domain will show that adequate practice and experiences are available.

It is well understood that the ability to merely decode the words and sentences in a text is not a mark of a successful reader beyond basic reading. Coles (1998,

2000); Street (1995); the New London Group (1996) and Gee (2003) have argued that reading texts has to include the relevant literacy and social practices, knowing the semiotic domain, and having embodied experiences. Gee (2003) defines a semiotic domain as the collective consciousness shared by people with similar interests, attributes, or skill sets. In addition, he claims that the opportunity to experience the semiotic domain (in and out of the classroom) in terms of active and critical learning is necessary in terms of "the full range of verbal and nonverbal meaning resources." He illustrates the concept this way: If two students are reading a text in biology and basketball and one student was able "to 'do' biology or basketball (see them, produce them, or simulate them, whatever the case may be) and another student has only read texts about biology (or basketball), the students have not had equivalent opportunities to learn" (p. 33).

Writing with specific reference to assessment, Gee (2003) decries the focus of reading assessments on "general, factual and dictionary-like questions about various texts" (p. 30). He develops six principles based on concepts such as "literacy is more than reading and writing," "understanding semiotic domains, social languages," and "situated and embodied meanings."

His first principle is stated as follows:

> People (children or adults) have not had the same Opportunity-to-Learn based solely on how much or how little they have read 'in general', but in terms of how equivalent their experience has been with reading specific types of text in specific sorts of ways. They must also have had equivalent experience with the social practices associated with reading these specific types of text in these specific ways. Finally, they must have had equivalent experiences in being producers and not just consumers of texts of that type read in that way.
> *(p. 31)*

This is a critical point that targets assessments like the CST that reduce listening, speaking, reading, or writing to facts and figures. It is more so in the case of reading assessments with selected-response formats like multiple-choice response and true-false formats. Such tests may not engage the test taker in the relevant semiotic domain or the embodied experiences of the test taker.

Illustrative OTL Studies

OTL in Schools

Two illustrative studies regarding OTL are presented and discussed here: Herman et al. (2000) examined OTL at the school level and Abedi et al. (2006) examined OTL for English language learner and non-English language learner groups in U.S. public schools. Claims, sub-claims, and warrants are presented first. The discussion of the findings gives us information about the backing for the claim(s). Finally, conclusions regarding the claim(s) are made.

OTL in School Classrooms: Herman, Klein, and Abedi (2000)

Claim: OTL is available in U.S. school classrooms.

Sub-claim: OTL is available in U.S. school-level instruction and assessment in terms of coverage of curriculum content, use of instructional strategies, and access to instructional resources.

Warrant: Research from surveys to students and teachers in Grade 8 should provide evidence to support the claim for OTL.

Herman et al.'s (2000) study examined the concept of OTL in the context of school-level instruction and assessment in the U.S. in terms of three variables: coverage of curriculum content, use of instructional strategies, and access to instructional resources. They collected data for this study in middle school mathematics classrooms through teacher interviews, student surveys, and classroom artifacts such as typical assignments and assessments. They surveyed 36 classrooms, 27 teachers, and 800 Grade 8 students from 13 schools (of which 9 were urban schools). Herman et al.'s main research questions were:

- What is the extent to which students have been exposed to the specific subjects and topics which are essential to attaining particular standards or which are directly assessed?
- Have students been exposed to the kind of teaching and instructional experiences that would prepare them for success?
- Do students have experience with the kinds of tasks by which their performance is to be judged?
- Are there appropriate resources to prepare students for success on standards? (In terms of) teacher preparation, such as educational experience (e.g., college degree), amount and type of teaching experience, participation in relevant in-service education, and attitudes toward mathematics instruction.

(p. 17)

The results, which were aggregated to the classroom level, showed that in terms of how much time teachers spent on a specific mathematical topic (such as area, fractions, perimeter, graphing, etc.), teacher responses were uniformly much higher than the student responses. In other words, students felt that the time spent on each of the topics was much less than what teachers thought. Correlations on how well teachers and students agreed on the four OTL measures (i.e., content preparation, instructional strategies, general preparation, and accessibility of instructional tools) showed that teacher responses and student responses had no relationship among them ($r = 0.02$), and for individual topics (e.g., fractions) correlations between teacher and student responses were very low except for the topic of distance/time problems ($r = 0.51, p < 0.01$). However, correlations were much higher between teacher and student responses on instructional strategies presented in the classroom ($r = 0.52, p < 0.002$). Similarly, correlations were moderately high between the researcher-coded classroom artifacts and the teacher

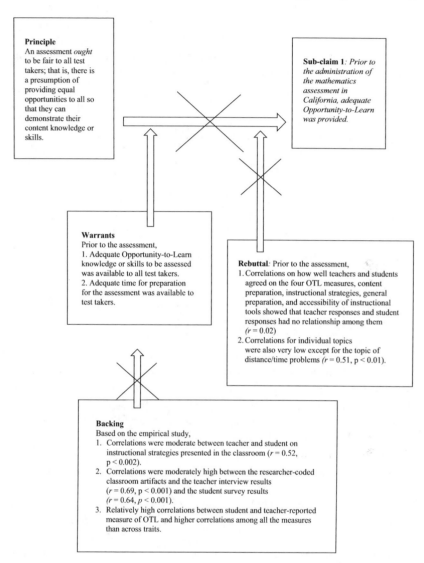

Principle
An assessment *ought* to be fair to all test takers; that is, there is a presumption of providing equal opportunities to all so that they can demonstrate their content knowledge or skills.

Sub-claim 1: *Prior to the administration of the mathematics assessment in California, adequate Opportunity-to-Learn was provided.*

Warrants
Prior to the assessment,
1. Adequate Opportunity-to-Learn knowledge or skills to be assessed was available to all test takers.
2. Adequate time for preparation for the assessment was available to test takers.

Rebuttal: Prior to the assessment,
1. Correlations on how well teachers and students agreed on the four OTL measures, content preparation, instructional strategies, general preparation, and accessibility of instructional tools showed that teacher responses and student responses had no relationship among them *(r = 0.02)*
2. Correlations for individual topics were also very low except for the topic of distance/time problems *(r = 0.51, p < 0.01).*

Backing
Based on the empirical study,
1. Correlations were moderate between teacher and student on instructional strategies presented in the classroom (r = 0.52, p < 0.002).
2. Correlations were moderately high between the researcher-coded classroom artifacts and the teacher interview results (r = 0.69, p < 0.001) and the student survey results (r = 0.64, *p* < 0.001).
3. Relatively high correlations between student and teacher-reported measure of OTL and higher correlations among all the measures than across traits.

FIGURE 5.3   Mapping Herman et al.'s (2000) findings on the OTL claim with rebuttal. Note the X marks on the sub-claim and on the arrow from the backing to warrants to claim indicates that the claim cannot be supported.

interview results ($r = 0.69$, $p < 0.001$) and between the teacher survey results and the student survey results ($r = 0.64$, $p < 0.001$).

Backing and rebuttal: Based on these findings, an argument for the sub-claim of adequate Opportunity-to-Learn can be made by mapping the results onto the Toulmin argumentation framework. Figure 5.3 presents this mapping of the results. The warrants relevant to the study are presented in the warrants box; the backing from the study is in the box below that leads to the warrants. But as the results are divergent, a rebuttal of the claim is possible. Therefore, in this case, in evaluating the argument for the sub-claim, there is insufficient convergent evidence to accept the claim—both in support of the claim and against the claim. In this type of event, the rebuttal of the claim ensures that the claim cannot be supported with currently available evidence. The X mark in the claims box and flow of backing and warrants going to the claims from the principle shows that the claims are invalidated or cancelled for now. Therefore, a deferred judgment pending additional backing from further empirical studies is the most logical conclusion.

OTL for English Language Learners: Abedi, Courtney, Leon, Kao, and Azzam (2006)

> *Claim:* OTL for English language learners is available in U.S. school classrooms.
>
> *Sub-claim:* OTL for English language learners is available in U.S. school-level instruction in terms of content coverage, teacher content knowledge, and student prior math ability.
>
> *Warrant:* Research from surveys to students and teachers in Grade 8 should provide evidence to support the claim for OTL.

Abedi et al.'s (2006) study investigated the OTL among English language learners (ELLs) in terms of mathematics achievement and the use of accommodations. Although this study did not directly examine the effects of OTL on assessment, it presents findings regarding OTL and ELLs, an important concern in subject-matter tests (like mathematics and science) for ELLs. A total of 21 rural and urban schools with 51 teachers in 98 algebra classes in Southern California participated in their study. There were 2367 Grade 8 students, 50 percent female and 50 percent male, with school student data that showed 32 percent as ELL and 68 percent as non-ELL.

The main goals of the study can be grouped into three categories, with many research questions for each goal (only the OTL-related ones are discussed here):

(1) *Opportunity-to-Learn/Accommodation/Language Proficiency Effects:* Do the three class-level components of OTL (i.e., content coverage, teacher content knowledge, and student prior math ability) affect students' math performance? Do these three components of OTL differentially affect the math performance of students with varying degrees of English language proficiency?

(2) *Language Proficiency and Opportunity-to-Learn:* Do students of varying English language proficiency receive the same level of OTL? Do students who scored lower on the TIMER test and lower on CAT/6 reading percentile ranking receive the same level of OTL? Do ELL students receive the same amount of OTL as compared to non-ELL students?

(3) *Class Participation OTL:* Are there any differences between ELL and non-ELL students in the level of class participation/teacher–student interaction?

Is there a relationship between students' class participation and their math performance?

(pp. 19–20)

Abedi et al. (2006) used many instruments and protocols in their study, including (1) a mathematics performance measure, (2) an English reading proficiency measure, (3) content coverage OTL measure, (4) a teacher content knowledge measure, (5) a class prior math ability OTL, (6) student background data, (7) state reading test scores, (8) teacher observation reports, and (9) teacher–student interaction observation reports.

The main findings were:

(1) All three measures of class-level OTL had a significant relationship with improved math performance when prior math ability was controlled for ELL status and test accommodations at the student level. All class-level OTL components were significantly associated with math performance, but they did not have a differential impact on ELL students (both ELL and non-ELL students benefited similarly).

(2) Overall, ELL students received less OTL than non-ELL students; the greatest disparity between ELL and non-ELL students occurred based on prior class math ability; students who performed in the bottom third of the TIMER test reported less class-level content coverage than students who performed in the top third; and students in the lower CAT/6 reading percentile ranking reported less class-level content coverage than students with a higher ranking.

(3) There were no differences between ELL and non-ELL students in level of participation or in teacher–student interaction; student-initiated classroom participation was significantly related to math performance while controlling for prior math ability at both the individual and classroom levels, but teacher-initiated classroom participation was not significantly related to math performance.

Backing and rebuttal: Based on these findings, especially in (2), where ELLs received less OTL than non-ELLs, there could be a rebuttal of the claim that ELL and non-ELL students received adequate OTL in their math classes. Similarly, as students in the lower third in both tests received less content coverage, there could be a rebuttal that students of all proficiency groups are receiving adequate content coverage. As there were no specific claims made by school authorities directly or indirectly, the Toulmin argumentation model with principles, claims, warrants, and backing are not presented in a figure.

OTL in the Classroom

OTL can also be considered a critical component of the teaching–learning–assessing model in the classroom. In traditional teacher-directed classes of writing, teachers are expected to provide diagnostic feedback for student essays (or other constructed responses) to help in the revision process. This type of feedback can be also considered OTL, as student writers traditionally benefit from teacher feedback in their essay revisions. In the last decade or so, computer-assisted instructional tools have been developed as part of automated essay evaluation (AEE) programs. AEE programs such as *MyAccess* (developed by Vantage Learning) and *WriteToLearn* (developed by Pearson) claim to provide automated diagnostic feedback that is comparable to human raters. For example, student writers who submit their essays to these software programs (on topics that the software have been trained) would expect to receive automated diagnostic feedback. Research studies on the comparability of the automated feedback when compared to human rater feedback are presented now.

Examining MyAccess: Hoang and Kunnan (2016)

> *Claim: MyAccess* provides scoring and diagnostic feedback to students that is similar to human scoring and feedback.
>
> *Sub-claim 1a:* Essay scoring provided by *MyAccess* of off-topic essays is similar to human scoring.
>
> *Warrant 1a:* Research on off-topic essays will provide evidence to support the comparability of *MyAccess* scoring and human scoring.
>
> *Sub-claim 1b:* Diagnostic feedback provided by *MyAccess* to students is similar to human scoring.
>
> *Warrant 1b:* Research on diagnostic feedback will provide evidence to support the comparability of *MyAccess* feedback and human feedback.

Hoang and Kunnan (2016) examined *MyAccess* in terms of its comparability of automated scoring with human ratings and its comparability of automated diagnostic feedback with trained human raters. I will focus only on the latter in this chapter. With data collected from 105 ESL writers in California and Vietnam, the authors compared *MyAccess'* diagnostic feedback with those provided by human essay raters in terms of off-topic essays and general diagnostic feedback.

Off-Topic Essays

In terms of off-topic essays, Hoang and Kunnan found *MyAccess* was unable to identify or read off-topic essays when compared to human raters. Table 5.1 presents the mismatches between human ratings and *MyAccess* ratings for off-topic essays. In addition, the ratings assigned by *MyAccess* are much higher than human ratings for all off-topic essays.

Diagnostic Feedback

In terms of diagnostic feedback, the authors examined 15 randomly selected essays for error analysis. The human raters focused on *grammar*, *usage*, and *mechanics*. The human raters used the exact same system of error tagging as *MyAccess* did to give feedback. Table 5.2 presents the human raters' list and frequency of identified errors compared to *MyAccess'* frequency of error identification. The column-wise information is in terms of error type (Column 1; spelling, articles, etc.), human feedback (Column 2; rater feedback), *MyAccess* feedback (Column 3; automated feedback), *precision hits* and percentages (Columns 4 and 5), and *recall* percentages (Column 6). Precision hits are defined as the number of cases in which human raters agree that the error rated by the software (in this case, *MyAccess*) was a true error, and recall is defined as the software's coverage of errors in terms of human rater feedback. Precision hits percentages and recall percentages are calculated in the following way: Precision % = Hits divided by software's total (for example, the precision of articles: 31 ÷ 32 = 96.9); Recall % = Hits divided by human rater's feedback's total (For example, the recall of articles: 31 ÷ 124 = 25.0).

The essay writers made a total of 465 errors (see Column 1 total); far more errors with articles (124 errors) than with any other error type; punctuations (39) and run-on sentences (39) were next, subject–verb agreement (37) was fourth, and preposition (36) was the fifth problematic area. The number of errors found in each of the other types ranged from 0 to 26. *MyAccess'* overall error detection was inadequate and uneven. It was most precise in its identification of open or closed spelling errors, although in this sample, it corrected only two cases (*part time* to *part-time* and *everyday* to *every day*), both of which matched the human rater. However, *MyAccess* missed many open/closed spelling cases that needed correction with the 28.6 percent *recall* (Column 6), which meant it missed 71.4 percent of the total human readers' flagged cases.

MyAccess did well with article errors, with 96.9 percent *precision* (Column 5); however, similar to open/closed spelling errors, the system identified only 25 percent, which means it missed 75 percent errors of this type that the human rater identified. Capitalization (90 percent) and run-on sentences (82 percent) were two error types that showed a similar pattern: over 80 percent *precision* in error identification, but with a recall of 45 percent and 56 percent, respectively (Column 6), when compared to errors flagged by human raters. Spelling and subject–verb agreement consistency, which combined the two sub-types of verb group consistency and noun phrase consistency errors, exhibited the smallest number of

TABLE 5.1 Comparison of human ratings and *MyAccess* on off-topic essays (0–6 scale)

Essay	HR 1	HR 2	MyAccess rating
ESL1–4	2.5	1.0	4.9
ESL1–5	2.0	2.5	4.2
EFL1–37	2.3	3.5	4.0
EFL2–27	3.8	4.0	4.6

Note: HR = Human Rating; scale is 0–6 points
Source: Hoang and Kunnan (2016)

cases overlooked by *MyAccess*, with 76.9 percent and 70.2 percent (Column 5), respectively, but also with recall of only 51 percent and 49 percent (Column 6).

Further, *MyAccess* failed to identify errors at the word, sentence, and discourse levels. It was least precise with its diagnosis of confused word errors, with 28.6 percent *precision* and 11.1 percent *recall* (Columns 5 and 6). This means that of all errors in this category flagged by *MyAccess*, only 28.6 percent were errors—the rest were false positives—and that it missed almost 89 percent cases of this type compared to the human rater.

Overall, *MyAccess* was 73 percent precise (Column 5) in flagging errors of the 16 error types designated for this analysis and covered 39.6 percent (Column 6) of errors the human rater flagged. In other words, it missed 60.4 percent of errors. Researchers on error feedback tools maintain that they would choose to err on the side of *precision* over *recall* (Burstein, Chodorow, & Leacock, 2003; Chodorow, Gamon, & Tetreault, 2010), which "means that we [they] would rather miss an error than tell the student that a well-formed construction is ill-formed" (Burstein, Chodorow, & Leacock, 2003, p. 6). In studying *Criterion*, (another AEE system), Burstein, Chodorow, and Leacock (2003) set the minimum threshold of 90 percent precision for the software to be useful for students. Judged by this criterion, *MyAccess* would fall short.

In terms of qualitative analysis, *MyAccess* provided some confusing comments and revision ideas, for example, double flagging of errors. Here are a few examples with flagging of errors shown between < > signs.

TABLE 5.2 Comparison between human and *MyAccess'* error feedback

Error type	Human reader feedback Total	MyAccess feedback			
		Total	Hits	Precision %	Recall %
Spelling 1	7	2	2	100	28.6
Articles	124	32	31	96.9	25.0
Capitalization	38	19	17	89.5	44.7
Spelling 2	26	24	20	83.3	76.9
Run-ons	39	27	22	81.5	56.4
Preposition	36	9	7	77.8	19.4
Contractions	18	9	7	77.8	38.9
Punctuation	39	26	20	76.9	51.3
Fragments	25	16	12	75.0	48.0
S–V agreement	37	25	18	72.0	48.6
Word form	24	11	4	36.4	16.7
Mass/count Ns	5	10	3	30.0	60.0
Wrong words	18	7	2	28.6	11.1
Comparatives	5	0	0	NA	0
Total	465	252	184	73	39.6

Note: Spelling 1 = open/closed spelling; Spelling 2= other spelling
Source: Hoang and Kunnan (2016)

Double Flagging of Errors

(1) It is sure that there are many <Mass vs. count errors> conflict <Noun phrase consistency errors>.

(2) There are many <Mass vs. count errors> reason <Noun phrase consistency errors> why three milestones are important.

(3) Argument <Subject–verb agreement errors; it is suggested that *argument* be changed to *arguments* to agree with the plural verb form *take* > take <Subject–verb agreement errors; it is suggested that *take* be changed to *takes* to agree with the original subject noun *argument*> place.

In example (1), the word *conflict* in the earlier sentence should agree in number with its plural determiner *many*. Therefore, labeling it as <noun phrase consistency> (implying inconsistent number agreement) is the best way to draw the student's attention to his or her mistake. In example (2), the first label <mass vs. count errors> on the same word suggesting "if the sentence requires a singular noun, consider [much] or [many a] instead of 'many'" goes against the second suggestion of consistency. In example (3), two errors are pointed out again—argument and take. But if the first is fixed, the second does not need to be fixed. Therefore, such conflicting comments can confuse writers who may think that they need to fix two errors.

Word Choice Errors

Example (3) shows a word choice error that was falsely flagged.

(3) It is conspicuous that the <u>effects</u> not only exist among adults, but also exist among children.[3]

WriteToLearn's feedback: Consider using "affects" instead of "effects" here.

Additionally, *WriteToLearn* missed a lot of word choice errors detected by human raters, as shown in Example (4):

(4) First and foremost, having jobs while studying is an effective way to <u>adopt</u> ourselves to social life. (E24_P2)

WriteToLearn's feedback: no feedback.

In Example (4), the student should have used the word "adapt" instead of "adopt." Such word choice errors were frequently found in this study; *WriteToLearn* did not identify these errors.

But punctuation was the error type that *WriteToLearn* identified with the highest frequency when compared to the human rater. Most of the errors identified were improper use of commas. Example (4) illustrates comma errors correctly detected and useful feedback provided:

(5)   The Internet also bring a lot of pleasure to children ^ which can let children feel relaxed.

   WriteToLearn's feedback: Comma may be missing before or after a non-restrictive element. "Which" is used to introduce a word, phrase, or clause that is not essential to the meaning of the sentence. Set the element apart using a comma, or use "that" instead of "which."

Backing

The backing for this study is added to the backing for the Liu and Kunnan (2016) study that is discussed next.

Examining WriteToLearn: Liu and Kunnan (2016)

   Claim: WriteToLearn provides diagnostic feedback to students that is similar to human scoring and feedback.
   Warrant: Research on diagnostic feedback will provide evidence to support the comparability of *WriteToLearn* feedback and human feedback.

Liu and Kunnan examined *WriteToLearn* in terms of its scoring agreement with human ratings and its comparable diagnostic feedback with human feedback. I will focus only on the latter in this section. With data collected from 163 ESL writers in China, the authors compared *WriteToLearn's* diagnostic feedback with those provided by human readers in terms of diagnostic feedback to students.

Table 5.3 presents the results of the accuracy analysis of *WriteToLearn's* feedback. Column 1 has the list of 22 error types and Column 2 the total number of errors of each type identified by human raters in the sub-sample of 60 essays. Among the 22 error types, the three most frequent errors flagged by human raters were word choice (125), capitalization (115), and article errors (115). Students also made a lot of singular/plural (86), preposition (79), expression (78), and pronoun (60) errors. The number of the errors found in each of the other types ranged from 4 to 54.

The four columns (Columns 3 to 6) under *WriteToLearn* display the results of the evaluation of its error detection ability. Column 3 shows the total number of each error type identified by *WriteToLearn*. The software detected 15 out of 22 error types identified by human raters and missed the other 7 types of errors, including expression, modal verbs, passive voice, sentence structure, verb tense, word form, and word order. Among the 15 error types it did identify, more capitalization ($n = 104$), spelling ($n = 93$), and punctuation ($n = 92$) errors were detected than detected by human raters. Other error types were largely ignored

TABLE 5.3 Comparison between human reader and *WriteToLearn* error feedback

Error type	Human reader feedback Total	WriteToLearn feedback			
		Total	Hits	Precision %	Recall %
Connecting words	18	1	1	100	5.6
Capitalization	115	104	96	92.3	83.5
Subj–verb agreement	42	19	15	79	35.7
Comma splice	10	8	6	75	60
Singular/plural	86	12	9	75	10.5
Article	115	10	7	70	6.1
Run-on sentences	8	14	6	42.9	75
Punctuation	54	92	34	37	63
Spelling	52	93	18	19.4	34.7
Pronoun	60	7	1	14.3	1.7
Fragment	13	5	0	0	0
Possessive case	4	6	0	0	0
Preposition	79	1	0	0	0
Verb form	33	5	0	0	0
Word Choice	125	7	0	0	0
Expression	78	0	0	N/A	0
Modal verbs	10	0	0	N/A	0
Passive voice	12	0	0	N/A	0
Sentence structure	47	0	0	N/A	0
Verb tense	15	0	0	N/A	0
Word form	41	0	0	N/A	0
Word order	15	0	0	N/A	0
Total	1032	394	193	49	18.7

Note: Precision = Hits divided by *WriteToLearn* total (for example, the precision of capitalization: 96 ÷ 104 = 92.3); Recall = Hits divided by human reader total (for example, the recall of capitalization: 96 ÷115 = 83.5).

by the software, with the number of errors ranging from 1 to 19. Specifically, punctuation was identified with the highest frequency relative to human raters.

Column 2 under *WriteToLearn* reports its hits. Except for capitalization, punctuation, spelling, and subject–verb agreement, few errors of other error types were correctly identified. Additionally, five error types were totally misidentified, including fragment, possessive case, preposition, verb form, and word choice. Many error types misidentified by *WriteToLearn* are the most common mistakes committed by ELL students. For example, word choice is the most salient error type in terms of its high frequency, and *WriteToLearn* failed to detect such errors. *WriteToLearn* identified 7 errors against human raters' 125 word choice errors. Further, none of them were correctly identified. Additionally, *WriteToLearn* missed many word choice errors detected by human raters. Closely related with word choice errors, problematic expressions, including both non–idiomatic and unclear expressions (which are difficult for human raters to decipher the meaning of), were found; in total, human raters identified 78 such expression errors, none of which were detected by *WriteToLearn*.

Columns 3 and 4 under *WriteToLearn* present the precision and recall of its error feedback. *WriteToLearn* was most precise in detecting connecting word errors, as indicated by 100 percent precision. However, its recall was only 5.6 percent, indicating that it missed 94.4 percent of the errors identified by human raters. It was also highly precise in detecting capitalization errors, with a 92.3 percent precision and 83.5 percent recall. It demonstrated a similar pattern in identifying subject–verb agreement, comma splice, and singular/plural nouns and article errors with precision varying between 70 percent and 79 percent and recall below 50 percent (the only exception was comma splice with its recall of 60 percent). In its identification of run-on sentences, punctuation, spelling, and pronoun errors, *WriteToLearn* demonstrated less ability to identify errors with precision rates below 50 percent and recall rates ranging from 1.7 percent to 75 percent. Its precision and recall of fragment, possessive case, preposition, verb form, and word choice errors were 0 percent because it misidentified all five of these types of errors (as shown in the Hits column). *WriteToLearn*'s overall precision and recall in detecting errors out of the 22 error types were 49 percent and 18.7 percent respectively, meaning that it missed 81.3 percent errors that were identified by human raters and only 49 percent of the errors detected were true errors.

With these results, its overall performance did not meet the threshold of 90 percent precision suggested by previous researchers (Burstein et al., 2003) and, therefore, its automated feedback is not highly useful to students in their revision process. Specifically, *WriteToLearn* misidentified or failed to detect the error types that stand out as particularly salient in the writing samples of Chinese undergraduate English majors.

Compared to *MyAccess*'s overall precision and recall of 73 percent and 29.6 percent (described earlier), *WriteToLearn*'s overall performance in detecting errors committed by ELL students was poorer. *WriteToLearn* was less accurate in identifying article errors with its precision and recall of 70 percent and 6.1 percent when compared to *Criterion*'s 90 percent and 40 percent (see Han et al., 2006). It performed very poorly in detecting preposition errors (with both precision and recall of 0 percent) in strong contrast with *Criterion*'s 84 percent and 19 percent (see Tetreault & Chodorow, 2008a) and *MyAccess*'s 78 percent and 19 percent.

In terms of qualitative analysis, *WriteToLearn* failed to detect many word choice errors. It only identified 7 errors against human raters' 125 errors; in addition, none of them were correctly identified. Here are a few examples:

(1) First and foremost, having jobs while studying is an effective way to adopt ourselves to social life.
    No identification of the error in the word "adopt" and to use "adopting."
(2) It is conspicuous that the effects not only exist among adults, but also exist among children.

WriteToLearn's feedback: Considering using "affects" instead of "effects" here. No mention of placement of not only before its referent? Or the redundancy of the second "exists."

Backing and Rebuttal from MyAccess and WritetoLearn Studies

Findings from Hoang and Kunnan and Liu and Kunnan can be mapped onto the Toulmin argument structure in terms of the sub-claim of adequate Opportunity-to-Learn. Figure 5.4 presents this mapping of the results. This figure shows the principle and sub-claims of the Hoang and Kunnan and Liu and Kunnan studies and the relevant warrants and backing. In these two studies, there is insufficient convergent backing in support of the claim of OTL. The results are divergent; therefore, there is a rebuttal of the claim. In this type of event, the rebuttal of the claim invalidates or cancels the claim for now. A deferred judgment pending additional backing from further empirical studies is the most logical conclusion.

Opportunity for Success

Although OTL is particularly relevant to the school context, there are high-stakes, large-scale assessments outside the school context where a similar concept would be relevant. This concept is called Opportunity-for-Success (OFS), a way of thinking of how assessment agencies or institutions can ensure fair assessments to all test takers (Phillips, 1995). Phillips (1995) argues that the concept of OFS should be a fundamental fairness requirement, as it would provide all test takers a chance to succeed equally. The 14th Amendment of the U.S. Constitution's substantive due process clause discussed earlier indicates that assessments should not be unfair, arbitrary, or capricious. This means that there should be standardized conditions in assessment with equal opportunity for success and that no one is disadvantaged or penalized. The basic concept is that all test takers ought to be provided the opportunity to know what the assessment is about; to know the procedures, facilities, and equipment related to the assessment; to know the rules and regulations; to know the possible consequences of the assessment; and to know the opportunities for appeal, remedies, and legal recourse. OFS can thus be seen as a corollary of OTL and fitting well within the meaning of the substantive due process clause.

For example, although OTL criteria may be met by an assessment agency, it is also necessary for an assessment system to make its test takers succeed as much as possible (much like how a teacher attempts to make all her students successful). Thus, OFS goes beyond OTL in providing, for example, additional adequate opportunity in the relevant literacy and semiotic domains, social practices, and embodied experiences. The APA, AERA, and NCME *Standards* (1985, 1999 and 2014) and the many Codes of Fair Testing Practices (1988) and various other Codes of Ethics, Practice, and Guidelines discussed in Chapter 2 have also endorsed this general view of Opportunity-for-Success.

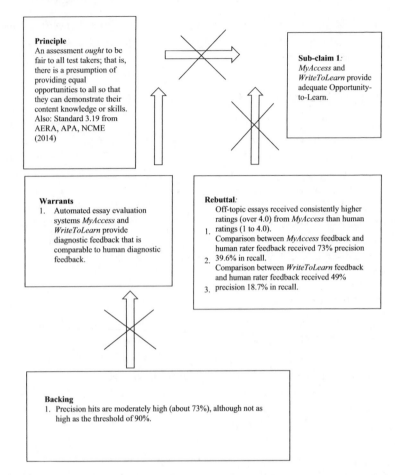

Principle
An assessment *ought* to be fair to all test takers; that is, there is a presumption of providing equal opportunities to all so that they can demonstrate their content knowledge or skills. Also: Standard 3.19 from AERA, APA, NCME (2014)

Sub-claim 1:
MyAccess and *WriteToLearn* provide adequate Opportunity-to-Learn.

Warrants
1. Automated essay evaluation systems *MyAccess* and *WriteToLearn* provide diagnostic feedback that is comparable to human diagnostic feedback.

Rebuttal:
Off-topic essays received consistently higher ratings (over 4.0) from *MyAccess* than human
1. ratings (1 to 4.0).
Comparison between *MyAccess* feedback and human rater feedback received 73% precision
2. 39.6% in recall.
Comparison between *WriteToLearn* feedback and human rater feedback received 49%
3. precision 18.7% in recall.

Backing
1. Precision hits are moderately high (about 73%), although not as high as the threshold of 90%.

FIGURE 5.4 Mapping Hoang and Kunnan's (2016) and Liu and Kunnan's (2016) findings on OTL claims with rebuttal. Note the X marks on the sub-claim and on the arrow from the backing to warrants to claim indicates that the claim cannot be supported.

Phillips (1995) pointed out that "the potential for violation of the Opportunity-for-Success requirement is of particular concern in the administration of high-stakes performance assessments" (p. 385). For example, suppose an assessment agency provided the option of using computers for typing in written responses to essay prompts. It is possible that some test takers would prefer this option as they may have been using computers prior to the assessment, but others may prefer to hand-write their answers as they may have had experience only with hand-writing their essays. Would the assessment agency provide both options? Therefore, in the Taylor and Kirsch (1998) study of TOEFL sample test takers, using the Opportunity-for-Success concept would have resulted in allowing both computer-based testing and the paper-and-pencil method based on personal test taker preference rather than for the test takers to have been forced to type in responses in the computer-based TOEFL.

Similarly, suppose an agency provided the option of using calculators for a high-stakes assessment but required all test takers to only use a particular brand and model. It is likely that some test takers who have used other brands or models prior to the assessment would be disadvantaged if they did not have sufficient familiarity and practice on the brand allowed in the assessment. Would the assessment agency allow many brands and models?

In these example cases, the Opportunity-for-Success may be interpreted differently for different test takers. At the same time assessment agencies should be responsible enough to provide equivalent conditions for all test takers and not conditions that disadvantage some test takers and violate the fundamental fairness requirement. Specific principles and claims and warrants and backing can be articulated for OFS. These arguments can then be evaluated in the same way as OTL warrants were examined.

OTL after the Assessment

The concept of OTL has focused on the opportunity that test takers need prior to taking an assessment. OFS is concerned with appropriate opportunities in an assessment itself. But there is another equally important aspect: OTL after the assessment.

It is always acknowledged in educational pedagogy that assessment should assist in the teaching–learning process. Therefore, in the classroom context, it is critical that students have the Opportunity-to-Learn from an assessment—particularly from their performances so that they can understand their strengths and weaknesses. This is often an overlooked aspect of assessment systems in schools, as they hardly provide direct feedback to individual students in a timely manner, although they may provide feedback to teachers, school administrators, and district or state officials.

Here is an egregious example from the *California Standards Test*. In this system, grade-level (Grades 3 to 8) assessments are administered to students in English, mathematics, and science in the month of March or April through a large-scale statewide assessment. But the assessment test performance results (and diagnostic information) are only available in June or July when students and teachers are on summer holidays. When students and teachers return to school in August, students have moved on to the next grade, and they will most probably have new teachers who may or may not have access to their new students' past year performances. It is also too late for students to meaningfully use their assessment results as they are in a new grade. Thus, OTL in its broadest sense is not available to students directly. Such assessment practices may not be uncommon in many school and college systems around the world.

Conclusion

In this chapter, the concept of OTL was presented and discussed as part of Principle 1, Fairness: Opportunity-to-Learn. The first type of OTL examined was primarily from the point of view of the school context, where it plays a significant factor in how it affects assessment performance in terms of content coverage, teacher competence, and instructional strategies and resources. The two illustrative studies presented found that OTL is a critical factor in student achievement in terms of proficiency and language status (ELL vs. non-ELL). The second type of OTL, providing adequate time in terms of notice and preparation, is also important in school contexts, where new assessments are being developed and launched in provinces or states. The third type of OTL, providing sufficient practice time with new technologies prior to the assessment, connects with the concept of Opportunity-for-Success. The fourth type of OTL, providing adequate opportunity in the relevant literacy and semiotic domains, social practices, and embodied experiences, goes beyond OTL into OFS matters. Further, OTL after the assessment is a neglected aspect of assessments despite what educational pedagogy promotes—that assessment can assist with the teaching–learning process.

The illustrative studies highlighted ways in which OTL can be examined and the kinds of information that assessment developers and reviewers and evaluators could use in their work. Results from the Herman et al. (2000) study examined the concept of OTL in the context of school-level instruction and assessment in the U.S. in terms of three variables: curriculum content, instructional strategies, and instructional resources. Results were also mapped onto the argumentation model in order to demonstrate how empirical findings can be fitted into the system. Two additional studies investigated the diagnostic feedback of two AEE systems (*MyAccess* and *WriteToLearn*) and found that there is divergent evidence in terms of whether they are offering adequate and appropriate feedback to student essay writers. As the results of these studies were not convergent, a claims argument and a rebuttal argument could be both presented, leading possibly to deferred judgments awaiting further empirical findings in support of either the original claims or the rebuttals. The next chapter will take up arguments for the meaningfulness (or validity) of an assessment.

Notes

1 From website: www.otlstatereport.org/national/summary/state-comparisons#.
2 Assessment agencies may articulate different sub-claims and warrants tailored to their needs: assessment for young children as opposed to young adults, or for university selection purposes as opposed to course placement purpose, etc.
3 In examples 3 to 5, words underlined are by the author to highlight the error; these are not underlined by the software.

References

Abedi, J., Courtney, M., Leon, S., Kao, J., & Azzam, T. (2006). *English language learners and math achievement: A study of opportunity to learn and language accommodation (Report No. 702).* Retrieved from the National Center for Research on Evaluation, Standards, and Student Testing (CRESST). Retrieved from: http://cresst.org/wp-content/uploads/R702.pdf

American Educational Research Association, American Psychological Association, the National Council on Measurement in Education. (1985). *Standards for educational and psychological testing.* Washington, DC: Author.

American Educational Research Association, American Psychological Association, the National Council on Measurement in Education. (1999). *Standards for educational and psychological testing.* Washington, DC: Author.

American Educational Research Association, American Psychological Association, the National Council on Measurement in Education. (2014). *Standards for educational and psychological testing.* Washington, DC: Author.

Banicky, L. A. (2000). *Opportunity to learn: Education Policy Brief 7.* Retrieved from: http://dspace.udel.edu/bitstream/handle/19716/2446/opp%20to%20learn.pdf?sequence=1&isAllowed=y

Burstein, J., Chodorow, M., & Leacock, C. (2003). *Criterion^{SM} online essay evaluation: An application for automated evaluation of student essays.* Palo Alto, CA: American Association for Artificial Intelligence.

Chodorow, M., Gamon, M., & Tetreault, J. (2010). The utility of article and preposition error correction systems for English language learners: Feedback and assessment. *Language Testing, 27,* 419–436.

Coles, G. (1998). *Reading lessons: The debate over literacy.* New York: Macmillan.

Coles, G. (2000). Commentary: "Direct, explicit, and systematic": Bad reading science. *Language Arts, 77,* 543–545.

Debra P. v. Turlington, 644 F.2d 397 (5th Cir. 1981), 730 F.2d 1405 (11th Cir. 1984). *Educational Researcher, 24,* 5–12.

Fourteenth Amendment to the United States Constitution. (1868, July 9). *Equal protection and due process clauses of the 14th Amendment of the U.S. Constitution.* Washington, DC: Constitution of the United States of America.

Gee, J. P. (2003). Opportunity to Learn: A language-based perspective on assessment. *Assessment in Education: Principles, Policy & Practice, 10,* 27–46.

Han, N. R., Chodorow, M., & Leacock, C. (2006). Detecting errors in English article usage by non-native speakers. *Natural Language Engineering, 12,* 115–129.

Herman, J. L., Klein, D. C. D., & Abedi, J. (2000). Assessing students' opportunity to learn: Teacher and student perspectives. *Educational Measurement, 19,* 16–24.

Hoang, G. T. L., & Kunnan, A. J. (2016). Automated essay evaluation for English language learners: A case study of MY Access. *Language Assessment Quarterly, 13,* 359–376.

Joint Committee on Testing Practices. (1988). *Code of fair testing practices in education.* Washington, DC: Author.

Kirsch, I., Jamieson, J., Taylor, C., & Eignor, D. (1998). *Computer familiarity among TOEFL examinees. Research Report 59.* Princeton, NJ: Educational Testing Service.

Kunnan, A. J. (2000). Fairness and justice for all. In A. J. Kunnan (Ed.), *Fairness and validation in language assessment* (pp. 1–13). Cambridge, UK: Cambridge University Press.

Liu, S., & Kunnan, A. J. (2016). Investigating the application of automated writing evaluation to Chinese undergraduate English majors: A case study of WriteToLearn. *CALICO, 33,* 71–91.

Moss, P. A., Pullin, D. C., Gee, J. P., Haertel, E. H., & Young, L. J. (2008). *Assessment, equity, and opportunity to learn.* Cambridge, UK: Cambridge University Press.

National Council of Teachers of English (NCTE). (1994). *Opportunity-to-learn standards.* Retrieved from: www.ncte.org/positions/statements/opptolearnstandards

The New London Group. (1996). A pedagogy of multiliteracies: Designing social futures. *Harvard Educational Review, 66,* 60–93.

Phillips, D. C. (1995). The good, the bad, and the ugly: The many faces of constructivism. *Educational Researcher, 24*, 5–12.

Porter, A. (1993). *Opportunity to learn: Brief No. 7.* Washington, DC: Office of Educational Research and Improvement.

The Schott Foundation for Public Education in Cambridge, Massachusetts. (2009). *Lost opportunity: 50 State Report: Executive summary.* Retrieved from: http://schottfound ation.org/resources/lost-opportunity-50-state-report

Schwartz, W. (1995). *Opportunity to learn standards: Their impact on urban students: Digest No. 110.* New York: ERIC Clearinghouse on Urban Education.

Street, B. (1995). *Social literacies: Critical approaches to literacy in education, development and ethnography.* London, UK: Longman.

Taylor, C., Jamieson, J., Eignor, D., & Kirsch, I. (1998). *The relationship between computer familiarity and performance on computer-based TOEFL test tasks.* (TOEFL Research Report No. 61). Princeton, NJ: Educational Testing Service.

Tetreault, J., & Chodorow, M. (2008a). *The ups and downs of preposition error detection in ESL.* Manchester, UK: COLING.

The UCLA Institute for Democracy, Education and Access. (2003). *Opportunity to Learn: Does California's school system measure up?* Retrieved from: http://justschools.gseis.ucla. edu/solution/pdfs/OTL.pdf

6

MEANINGFULNESS

Introduction

One of the most critical questions asked regarding an assessment and related assessment practice is whether the assessment and its score interpretation are valid for the specific purpose for which they were designed. More specifically, an assessment and assessment practice are generally queried or examined for evidence that can be collected in terms of the validity of its content, criteria, construct, and consequences. Bachman and Palmer (2010) used the term "meaningfulness" as an alternative to validity, as the term is not technical and thus could be clearer than validity to teachers, students, and other stakeholders. The term "meaningfulness" will be used in this chapter interchangeably with validity as theorists still use the latter term.

In the previous chapter, arguments related to the sub-claim of Opportunity-to-Learn were presented. In this chapter, arguments related to the sub-claim of meaningfulness are discussed. The sub-claim is illustrated with warrants and backing and with brief descriptions of findings from relevant empirical studies.

Defining Meaningfulness

The *meaningfulness* of an assessment is traditionally known as the validity of an assessment—or evidence from its content, criterion, construct, and consequences.[1] The four aspects of meaningfulness included in this discussion are (1) content-related evidence for meaningfulness, including its blueprint, specifications, curricula objectives, and items and tasks including task prompts for speaking and writing and listening and reading material; (2) criterion-related evidence, including whether test taker performance can predict future real-world performance in a similar domain; (3) construct-related evidence, including a theory of knowledge or ability at a particular level for a particular purpose, test taker performance, scoring, standard setting, and decision-making; and (4) the consequences of an assessment, including both micro and macro effects of an assessment on the teaching–learning context as well as on the community. In other words, the term meaningfulness is a cover-all term that is used interchangeably with validity.

In describing the different conceptualizations of meaningfulness or validity, Kane (2006a) classified the meanings, interpretations, and consequences—collectively considered conceptions of validation—into three developmental periods. He argued that the first period in the 1950s was dominated by the criterion model—both concurrent and predictive in which validity was defined in terms of "the correlation between the actual test scores and the 'true' criterion score" (Cureton, 1951, p. 623). The criterion model for concurrent validation resulted in finding score estimates of a criterion assessment at the same time as the estimates for a new assessment that is being validated. For predictive validation, the interest was in predicting future performance (in college, in the workplace, etc.) from score estimates from an assessment.

Dissatisfied with difficulties in defining the criterion, researchers in the 1970s turned to the content of the assessment. Their thinking was that, surely, if the content of an assessment was from a pool of tasks in the domain of interest, content validity could be ensured. However, researchers found that there were difficulties in judging whether there was sufficient content representativeness in an assessment from the domain of interest. And without any test taker performance data, content analysis information was limited (Cronbach, 1971). Messick (1989) summed up this problem best when he argued that content-based validity evidence was useful in providing domain representativeness and relevance, but did not provide direct evidence "for the inferences to be made from test scores" (p. 17).

As inadequacies of both criterion and content validation were highlighted, Loevinger (1957) argued that "since predictive, concurrent, and content validities are all essentially ad hoc, construct validity is the whole of validity from a scientific point of view" (p. 636). This construct model in the 1980s was the start of the second period, but gained popularity only when Messick (1989) proposed construct validity as a unified notion in his landmark essay. He proposed that the previous view of three types or aspects of validity (content, criterion, and construct) could be seen as different pieces of evidence toward construct validity. Messick (1989) stated that validity is

> an integrated evaluative judgment of the degree to which empirical evidence and theoretical rationales support the *adequacy* and *appropriateness of inferences* and *actions* based on test scores or other modes of assessment.
>
> *(p. 13; italics in original)*

He conceptualized in a 2 × 2 matrix that validity included two interconnected facets of validity: the *justification* of an assessment through the evidential or consequential basis and the *function or outcome* of an assessment in terms of score interpretation and score use. Placing both types of evidence in equal part of an assessment's validation process was an innovative way of thinking of assessment validity.

In the later part of the 1990s, researchers built on Cronbach's (1988) notion of an evaluation argument. Thus, in the third period in the 1990s, the notion of an argument-based approach to validity was postulated by various researchers such as Bachman (2005); Kane (1992, 2006b); and Crooks, Kane, and Cohen (1996). Bachman and Palmer (2010) have made a case for this approach to validation by proposing an "Assessment Use Argument" approach using the Toulmin argumentation model.

Argumentation for Meaningfulness

Argumentation for meaningfulness should proceed in previously indicated ways: principles should lead to claims, and these claims need to be supported through warrants and backing. In order to find appropriate backing, a number of analyses need to be conducted. They include (1) *Analysis of content and construct* (e.g., assessment blueprints, specifications, content, and performance standards; the actual test item or tasks or prompts; rubrics; and scoring guidelines); (2) *Analysis of cognitive process* (e.g., the behaviors used in responding to tasks, strategy use); (3) *Analysis of the items and the test* in terms of its consistency (e.g., internal consistency, inter-rater consistency, reliability/dependability); (4) *Analysis of test performance* (e.g., test performance in terms of answers provided in both selected and constructed-response formats as well as written and spoken performance; internal structure); (5) *Analysis of consequences* (e.g., scoring, standard setting and decision-making, washback, and beneficence).

But as assessments for different purposes may have different claims, analyses will need to be tailored to the specific claims and evidence from different analyses brought together. Cronbach (1971) made this point decades earlier:

> Validation of an assessment calls for an integration of many kinds of evidence. The varieties of investigations are not alternatives any one of which would be adequate. The investigations supplement one another. . . For purposes of exposition, it is necessary to subdivide *what in the end must be a comprehensive, integrated evaluation of the test.*
>
> *(p. 445; italics in original)*

With this brief background and specific analyses needed for argumentation in support of claims, the APA, AERA, and NCME *Standards* (2014) for meaningfulness (validity) are presented.

Standards *for Meaningfulness (Validity)*

The well-known APA, AERA, and NCME *Standards* (2014) listed 25 different standards that assessment agencies ought to meet under three clusters: (1) establishing intended uses and interpretations, (2) samples and settings, and (3) forms of validity evidence. The overarching standard is designed to convey the primary focus of the standard, and the specific standards refer to the three clusters.

Validity

Standard 1.0

Clear articulation of each intended test score interpretation for a specified use should be set forth, and appropriate validity evidence in support of each intended interpretation should be provided.

(p. 23)

Cluster 1: Establishing intended uses and interpretations

Standard 1.1

The test developer should set forth clearly how test scores are intended to be interpreted and consequently used. The population(s) for which a test is intended should be delimited clearly, and the construct or constructs that the test is intended to assess should be described clearly.

(p. 23)

Standard 1.4

If a test score is interpreted for a given use in a way that has not been validated, it is incumbent on the user to justify the new interpretation for that use, providing a rationale and collecting new evidence, if necessary.

(p. 24)

Cluster 3: Specific forms of validity evidence

(a)   Content-oriented evidence

Standard 1.11

When the rationale for test score interpretation for a given use rests in part on the appropriateness of test content, the procedures followed in specifying and generating test content should be described and justified in reference to the intended population to be tested and the construct the test is intended to measure or the domain it is intended to represent.

(p. 26)

(b)   Evidence regarding internal structure

Standard 1.13

If the rationale for a test score interpretation for a given test depends on premises about the relationships among test items or among parts of the test, evidence concerning the internal structure of the test should be provided.

(pp. 26–27)

The APA, AERA, and NCME *Standards* (2014) also documented its thinking on consistency in terms of reliability/precision and errors of measurement. It listed 20 different standards that assessment agencies ought to meet in eight clusters: (1) specifications for replications of the testing procedure, (2) evaluating reliability/precision, (3) reliability/generalizability coefficients, (4) factors affecting reliability/precision, (5) standard errors of measurement, (6) decision consistency, (7) reliability/precision of group means, and (8) documenting reliability/precision. The overarching standard is designed to convey the primary focus of the standard and specific standards that are related to each of the clusters.

Reliability/Precision and Errors of Measurement

Standard 2.0

Appropriate evidence of reliability/precision should be provided for the interpretation for each intended score use.

(p. 42)

Cluster 2: Evaluating reliability/precision

Standard 2.3

For each total score, subscore, or combination of scores that is to be interpreted, estimates of relevant indices of reliability/precision should be reported.

(p. 43)

Standard 2.5

Reliability estimation procedure should be consistent with the structure of the test.

(p. 43)

Cluster 3: Reliability/generalizability coefficients

Standard 2.6

A reliability or generalizability coefficient (or standard error) that addresses one kind of variability should not be interpreted as interchangeable with indices that address other kinds of variability, unless their definitions of measurement error can be considered equivalent.

Comment: Internal-consistency, alternate-form, and test-retest coefficients should not be considered equivalent, as each incorporates a unique definition of measurement error.

A relevant standard that addressed the issues related to test specifications and blueprints was under the standards for test design and development. This standard was separated into four thematic clusters: (1) standards for test specifications, (2) standards for test development and review, (3) standards for developing test administration and scoring procedure and materials, and (4) standards for test revision. The overarching standard is presented here, followed by a few specific standards relevant to this discussion.

Test Design and Development

Standard 4.0

Tests and testing programs should be designed and developed in a way that supports the validity of interpretations of the test scores for their intended uses. Test developers and publishers should document steps taken during the design and development process to provide evidence of fairness, reliability, and validity of intended uses for individuals in the intended examinee population.

Cluster 1: Standards for test specifications

Standard 4.1

Test specifications should describe the purpose(s) of the test, the definition of the construct or domain measured [in] the intended examinee population, and interpretation for intended use. The specifications should include a rationale supporting the interpretations and uses of test results for the intended purpose(s).

(p. 85)

Standard 4.2

In addition to describing intended uses of the test, the test specifications should define the content of the test, the proposed test length, the item formats, the desired psychometric properties of the test items and the test, and the ordering of items and sections. Test specifications should also specify the amount of time allowed for testing; directions for the test takers; procedures to be used for test administrations, including permissible variations; any materials to be used; and scoring and reporting procedures.

(p. 86)

The listed standards for validity and reliability/precision together constitute the meaningfulness of an assessment. These standards, along with principles of fairness, can be used to build an argument for meaningfulness through claims and sub-claims.

Building an Argument for Meaningfulness

Principles

Keeping in mind the definition and analyses of meaningfulness and limiting its focus to the *Standards* listed earlier, the general principle of fairness is articulated and followed with specific claims.

Principle 1: Fairness

Principle: An assessment *ought* to be fair to all test takers by being meaningful in terms of what is meant to be assessed.

Claims, Warrants, and Backing

A general claim regarding meaningfulness of an assessment and sub-claims could be operationalized into key warrants that can be articulated as illustrated in Extract 6.1 and Figure 6.1. The examples used in this chapter all relate to school and college assessments. A presentation of the general principle, then the claims and sub-claims and warrants and backing follow.

EXTRACT 6.1   FAIRNESS ARGUMENT FOR MEANINGFULNESS

Principle: Fairness

An assessment *ought* to be fair to all test takers by being meaningful in terms of what is meant to be assessed.

General Claim: A classroom language assessment or a college entrance assessment is fair to all test takers.

Sub-claim 1a: A classroom or college language assessment is meaningful in terms of the blueprint and specifications and content standards, and language, content, and topics are based on curriculum objectives, standards, or theory of knowledge.
Warrant 1a: Research on a classroom or college language assessment will show that the assessment is meaningful in terms of the blueprint and specifications and content standards, and language, content, and topics are based on curriculum objectives, standards, or theory of knowledge.

Sub-claim 1b: A classroom or college language assessment contributes to meaningfulness through its consistency.
Warrant 1b: Research on a classroom or college language assessment will show that the assessment contributes to meaningfulness through its consistency.

Sub-claim 1c: A classroom college language assessment is meaningful in terms of its internal factor structure.
Warrant 1c. Research on a classroom college language assessment will show that the assessment is meaningful in terms of its internal factor structure.

Also: see *Standards 1.0, 2.0, 3.0, 4.0* from AERA, APA, NCME (2014)

Sub-claim 1a: A classroom or college language assessment is meaningful in terms of the blueprint and specifications and content standards and language, content, and topics are based on curriculum objectives, standards, or theory of knowledge.

Warrant 1a: Research on a classroom or college language assessment will show that the assessment is meaningful in terms of the blueprint and specifications and content standards, and language, content, and topics are based on curriculum objectives, standards, or theory of knowledge.

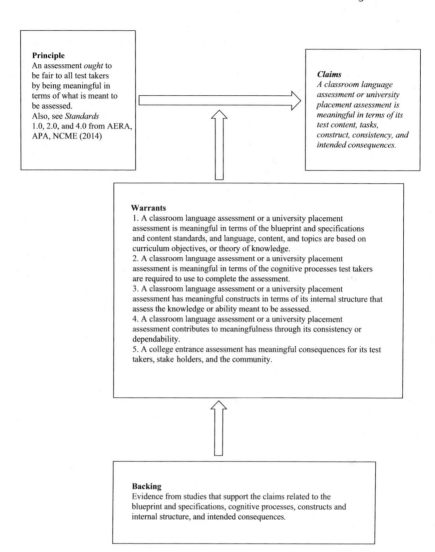

Principle
An assessment *ought* to be fair to all test takers by being meaningful in terms of what is meant to be assessed.
Also, see *Standards* 1.0, 2.0, and 4.0 from AERA, APA, NCME (2014)

Claims
A classroom language assessment or university placement assessment is meaningful in terms of its test content, tasks, construct, consistency, and intended consequences.

Warrants
1. A classroom language assessment or a university placement assessment is meaningful in terms of the blueprint and specifications and content standards, and language, content, and topics are based on curriculum objectives, or theory of knowledge.
2. A classroom language assessment or a university placement assessment is meaningful in terms of the cognitive processes test takers are required to use to complete the assessment.
3. A classroom language assessment or a university placement assessment has meaningful constructs in terms of its internal structure that assess the knowledge or ability meant to be assessed.
4. A classroom language assessment or a university placement assessment contributes to meaningfulness through its consistency or dependability.
5. A college entrance assessment has meaningful consequences for its test takers, stake holders, and the community.

Backing
Evidence from studies that support the claims related to the blueprint and specifications, cognitive processes, constructs and internal structure, and intended consequences.

FIGURE 6.1   Generic structure of principle, claims warrants, and backing for Principle 1, Fairness—Meaningfulness

As this is most often one of the first steps in assessment development, there needs to be a clear domain description of target language use so that the blueprint, specifications, language, content, and topics are based on content standards, curriculum objectives, or a theory of language knowledge. Although the terms blueprint and specifications are used interchangeably sometimes, in this chapter a blueprint is the overall plan for the assessment, and specifications provide details regarding item/task, content, and topic coverage and are representative of the domain or content. Some researchers consider specifications narrowly and only consider guidelines for writing test items and the test items themselves as part of specifications, but others consider specifications to include everything in the test development process. Here are a few views.

Lynch and Davidson (1994) discussed a criterion-referenced test specification (or test specs) model using Popham's five components in test development: (1) mandate select skill, (2) write spec, (3) write item/task from spec, (4) assemble test and pilot/trial, and (5) finalize operational measure. However, a more comprehensive test development process was later proposed by Fulcher and Davidson (2009), who compared test development to architectural design and building with three layers of documentation: models, frameworks, and test specifications. According to this view, as outlined in Kim and Davidson (2015),

> models provide theoretical foundations of knowledge skills, and abilities that are necessary for successful performance in a domain of interest, frameworks state test purposes, lay out constructs to be tested, and explain how to elicit the evidence for the constructs and to translate the observation of the evidence into a score... test specs are generative documents from which equivalent test items or tasks can be built... they are like the production blueprints that a builder would use during construction.
>
> *(p. 788)*

Schmeiser and Welch (2006) took a much broader view and argued for a test philosophy prior to test design so that the test has a firm foundation. Under philosophy, they include, "an explicit linkage between test purpose and the criterion that defines the test domain, that is, what will and will not be measured in the test (p. 314)." The purpose of test specification, they argued, is

> to provide direction for construction... Derived directly from test philosophy, test purpose and use, test audience, and empirical validity evidence gathered for the test, test specifications delineate the requirements for the subsequent stages of development, review, field testing, assembly, and evaluation of the end product.
>
> *(p. 314)*

Webb et al. (2006) argued from a researcher's perspective that a well-delineated test specifications can help in ensuring that valid inferences can be made from test results. Judging from the views and the overarching *Standards* 4.0 listed earlier, there is no doubt that test specifications play a significant role in providing guidance for an overall plan of an assessment, for assessment development, for documenting the development process, and for the validation process. Content analyses of all the assessment materials mentioned earlier would provide evidence for the backing for the claim and sub-claims.

Sub-claim 1b: A classroom or college language assessment contributes to meaningfulness through its consistency.

Warrant 1b: Research on a classroom or college language assessment will show that the assessment contributes to meaningfulness through its consistency.

Assessment scores need to be analyzed in terms of their consistency or reliability, dependability, and generalizability. In a norm-referenced test (NRT), the concern is with the consistency of scores (technically, consistency of ranking, but in practice it is generally treated as consistency of scoring), which is referred to as reliability. In a criterion-referenced test (CRT), the concern is with two areas of consistency, both referred to as dependability. The first is the dependability of scores, and the second is the dependability of classification. In general, however, it is important to provide an index of score consistency (and classification consistency, for CRT), as well as an estimate of the margin of error associated with the estimate (for NRT, the standard error of measurement; for CRT, the criterion-referenced confidence interval) (see Bachman, 1990; Brown, 2014, for details).

NRT and CRT performance data can be used to analyze the internal consistency of a test section or for the whole test when there is only one test administration. Cronbach's alpha can serve as an estimate of this type of internal consistency. This procedure provides assurance that the test items in a section or in the whole test are consistently measuring the construct of interest.

When analyzing scores based on ratings, there is interest in finding out whether a rater would give the same score at different times or occasions. Thus, both inter-rater consistency (consistency of ratings from different raters) and intra-rater consistency (consistency of each rater) are important. The simplest approach is to estimate the consistency of ratings through a correlation of the sets of ratings. This correlation is often reported by itself, but to be used as a reliability estimate, it should be adjusted using the Spearman–Brown prophecy formula.

Two alternative paradigms for examining measurement consistency developed in the last few decades are generalizability theory (G theory) and item response theory (IRT). G theory can be used to analyze rated performances, as in tests of speaking or writing, and to identify which facets of the measurement process are contributing most to unreliability. G theory also provides estimates of the margin of error for test scores, as well as classification consistency for CRTs. IRT is particularly suited for working with large (i.e., numbering hundreds or thousands) test-taker groups and an IRT variant known as the Many-Faceted Rasch model, which is useful with rated performances. Its advantages are that it provides ability estimates for each test taker and difficulty or severity estimates for each rater, task, or rubric sub-scale.

Sub-claim 1c: A classroom college language assessment is meaningful in terms of its internal factor structure.

Warrant 1c: Research on a classroom college language assessment will show that the assessment is meaningful in terms of its internal factor structure.

Constructs (or latent variables) are the basis for the operationalization of test items and tasks in an assessment. Bachman and Palmer (1996) defined construct "as the specific definition of an ability that provides the basis of a given test or test task and interpreting scores based on this task" (p. 66). These constructs could be based on a theoretical model of language like Canale and Swain's (1980) communicative language ability model or Bachman (1990) and Bachman and Palmer's (1996) Communicative Language Ability (CLA).

Quantitative analyses such as exploratory factor analysis (EFA) or confirmatory factor analysis (CFA) of test performance data could identify a parsimonious and interpretable structure of an assessment, which can reveal the constructs used in an assessment. For example, if the test performance data analysis of a reading and listening assessment revealed that a two-factor structure was the best solution with items of a reading assessment loading on one factor and items of a listening assessment loading on another factor, then the internal structure matches the design of the assessment. Thus, it can be said that the internal structure of the assessment is consistent with the design of the assessment, and the evidence supports the two constructs. But if the factor structure does not match the design of the assessment, as there is a different factor structure when compared to the test design (with little or no discernible pattern with the loadings of items and factors), it can be said that the internal structure of the assessment is not consistent with the design of the assessment. The evidence in this case does not support the two constructs, and a rebuttal can be staged. Thus, test performance analyses could provide evidence for this warrant and could contribute to the backing for this sub-claim.

Illustrative Studies

Several studies that focus on the meaningfulness of an assessment are presented here. The studies are related to test blueprints and specifications, assessment consistency or dependability, and internal structure.

Blueprints and Specifications

Blueprint and Test Specifications: Johnstone, Moen, Thurlow, Matchett, Hausmann, and Scullin (2007)

Claim: Blueprints and specifications adequately represent the reading assessment in U.S. schools and therefore the assessment is meaningful.

Sub-claim: Blueprints and specifications adequately represent the reading assessment in schools in 49 states of the U.S.

Sub-claim 1a: The themes related to the purposes and constructs of assessments are adequately represented.

Sub-claim 1b: How the themes are related to the purposes and constructs of assessments is adequate.

Sub-claim 1c: The number of items assigned to particular constructs adequately represents the constructs of the assessment.

Warrants 1a to 1c: Research from a large-scale survey of U.S. surveys of 49 states will provide evidence to support sub-claims 1a to 1c.

This study is a large-scale survey of the blueprints and specifications related to reading assessments in all states in the U.S. This subject in U.S. schools is called language arts and is meant for students who have first-language–level proficiency in English. The survey involved examining assessment blueprints or test specifications from four perspectives: "(1) themes related to the purposes and constructs of assessments, (2) how those themes related to state standards, (3) the number of items assigned to particular constructs, and (4) the types of items typically found in state-wide assessments" (p. 1). Only the first of the three studies is reported here. In terms of claims, the general claims could be that all the state blueprints or specifications specifically mention reading skills to be assessed in both grade levels and that there is a match between states' constructs standards and assessment blueprints (see APA, AERA, and NCME *Standards* 4.0, 2014).

The first part of this study was conducted by examining school-level documents related to Grades 4 and 8. These levels were selected by the authors as they represented the early years of No Child Left Behind legislation in which the National Assessment of Educational Progress was administered. The document analysis method involved reading each of the 49 state blueprints, which explicitly identified the constructs to be assessed in the state assessment. Each of the blueprints or specifications reviewed indicated that states assessed a wide variety of skills on their reading assessments. These skills were coded into three categories: (1) foundational skills, (2) comprehension, and (3) analysis and interpretation of text. Sub-categories were also distinguished within each of these categories. The number and percentage of states that directly assessed each sub-category of foundational skills, comprehension, and analysis and interpretation is presented in Table 6.1. The only noticeable difference was in word identification in terms of both the number and percentage of states that addressed this skill across Grades 4 and 8 (14 vs. 6; 29 percent vs. 12 percent). All other skill areas were addressed by the states in similar numbers. However, only reading comprehension was addressed by most states across the grade levels (28 and 29; 57 percent vs. 58 percent).

Table 6.2 presents the presence of the constructs listed in the state standards documents and in the reading assessment blueprints in the states. Here, there is a close match in the two columns in the 27 areas, but a noticeable absence in 5 areas: personal growth through reading, reflection upon culture through reading, reflection upon self through reading, relate to real life, and socialization into literary communities. Further, four other areas with Xs next to the constructs in Column

1 instead of Xs in Column 2 are areas in which they are "assessed in a manner substantially different from that indicated in state standards" (Johnstone et al., 2007; website: www.cehd.umn.edu/NCEO/onlinepubs/PARA/blueprint/).

According to Johnstone et al. (2007), the findings are a mixed bag:

> In sum, according to state test specifications and blueprints, most state stand-ards are assessed in some way on state assessments. Standards related to the personal development of children are not currently measured in large-scale assessments. Likewise, standards that require authentic research activities are limited to the information provided in the test itself. Of the 27 themes Thompson et al. found in state reading standards, 22 are found in state test blueprints and assessments at least to some extent. Four of these 22 are assessed in a manner substantially different from that indicated in state standards.
>
> *[www.cehd.umn.edu/NCEO/onlinepubs/PARA/blueprint/]*

Backing

In terms of backing, as the findings are not entirely positive, the claim that assess-ment blueprints or specifications for reading are adequately represented in the 49-state survey cannot be supported. In this type of event, the rebuttal of the claim invalidates or cancels the claim for now. In this type of situation, a deferred judgment, pending additional backing from further empirical studies, is the most logical conclusion. The Toulmin argumentation model is not presented for this study as the state authorities did not have direct claims.

TABLE 6.1 Percentage of state blueprints or specifications dedicated to assessment purposes (based on 49 states) in Grades 4 and 8

Purpose (Construct)	Grade 4		Grade 8	
	Count	%	Count	%
Foundational skills				
Vocabulary	17	35	17	35
Word identification	14	29	6	12
Word analysis	8	16	8	16
Fluency	4	8	4	8
Comprehension				
Reading comprehension	28	57	29	59
Comprehension: Literary text	12	24	13	27
Comprehension: Expository text	8	16	11	22
Analysis and interpretation				
Analysis and interpretation (general)	18	37	18	37
Analysis: Literary text	12	24	13	27
Analysis: Expository text	10	20	10	20

Consistency or Dependability of a Criterion-Referenced Test: Kunnan (1992)

Claim: The CRT is meaningful to test takers, as it is consistent.

Sub-claim 1a: The CRT is meaningful to test takers, as the agreement of placement classification decisions is consistent.

Warrant 1a: Research on the CRT is meaningful to test takers, as the agreement of placement classification decisions will show that the assessment is consistent.

Sub-claim 1b: The CRT is meaningful to test takers, as the agreement of decisions at cut scores is consistent.

Warrant 1b: Research on the CRT is meaningful to test takers, as the agreement of decisions at cut scores will show that the assessment is consistent.

Sub-claim 1c: The CRT is meaningful to test takers, as the dependability of domain scores of the assessment is consistent.

Warrant 1c: Research on the CRT is meaningful to test takers, as the dependability of domain scores of the assessment will show that the assessment is consistent.

TABLE 6.2 Constructs found in state standards vs. state reading assessment blueprints

Construct	Standards	Blueprints
Compare	x	x
Context	x	x
Critical analysis	x	x
Expository elements	x	x
Fluency	x	x
Following instructions	x★★	x
Higher-order thinking	x	x
Inferential comprehension	x	x
Language conventions	x	x
Literal comprehension	x	x
Literary elements	x	x
Meta literacy	x	x
Mine information	x★★	x
Organize information	x★★	x
Personal growth through reading	x	
Phonemic knowledge	x	x
Problem solving	x★★	x
Question authors	x	x
Reflection upon print	x	x
Reflection upon culture through reading	x	
Reflection upon self through reading	x	
Relate to real life	x	
Respond to text	x	x
Socialization into literary communities	x	

(Continued)

TABLE 6.2 (Continued)

Construct	Standards	Blueprints
Strategic, non-phonemic skills	x	x
Vocabulary	x	x
Word recognition	x	x

Notes: "x" means that at least one state had the particular construct represented in its standards or blueprints; ★★ means standards were intended for authentic research activities that may or may not be reflected in large-scale assessments.

The purpose of this study was to investigate the consistency or dependability of a CRT—the New ESL Placement Exam (NESLPE, for short) used for placing international students into ESL classes at UCLA. The main research question was: What was the consistency or dependability of the NESLPE across the four ESL classes (33A, 33B, 33C, and 35 and Exempt) as well as for the total class group?

The study subjects were 390 non-native speakers of English who had been required to take the NESLPE as part of the admission and placement procedures at UCLA. All the subjects were given Form A of the NESLPE. The NESLPE followed Popham's (1978) principles of criterion-referenced test development. The test had 100 multiple-choice and true/false items in all: 30 in the listening section, 40 in the reading and vocabulary section, 30 in the grammar section, and an additional composition writing section. However, this study will only consider 90 of the multiple-choice and true/false items: 30 from each section. This was necessary so that the GENOVA software program (Crick and Brennan, 1982), which requires a balanced design for all sections (30 items in each of the three sections) for computing generalizability statistics, could be used.

Criterion-referenced estimates of dependability were classified by Hambelton, Swaminathan, Algina, and Coulson (1978) into three different dependability concepts: (a) agreement of mastery classification decisions (placement classifications, for this study); (b) agreement of decisions at cut scores; and (c) dependability of domain scores. The first concept is concerned with the consistency of placement decisions, the second concept with the deviations of student scores about the cut-off scores and the consistency of these deviations across forms, and the third concept with the consistency of the individual's score.

Agreement of Placement Classification Decisions

Two threshold-loss agreement indices were computed to provide coefficients that estimate the agreement of placement classification decisions. In the case of the abbreviated NESLPE, students who were exempted from any ESL class are those who secured total scores of 80 percent or above (the cut score was 72). Students who scored less than 80 percent were placed in ESL classes that matched their overall ability in terms of the score. Table 6.3 provides the ESL class group, the score range, and the cut score for each level. In addition, it presents the dependability indices

TABLE 6.3 Dependability of placement classification decisions

Group	Range	Cut score		Coefficients	
		Raw	Proportion	p_o	$\hat{K}$
★	0–46	–	–	–	–
33A	47–55	47	.52	.98	.58
33B	56–64	56	.62	.95	.63
33C	65–71	65	.72	.90	.68
35 & Ex.	72–90	72	.80	.86	.71

★ Low for regular UCLA placement

(p_o and $\hat{K}$) for each of these placement classification decisions for all groups: 33A, 33B, 33C, and 35 and exempt groups. The p_o agreements are high for all groups, decreasing as the level goes higher. The dependability of placement classification decisions as the cut scores is quite high and more agreeable at 33A and 33B in comparison to 33C and 35 and exempt groups. Still, they are high, especially given the observation by Subkoviak (1980) that p_o agreement coefficients for one administration will be an underestimate of the values that would be obtained using two separate administrations. Coefficient p_o would therefore be best suited for the purpose of judging the dependability of placement classifications.

Coefficient $\hat{K}$ estimates are noticeably lower than the p_o coefficients because they are corrected for chance agreements (as though there were more than one administration). In addition, they are ordered differently from the fit coefficients for the different class groups, with the agreement higher for the high ability group and lower for the lower ability group.

Agreement of Decisions at Cut Scores

Although the p_o and $\hat{K}$ coefficients estimate the agreement of mastery/non-mastery decisions, treating these as categories, squared-error loss agreement indices do this with sensitivity along the score continuum. This approach, in other words, takes into consideration differences of students' scores from the cut score, that is, degrees of mastery or non-mastery, rather than the simple categorization.

Table 6.4 presents information from the D-studies for the whole group based on the fixed model design. This design sets the size of the object of measurement, P, at infinite; the test section facet (or T) to three; and the items facet (or I) to sizes of 20, 30, and 40. Reading Table 6.4 from left to right, it is apparent that there is a steady drop in Φ (λ) agreement coefficients from low to high cut scores: they are higher for lower scores and lower for the higher scores at the right end. For example, the first row shows a drop from 0.97 to 0.91. Comparing the Φ (λ) for differing numbers of items, it is clear that the coefficients increase as the number of items increases.

TABLE 6.4 Agreement of decisions at cut scores (from the D studies). Fixed model design: P = Indefinite, T = 3, I = 20, 30, 40

Group	33A	33B	33C	35 and Ex
Raw cut score	47	56	65	72
Items = 20 Φ (λ)	.97	.95	.91	.91
Items = 20 Φ (λ)	98	.96	.94	.94
Items = 40 Φ (λ)	.99	.97	.95	.95

Dependability of Domain Scores

Table 6.5 presents Brennan's Φ coefficient (1980), the index of domain score dependability, for the different groups with facet T fixed at 3 and facet I fixed at 30. These conditions reflected the present format of the NESLPE. Because the Φ coefficient can be interpreted as a general-purpose estimate of the dependability of a domain score of a CR test and the total group provides the highest coefficient, the NESLPE could be said to be best dependable for the total group. Brennan's Φ coefficients were high for the 33A group and for the total group, but dropped in the middle with the 33C group getting the lowest coefficients. As for the other groups, the 33A group had the next highest coefficient followed by the 33B group. The 33C group had a low coefficient, indicating the low dependability of the domain score for this group.

From this information, two observations could be made: One, that the NESLPE was not dependable to the same extent for all groups. A possible reason for this observation could be that the NESLPE was not able to assess the ability of students at all levels accurately because there was not enough item-to-specification congruence at all levels. In addition, if the specifications were more carefully laddered, they would have a better chance of assessing student ability at the different levels.

Backing

In terms of backing, the dependability estimates of the NESLPE showed that consistency or dependability for the total group was different from the estimates for

TABLE 6.5 Dependability of domain scores (from the D studies). Fixed model design P = Infinite, T = 3, I = 30

Group	Coefficient Φ
33A	.80
33B	.55
33C	.30
35 and Ex	.48
Total	.93

the four ESL class groups. Agreement indices also differed across cut scores. But although dependability indices for some groups were unacceptably low, agreement indices for all cut scores were generally above acceptable levels. Furthermore, it showed that the dependability of domain scores was the lowest for the 33C and 35 and exempt groups. Thus, this analysis showed that test scores were not equally dependable for all groups and were very undependable for two out of the four groups. These low-dependability estimates for the two groups could be due to less accurate item-to-specification congruence for those groups.

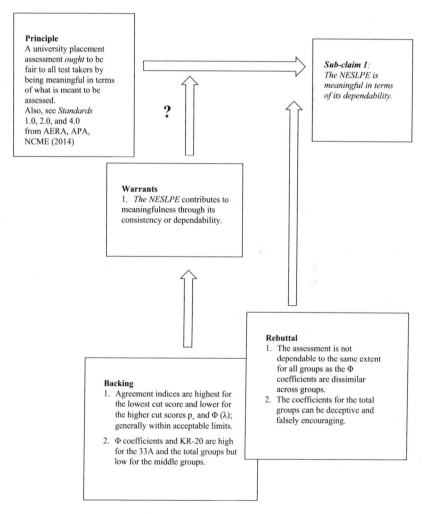

FIGURE 6.2 Principle, claims, warrants, and backing for Principle 1, Fairness, sub-claim 1 (dependability or consistency) with rebuttal. Note the question mark on the arrow from the warrants to the claim indicates doubts whether the claim can be supported.

Figure 6.2 presents the Toulmin argumentation model for the general claims and backing for the claim of consistency. As can be seen, the claim of consistency for a CRT is backed up by research findings from the dependability studies. But the results from these studies do not support the claim of consistency of the CRT fully. Hence, there was a rebuttal of the claim, although the backing for the rebuttal did not defeat the claim but only undercut it mildly. Therefore, a deferred judgment pending additional backing from further empirical studies is the most logical conclusion.

Internal Structure Analyses: Kunnan (1992)

Claim: The CRT is meaningful to test takers.

Sub-claim 1: The CRT is meaningful to test takers, as the internal structure of the assessment is similar to the assessment design.

Warrant 1: Research on the CRT will show that the assessment is meaningful to test takers, as the internal structure of the assessment is similar to the assessment design.

In Kunnan (1992), internal structure analyses of the NESLPE were conducted with the same data, N = 390, with 33A, 33B, 33C, 35, and Ex. classes as described for the consistency study earlier. This study was conducted with EFA; it was performed on the Pearson product–moment correlations for the six sections of the test data. These data were two sections of listening (LIST1 and LIST2), two sections of reading (READ1 and READ2), and two sections of grammar (GRAM1 and GRAM2).

All correlation matrices were examined for appropriateness of the common factor model. They satisfied Bartlett's test of sphericity; all group matrices had high values for this statistic, and the associated significance level was small. Another test used to examine the correlation matrices was the Kaiser–Meyer–Olkin measure of sampling adequacy. In this analysis, values ranged from 0.90 for the total group to 0.44 for the 33C group. All group matrices with values above 0.50 are said to have adequate sampling (Kaiser, 1974); only the 33B and 33C groups had marginally less adequate sampling.

Several EFA extraction methods were used for all the groups: the principal axes factoring, alpha factoring, and unweighted least squares. After initial factor matrices and rotated matrices of all extractions were examined, it was decided to use the alpha factoring method. After the alpha factoring method was chosen, the problem of number of factors to be extracted was addressed. The initial decision about the appropriate number of factors to be extracted was made after scrutinizing the eigenvalues obtained from the initial extraction using the criteria of substantive importance and the screen test. Several numbers of factors were then extracted, and oblique rotated factor structures were examined to determine if factors were correlated. For those solutions in which inter-factor correlations were small, orthogonal rotations were performed. The final determination regarding the number of factors and the best solution was made on the basis of three criteria: parsimony, simplicity, and interpretability. Parsimony refers to the least number of factors in acceptable factor solutions, simplicity was evaluated by examining the factor loadings for salient loadings, and interpretability was evaluated in terms of the extent to which salient factor loadings corresponded to the sections of the test. Only the final interpretable factor solutions and related statistics for the different groups are presented in Tables 6.6 and 6.7. Table 6.6 presents only the 33A group factor solution, as it is a correlated (oblique) solution. Table 6.7 presents uncorrelated orthogonal factor solutions for the 33B, 33C, 35, Ex., and Total groups.

For each of the four class groups and the total group, two-factor solutions were the most parsimonious and interpretable. All solutions except that for the 33A group were orthogonal. For the 33A group, the two-factor oblique solution showed that although the listening and grammar sub-tests loaded on the same factors, the two reading sub-tests loaded on separate factors. The inter-factor correlation was moderately high (0.424). For the 33B group, the two-factor orthogonal solution produced another pattern in which the listening sub-tests loaded on separate factors. The two-factor orthogonal solution for the 33C group showed that one sub-test of each of the listening and reading groups loaded on the second factor, and for the 35 and exempt groups, only one subtest of the grammar loaded on the second factor. At the bottom of the table, for the total group, the two sub-tests of listening loaded on one factor, whereas the reading and grammar sub-tests loaded on the other factor. From the point of view of the skills, the two listening sub-tests loaded on the same factor for four groups (33A, 35, exempt, and the total groups) but on separate factors for the 33B and the 33C groups. The reading sub-tests loaded on the same factor for all groups except for the 33A and 33C groups, and the grammar sub-tests loaded on the same factor for all groups except for the 35 and exempt groups.

Table 6.8 summarizes all solutions for all groups and shows the differences in factor structures of the NESLPE for the different groups. Two differences between the factor structures in the groups could be observed: first, only the 33A group had an oblique solution, and second, the variables that loaded on the factors for each of the groups was different. The first difference might indicate that students with lower-level ability (33A group) had inseparable skill ability as compared to students at higher levels of ability who have distinct skill abilities. The second difference seemed to indicate that the NESLPE did not measure the same abilities equally across all groups. In summary, EFA showed that although two-factor solutions were the best solutions for different groups, there were differences in the way the sub-tests loaded in the different groups, with progressively fewer sub-tests loading on the second factor as ability increased. This is consistent with the findings of Oltman and Stricker (1988) who found a greater test dimensionality of

TABLE 6.6 Exploratory factor analysis of 33A group, factor structure matrix (oblique rotation)

Variable	Factor 1	Factor 2
LIST1	.2598	**.4948**
LIST2	.0969	**.3025**
READ1	*.5856*	**.6484**
READ2	**.5580**	.1325
GRAM1	**.7399**	.4788
GRAM2	**.6896**	*.3959*
Factor correlations		
Factor 1	1.0	
Factor 2	.4236	1.0

Note: **Bolded** values are highest loadings for a variable on a factor; *italicized* values are next highest loadings for a variable on another factor that are above .3000.

TABLE 6.7 Exploratory factor analysis of 33B, 33C, 35 and Ex. group, rotated factor matrix (orthogonal rotation)

Variable	Factor 1	Factor 2	h^2
33B Group			
LIST1	**.7707**	.1889	.6297
LIST2	*.3622*	**.7335**	.6693
READ1	**.3742**	.0486	.1424
READ2	**.4888**	.2147	.2851
GRAM1	.0863	**.5218**	.2797
GRAM2	.0034	**.4019**	.1615
Eigenvalues	1.111	1.056	2.167
Tot. Var. %	18.53	17.60	36.13
33C Group			
LIST1	**.4350**	.0239	.1726
LIST2	.2304	**.7038**	.5485
READ1	.2324	**.4245**	.2342
READ2	**.4149**	.0142	.1723
GRAM1	**.7361**	.1407	.5617
GRAM2	**.5457**	*.3685*	.4337
Eigenvalues	1.344	.7692	2.113
Tot. Var. %	22.40	13.30	35.70
35 and Ex. group			
LIST1	**.4122**	.0519	.1726
LIST2	**.3769**	.1360	.1606
READ1	**.3088**	.1216	.1102
READ2	**.4752**	.1445	.2467
GRAM1	.1720	.0934	.0383

(Continued)

TABLE 6.7 (Continued)

Variable	Factor 1	Factor 2	h^2
GRAM2	.0966	**.7696**	.6016
Eigenvalues	.6722	.6579	1.330
Tot.Var. %	11.20	10.97	22.17
Total group			
LIST1	.4469	**.7039**	.6952
LIST2	.4225	**.7161**	.6914
READ1	**.5948**	.5144	.6185
READ2	**.6513**	.4932	.6677
GRAM1	**.7898**	.4568	.8325
GRAM2	**.7071**	.4069	.6656
Eigenvalues	3.998	.1824	4.181
Tot.Var. %	66.50	3.00	69.50

Note: **Bolded** values are highest loadings for a variable on a factor; *italicized* values are next highest loadings for a variable on another factor that are above .3000.

TABLE 6.8 Summary of factor solutions for all groups

Groups	Solutions	Factors	
		1	2
33A	2 factor oblique	READ2	LIST1
		GRAM1	LIST2
		GRAM2	READ1
33B	2 factor orthogonal	LIST1	LIST2
		READ1	GRAM1
		READ2	GRAM2
33C	2 factor orthogonal	LIST1	LIST2
		READ2	READ1
		GRAM1	
		GRAM2	
35 and Ex.	2 factor orthogonal	LIST1	GRAM2
		LIST2	
		READ1	
		READ2	
		GRAM1	
Total	2 factor orthogonal	READ1	LIST1
		READ2	LIST2
		GRAM1	
		GRAM2	

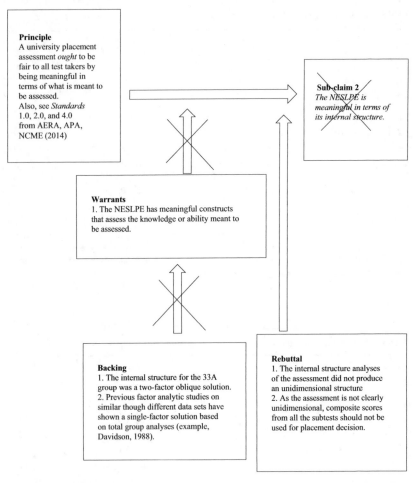

Principle
A university placement assessment *ought* to be fair to all test takers by being meaningful in terms of what is meant to be assessed.
Also, see *Standards* 1.0, 2.0, and 4.0 from AERA, APA, NCME (2014)

Sub-claim 2
The NESLPE is meaningful in terms of its internal structure.

Warrants
1. The NESLPE has meaningful constructs that assess the knowledge or ability meant to be assessed.

Backing
1. The internal structure for the 33A group was a two-factor oblique solution.
2. Previous factor analytic studies on similar though different data sets have shown a single-factor solution based on total group analyses (example, Davidson, 1988).

Rebuttal
1. The internal structure analyses of the assessment did not produce an unidimensional structure
2. As the assessment is not clearly unidimensional, composite scores from all the subtests should not be used for placement decision.

FIGURE 6.3 Principle, claims, warrants, and backing for Principle 1, Fairness, sub-claim 2 (internal structure) with rebuttal. Note the X marks on the sub-claim and on the arrow from the backing to warrant to the claim indicates that the claim cannot be supported.

ability at lower levels than at higher levels. These findings also indicated that the NESLPE was not unidimensional. This lack of unidimensionality raises a critical question: If the test is not unidimensional, then should placement decisions be based on a single composite score (based on all sub-test scores), which was supposed to represent a single indicator of language ability? Or if placement decisions are based on single composite scores, would there be any misclassification of students?

Previous factor analytic studies on similar though different data sets have shown a single-factor solution based on total group analyses (example, Davidson,

1988), and this has legitimatized placement decisions based on the single composite score. These single composite scores reflected the so-called unidimensional factor structure of the test. So administrators could add up all scores for sub-tests to make the single composite score. At UCLA, too, this single composite score, based on all the skills tested, was generally used to place students into ESL classes or to exempt them. In this type of procedure, a very low score would place a student into a low-level ESL class, like ESL 33A at UCLA, which could focus on listening and speaking skills. A higher score would place a student into a higher-level ESL class, like ESL 35 at UCLA, which could focus on reading and writing skills. Thus, at UCLA, the single composite score determined not only the level, but also the kind of class the student would place into. This can clearly be a disservice to many students. For example, a student with low listening section scores but with very high reading scores would be placed into a higher-level ESL class, which could focus on reading and writing skills and generally neglect listening and speaking skills.

Backing

In terms of backing, the claim that the NESLPE was unidimensional and therefore composite scores from all the sub-tests can be used for placement cannot be supported. Figure 6.3 shows the lack of backing from the research and therefore the cancellation of the link from backing to warrants and warrants to the claim. There can be a rebuttal of the claim based on EFA results. Therefore, a deferred judgment pending additional backing from further empirical studies is the most logical conclusion.

Conclusion

In this chapter, the concept of meaningfulness was presented and discussed as part of Principle 1, Fairness: Meaningfulness. There are many different aspects of meaningfulness from which evidence can be gathered for this principle. The first aspect examined was *in terms of the blueprint and specifications, etc.*, assembled by an assessment prior to assessment development. The second aspect examined was *in terms of the cognitive processes test takers use to complete the assessment.* The third aspect examined was that of *constructs that assess the knowledge or ability meant to be assessed.* The fourth aspect examined was *consequences of assessments for test takers, stakeholders, and the community.*

The illustrative studies presented showed how evidence can be gathered for their respective aspect of meaningfulness. The Johnson et al. study was a large-scale survey of the blueprints and specifications related to reading assessments in all the states in the U.S.; it included examining assessment blueprints or test specifications in terms of the purposes and constructs of assessments. The Kunnan studies examined the consistency or dependability of an assessment and the internal factor structure of the assessment. Results from these studies were mapped onto the Toulmin argumentation framework. As the results of the two Kunnan studies had divergent findings; the claim of meaningfulness in terms of dependability of the assessment is supported, but the claim of meaningfulness in terms of internal structure is not supported. The next chapter will take up arguments for the absence of bias of an assessment.

Note

1 Newton and Shaw (2014) present a discussion regarding the lack of consensus about the term "validity" in the first decade of the 21st century. The main points of debate are regarding what validity should encompass and what validity should apply to. One of the primary objections regarding what validity should encompass is whether social consequences (or consequential validity) should be part of a validity framework. At the same time, it does not seem reasonable to ignore the consequences of an assessment. Therefore, in this book, I'm side-stepping the debate and using the term "meaningfulness," following Bachman and Palmer (2010).

References

American Educational Research Association, American Psychological Association, the National Council on Measurement in Education. (2014). *Standards for educational and psychological testing*. Washington, DC: Author.

Bachman, L. F. (1990). *Fundamental considerations in language testing*. Oxford, UK: Oxford University Press.

Bachman, L. F., & Palmer, A. S. (1996). *Language testing in practice*. Oxford, UK: Oxford University Press.

Bachman, L. F., & Palmer, A. S. (2010). *Language assessment in practice*. Oxford, UK: Oxford University Press.

Brennan, R. L. (1980). Applications of generalizability theory. In R. A. Berk (Ed.), *Criterion-referenced measurement: The state of the art* (pp. 186–232). Baltimore, MD: The Johns Hopkins University Press.

Brown, J. D. (2014). *Mixed methods research for TESOL*. Edinburgh, UK: Edinburgh University Press.

Canale, M., & Swain, M. (1980). Theoretical bases of communicative approaches to second language teaching and testing. *Applied Linguistics, 1*, 1–47.

Crick, J. E., & Brennan, R. L. (1982). *GENOVA: A generalized analysis of variance system*. Dorchester, MA: University of Massachusetts at Boston.

Cronbach, L. J. (1971). Test validation. In R. L. Thorndike (Ed.), *Educational measurement* (pp. 443–507). Washington, DC: American Council on Education.

Cronbach, L. J. (1988). Five perspectives on validity argument. In W. Howard & H. I. Braun (Eds.), *Test validity* (pp. 1–14). Hillsdale, NJ: Lawrence Erlbaum.

Crooks, J. T., Kane, M. T., & Cohen, A. S. (1996). Threats to the valid use of assessments. *Assessment in Education, 3*, 265–286.

Cureton, E. E. (1951). Validity. In E. F. Lindquist (Ed.), *Educational measurement* (pp. 621–694). Washington, DC: American Council on Education.

Davidson, F. G. (1988). *An exploratory modeling survey of the trait structures of some existing language test datasets* (Doctoral dissertation, UCLA).

Hambelton, R. K., Swaminathan, H., Algina, J., & Coulson, D. B. (1978). Criterion-referenced testing and measurement: A review of technical issues and developments. *Review of Educational Research, 48,* 1–47.

Johnstone, C. J., Moen, R. E., Thurlow, M. L., Matchett, D., Hausmann, K. E., & Scullin, S. (2007). *What do state reading test specifications specify?* Minneapolis, MN: University of Minnesota, Partnership for Accessible Reading Assessment. Retrieved from: www.cehd.umn.edu/NCEO/onlinepubs/PARA/blueprint

Kaiser, H. F. (1974). An index of factorial simplicity. *Psychometrika, 39,* 31–36.

Kane, M. T. (1992). An argument-based approach to validity. *Psychological Bulletin, 112,* 527–535.

Kane, M. T. (2006a). Validating score interpretations and uses. *Language Testing, 29,* 3–17.

Kane, M. T. (2006b). Validation. In R. Brennan (Ed.), *Educational Measurement,* 4th Edn. (pp. 17–64). Westport, CT: American Council on Education and Praeger.

Kunnan, A. J. (1992). An investigation of a criterion-referenced test using G-theory, factor and cluster analyses. *Language Testing, 9,* 30–49.

Loevinger, J. (1957). Objective tests as instruments of psychological theory. *Psychological Reports, Monograph Supplement, 3,* 635–694.

Lynch, B. K., & Davidson, F. (1994). Criterion-referenced language test development: Linking curricula, teachers, and tests. *TESOL Quarterly, 28,* 727–743.

Messick, S. (1989). Validity. In R. Linn (Ed.), *Educational measurement* (pp. 13–103). London, UK: Macmillan.

Newton, P., & Shaw, S. (2014). *Validity in educational and psychological assessment.* Thousand Oaks, CA: Sage.

Oltman, P. K., Stricker, L. J., & Barrows, T. S. (1988). Native language, English proficiency, and the structure of the Test of English as a Foreign Language. *ETS Research Report Series, 1988* (1).

Popham, W.J. (1978). *Criterion-referenced measurement.* Englewood Cliffs, NJ: Prentice Hall.

Schmeiser, C. B., & Welch, C. J. (2006). Test development. In R. L. Brennan (Ed.), *Educational measurement,* 4th Edn. (pp. 307–353). Washington, DC: American Council on Education.

Subkoviak, M. (1980). Decision-consistency approaches. In Berk, R.A., editor, *Criterion-referenced measurement: the state of the art* (pp. 129–185). Baltimore, MD: The Johns Hopkins University Press.

7
ABSENCE OF BIAS

Introduction

In order to provide a level playing field to all test takers, assessments for any purpose anywhere in the world attempt to be free of bias against any test taker or test-taking group. But despite this goal, many assessments are not found to be free of bias by test takers, test score users, researchers, and the public. Therefore, assessments need to be evaluated so that assessments (or parts of assessments) that are biased are identified, removed, or modified, thus providing assessment agencies support for their claim that their assessments are free of bias.

A popular way of investigating this is to examine the assessment itself for bias in terms of dialect, content, topics, response format, etc. Another way is to analyze test performance data in terms of different test taker groups with specific backgrounds or attributes such as male/female, first language, nationality, race and ethnicity, age, rural/urban, religion, sexual orientation, household academic and professional background, socioeconomic level, disability, etc. Findings from both these analyses can be expected to identify biased items or tasks so that such items or tasks can be modified or removed from the assessment to make it free from bias. These actions can ensure that an assessment is free of bias in terms of its test design, tasks and items, administration, scoring, and reporting; free of bias from invalid test score interpretations; free of bias in terms of test takers with disabilities (in terms of providing appropriate accommodations); and free of bias by safeguarding against inappropriate score interpretations for specific test taker groups.

This chapter discusses arguments regarding absence of bias by examining claims and sub-claims with the relevant warrants and backing from relevant empirical studies.

Background

Defining Bias

An assessment can be said to be biased if there is systematic bias in the measurement of the ability that is being assessed, either in the assessment instrument caused by cognitive, affective, or physical sources of construct-irrelevant variance, or in the assessment performance, scoring, standard setting, and decision-making where test-taking groups of similar ability are not treated in the same manner. Jensen (1980) defined test bias this way: "a biased test is one that yields scores that have a different meaning for members of one group from their meaning for members of another" (p. 516).

Holland and Wainer (1993) suggested that assessment developers ought to be responsible for developing tests that measure the intended constructs and to eliminate or minimize construct-irrelevant characteristics in the tests in the form of linguistic, cognitive, cultural, physical, or other characteristics. This would require them to identify and eliminate language, symbols, words and phrases, content, and stereotyping of characters that are offensive or insulting to test takers of different racial, ethnic, gender, or other groups. They specifically outlined three relevant aspects to be routinely used to ensure test fairness:

> (1) Detailed reviews of test items by subject matter experts and members of the major subgroups in society (gender, ethnic, and linguistic) that, in prospect, will be represented in the examinee population; (2) Comparisons of the predictive validity of the test done separately for each of the major subgroups of examinees; and (3) Extensive statistical analyses of the relative performance of major subgroups of examinees on individual test items.
>
> *(p. xiii)*

Hambleton and Rodgers (1995) identified five areas in their review: fairness, content bias, language bias, item structure and format bias, and stereotyping. They suggested using a review form that worked as follows: each reviewer would receive a reading passage and related items (testlet) or other types (such as individual items or prompts). This testlet or other type would then be examined in terms of the checklist items. The checklist information from all the reviewers would be then collated and organized into a spreadsheet for further descriptive statistical analyses. If a testlet or other test type receives checks indicating bias on more than 25 percent of the checklist items, then such items might be flagged for modification, revision, or deletion.

Building on these ideas, the *ETS Guidelines* (2009) are particularly relevant to fairness reviews of language assessments. They require ETS staff to "ensure that symbols, language, and content that are generally regarded as sexist, racist, or offensive are eliminated except when necessary to meet the purpose of the assessments" (p. 2). These guidelines identified three sources of construct-irrelevant variance: cognitive, affective, or physical that leads to three guidelines for fairness reviews:

(1) *Cognitive sources of construct-irrelevant variance.* Avoid unnecessarily difficult language (dialect, grammatical structure, and vocabulary above the proficiency level of the assessment), military topics (especially wars, conflicts, battles, military strategy), language regionalisms (for example, hoagie instead of sandwich, or borough instead of county or province), specific sports (for example, T20 cricket or Rugby sevens), specific target language culture (for example, in U.S. English language assessment *cinco de mayo* celebrations), political affiliations and specific politicians and public figures, measurement systems (such as Fahrenheit, inches, pounds, etc.), and the practices of religions.

(2) *Affective sources of construct-irrelevant variance.* Avoid emotional reactions caused by inappropriate language that is contemptuous, derogatory, exclusionary, and insulting of any people. Further, personal questions are to be avoided. These include questions regarding family members, household income, political affiliation, contraception, religious beliefs, sexual practices, and substance abuse. Topics of concern include accidents, illnesses, natural disorders, death and dying, violence and suffering, and other controversial topics such as the death penalty, evolution, abortion, child marriage, prostitution, torture, slavery, rape, euthanasia, etc. In similar fashion, the document cautions staff in the use of humor, irony, and satire that are likely to offend some test takers. Representations and stereotypes of people to be avoided include people and their occupations or attributes (Chinese as laundry shop owners, Blacks as servants, women as secretaries, Hispanics as gardeners, Whites as racists, etc.), the use of names for people (such as Negro or Colored, handicap or cripple), and the representation of people (such as he or she, man or woman and not the generic he or man; chairperson instead of chairman, police officer or firefighter instead of policeman or fireman), and gender and racial and ethnic imbalance.

(3) *Physical sources of construct-irrelevant variance.* Avoid construct-irrelevant charts, maps, graphs, visual stimuli, equipment, computers, computer software, etc.

Empirical Studies

Here are a few empirical studies that offer clarity in terms of how absence of bias can be investigated.

Sensitivity Review

A well-documented sensitivity review process of all assessment materials was in place at Educational Testing Service as early as the 1980s based on the *ETS Test*

Sensitivity Review Process (1980) and the *ETS Standards for Quality and Fairness* (1987). When these standards were translated into practice, Ramsey (1993) documented it required all ETS documents and tests (a) to be balanced, (b) to not foster stereotypes, (c) to not contain ethnocentric or gender-based underlying assumptions, (d) to not be offensive from a test taker's perspective, (e) to not contain controversial material that the subject matter does not demand, and (f) to not be elitist or ethnocentric. Sensitivity reviews of tests used in most U.S. school and college districts include additional sensitivity to cultures, religions, socioeconomic groups, and disabilities. Over the decades, ETS formalized its sensitivity review processes to include development of the review guidelines, review forms, membership and training of review panels, and coordination and arbitration.

Most large-scale assessment programs such as the SAT (College Board), American College Testing, Graduate Management Achievement Test, and Iowa Tests of Basic Skills, Internet-based TOEFL conduct in-house sensitivity reviews in order to improve fairness and legal defensibility of their assessments. The *Standards for Educational and Psychological Testing* (AERA, APA, & NCME, 1999) also stated that "the test review process should include empirical analyses and, when appropriate, the use of expert judges to review items and response formats" (Standard 3.6). This standard has resulted in assessment agencies forming review panels that include members of their assessment development group along with review members who are from minority groups of the test-taking population. The assumption behind including minority members in the review panels is that minority members would be aware of social and cultural stereotypes and insensitivities in tasks, language, and other materials that are likely to be insensitive to minority test takers.

Accommodations for ELLs[1]

Abedi and Gandara (2007) discussed another aspect of bias that has to do with ELLs in mainstream U.S. classrooms. They stated, "Fairness demands equal educational opportunities for all students including ethnic minorities, students with disabilities, low-income students, and English language learners. However, these subgroups of students have historically lagged behind their mainstream peers on test scores" (p. 43). In a series of studies, Abedi made the case for appropriate accommodations for ELL test takers. In an earlier empirical study, Abedi and Lord (2001) examined the effects of the linguistic modification approach with 1031 8th grade students in Southern California. In this study, the National Assessment of Educational Progress (NAEP) mathematics assessment items were modified by reducing complex sentence structures and unfamiliar vocabulary with familiar words, keeping content-related words like mathematical terms. The results showed significant improvements in the scores of ELL and non-ELL students in low- and average-level mathematics classes, but no effect on scores among other non-ELL students. Other linguistic features that appeared to contribute to the differences were unfamiliar vocabulary and passive voice sentences.

In yet another study, Abedi, Courtney, and Leon (2003) examined 1594 8th grade students using assessment items from NAEP and The Trends in International Mathematics and Science Study (TIMSS). Students were given one of the following accommodations: a customized English dictionary (words were selected directly from assessment items), a bilingual glossary, a linguistically modified test version, or the standard test items. Only the linguistically modified version improved the ELL students' scores, but they did not affect the non–ELL students' scores.

In a more recent study, Abedi, Courtney, Leon, Kao, and Azzam (2006 p. 19) asked the question: "Do the dual-language test version and linguistic modification accommodations improve students' math performance?" Although their findings showed that linguistic modification made a significant difference, they expressed doubts about the value of these dual-language assessment accommodations:

> With respect to the dual-language test version accommodation, the results of our analyses did not show significant improvement on ELL student performance using this accommodation. That is, students who received the dual-language test version performed the same as those receiving the standard math test. This finding confirms previous research on dual-language testing, which found that while students preferred a dual-language format, no differences were detected in their performance.
>
> *(p. 2006)*

Pennock-Roman and Rivera (2011) examined this issue in depth in their study. Their objective was to empirically study the impact of different types of accommodations on performance in content tests such as mathematics. The meta-analysis included 14 U.S. studies that randomly assigned school-aged ELLs to test accommodation versus control conditions. Individual effect sizes were calculated for 50 groups of ELLs and 32 groups of non-ELLs. Findings suggested that accommodations that required extra printed materials needed generous time limits for both the accommodated and unaccommodated groups to ensure that they were effective. Computer-administered glossaries were effective even when time limits were restricted. Although the plain English accommodation had very small average effect sizes, inspection of individual effect sizes suggested that it may be much more effective for ELLs at intermediate levels of English language proficiency.

Differential Item Functioning (DIF) Studies

The primary focus of these studies has been on assessments (or parts of assessments) that function differently for different native-language, cultural, racial or ethnic, gender, or other test-taking groups. These studies are popularly known as test bias studies, but the term test bias is misleading and inaccurate. The term assumes that the researcher is examining tests or test items that are biased; however, what we know from test-taker responses is only that there are differences in performances that could be due to several reasons, only one of which is bias. A more accurate term, therefore, that has been used recently in testing literature is differential item/bundle functioning (DIF/DBF), referring to the way items or bundles of items function differently for test-taking groups who have similar abilities.

Holland and Wainer (1993) suggested that scores of different subgroups should ideally have similar predictive validity with an external criterion (such as workplace or university performance) for these sub-groups. When a comparison of sub-groups is conducted and there is a significant difference, then the assessment developer has to be sure that the difference is not due to the assessment itself. Specifically, if scores among sub-groups are significantly different, then assessment developers and score users are responsible for examining the evidence for validity of score interpretations for intended uses for test takers from subgroups.

Zumbo (2007) also makes this point succinctly:

> If the average test scores for such groups (e.g., men vs. women, Blacks vs. Whites) were found to be different, then the question arose as to whether the difference reflected bias in the test. Given that a test comprises items, questions soon emerged about which specific items might be the source of such bias.
>
> *(p. 224)*

To put it another way, when a test is fair, the expectation is that test takers in all subgroups will fare equally well. However, when test score differences occur among test taker subgroups (say, by gender, race/ethnicity, native language) of similar ability (as determined and matched by the total score), the question is why did the differences occur? Were the differences due to differences in ability of interest, or were the differences due to test items; more specifically, were the differences due to test content (reading passage, listening script), test format (multiple-choice, constructed responses), or some other irrelevant variable (say, typing skills) that were unfair to some groups?

Among the early DIF studies in language assessment was Chen and Henning (1985) who examined the 1985 version of the ESL Placement Examination (ESLPE) at UCLA to determine the nature, direction, and extent of bias present for test takers of the Spanish and the Chinese L1 groups. This was followed by a host of others: Zeidner (1986, 1987), who investigated the English Language Aptitude Test used routinely for student selection and placement in Israel; Spurling (1987), who studied the "fair use" of the Marin Community College English admissions and placement test; Hale (1988), who reported on the interaction of student academic major and text content in the reading comprehension section of the Test of English as a Foreign Language (TOEFL); and Angoff (1989), who tested the hypothesis that items of the TOEFL that contain references to people, places, regions, etc., of the U.S. tend to favor test takers who have spent some time living in the U.S. Kunnan and Sasaki (1989) extended the Chen and Henning (1985) study by including five L1 groups in their examination of the 1987 version of the ESLPE. Their study, like that of Chen and Henning (1985), identified several vocabulary and grammar items that favored certain native language groups.

In a similar vein, Ryan and Bachman (1992) investigated how items on the (retired) TOEFL and the First Certificate in English (FCE) function differently for Indo-European L1 and non–Indo-European L1 groups. They found that the non–Indo-European L1 group was favored on the TOEFL Listening Comprehension sub-test, whereas the Indo-European L1 group was favored on the TOEFL Reading and Vocabulary sub-test. On the TOEFL Structure and Written Expression sub-test, the same number of items favored the Indo-European or the non–Indo-European L1 groups, and the two groups were neither advantaged nor disadvantaged on the FCE vocabulary and reading items. A follow-up content analysis suggested that items that favored the non–Indo-European L1 group were associated with American culture and/or were more academic or technical material.

Kim and Jang (2009) investigated the extent to which reading item bundles or items on the Ontario Secondary School Literacy Test (OSSLT) functioned differentially for L1 and ELL students using the approach of the multidimensionality-based DIF method. Specifically, the authors examined the extent to which reading item bundles or items on the Ontario Secondary School Literacy Test functioned differently for Grade 10 students who spoke only or mostly English at home and those whose home language was other than English. The research questions were: (1) What reading sub-skills constitute the dimensionality structure of the OSSLT? and (2) To what extent do reading item bundles or items on the OSSLT function differentially for L1 and ELL students? From the content analysis, the five reviewers determined that the following six reading sub-skills represent the construct of the OSSLT: textual comprehension skill, inferencing skill, vocabulary knowledge, grammatical knowledge, summary skill, and integrated reading and writing skill. The evidence gathered in the DIF study indicated that items associated with vocabulary knowledge favored L1 students, whereas items requiring grammatical knowledge or integrated reading and writing skill favored ELL students. A full list of bias-related studies is presented in Table 7.1.

DIF Methodology

The methodology for conducting research on bias, accommodation, and internal structure has typically relied on post hoc studies—that is, studies conducted after an assessment is administered and test performance data are available for analysis. This approach has resulted in research on available test taker groups divided into focal and

TABLE 7.1 Empirical studies in language testing focusing on test bias (from 1980)

Author(s) and Year of Study	Specific Focus
Swinton and Powers (1980)	L1 language
Alderman and Holland (1981)	L1 language
Shohamy (1984)	Test method
Alderson and Urquhart (1985a)	Academic major
Chen and Henning (1985)	L1 language
Zeidner (1986, 1987)	Gender and minorities
Hale (1988)	Major field and test content
Oltman, Stricker, and Barrows (1988)	L1 language
Kunnan (1990, 1992)	L1 language, gender
Sasaki (1991)	L1 language
Shohamy and Inbar (1991)	Question type and listening
Ryan and Bachman (1992)	Gender
Kunnan (1995)	L1 language
Brown (1993)	Tape-mediated test
Ginther and Stevens (1998)	L1 language, ethnicity
Norton and Stein (1998)	Text content
J. D. Brown (1999)	L1 language
Takala and Kaftandjieva (2000)	L1 language
Lowenberg (2000)	Different Englishes
M. Kim (2001)	L1 language
T. Pae (2004a)	Academic major
T. Pae (2004b)	Gender
Ockey (2007)	L1 language
Roever (2007)	L1 language
Geranpayeh and Kunnan (2007)	Age
Kim and Jang (2009)	L1 language
Harding (2012)	L1 language
Aryadoust, Goh, and Kim (2011)	Gender
Banerjee and Papageorgiou (2016)	Age

reference groups—somewhat similar to convenience sampling for study participants. Experimental studies, on the other hand, with control and treatment groups followed by random selection of study participants and random assignment to groups is less common because of the difficulty in disrupting intact school and college classrooms. A more conceptual reason for the lack of experimental research is that researchers, until recently, for the most part did not use hypothesis-based testing.

Zumbo (2007) traces three generations of DIF research. The first generation involved "many of the early item bias methods (that) focused on (a) comparisons of only two groups of examinees; (b) terminology such as focal and reference groups to denote minority and majority groups, respectively; and (c) binary (rather than polytomous) scored items" (p. 224); the second generation focused on "(a) modeling item responses via contingency tables and/or regression models,

(b) item response theory (IRT), and (c) multidimensional models" (p. 225), and the third generation is focusing on "item characteristics such as item format and item content, which may influence students' performance on tests" (p. 229).

In third-generation research, Zumbo (2007) identified five uses: (1) fairness and equity, (2) threats to internal validity, (3) comparability of translated and/or adapted measures, (4) item response processes, and (5) lack of invariance. Although these uses provide a wide range of research possibilities, the lack of studies on what Zumbo calls (2007) contextual variables such as classroom size, socioeconomic status, teaching practices, and parental styles as possible explanations for and sources or causes of DIF is troubling.

For example, relevant hypotheses that utilize contextual variables include using subgroups of test takers in terms of their native languages such as Indo-European (IE) and non–Indian European (NIE) language subgroups relevant for international assessments. Thus, a hypothesis could be stated as a null hypothesis: There is no DIF or DTF in the IE or NIE subgroups or as a directional hypothesis: There is DIF/DTF for the IE group (or NIE group). A popular line of investigation is to examine DIF by gender subgroups, male and female. Another line of research could be subgroups formed by age groupings (for example, ages 16 to 25, 26 to 40, 41 to 60, 61 and above). Yet another research hypothesis could be formed based on whether ELL test takers with an accommodated assessment perform better than an assessment without accommodation.

These hypotheses may be based on previous research, theoretical foundation, anecdotal evidence, or the researcher's or test developer's hunches. The subsequent DIF/DTF analysis would reveal whether test performance of the two subgroups at the item or testlet level is affected by their grouping even when bands of test takers who have similar overall scores are matched and analyzed. As mentioned earlier, items and testlets that display DIF/DTF will then need to be examined by content experts for the source of the DIF/DTF, whether it is content, test format, or any form of bias. If the source of the DIF/DTF is determined to be construct-irrelevant variance, the item or testlet will need to be revised or removed.

Similar difficulties of addressing accommodations and standard setting through experimental research exist, but Abedi and collaborators have shown that advances can be made with non-experimental research methods as well.

Standards *for Absence of Bias*

The APA, AERA, and NCME *Standards* (2014) listed 20 different standards that assessment agencies ought to meet under four clusters: (1) *test design, development, administration, and scoring procedures* that minimize barriers to valid score interpretations for the widest possible range of individuals and relevant subgroups; (2) *validity of test score interpretations* for intended uses for the intended examinee population; (3) *accommodations to remove construct-irrelevant barriers* and support valid interpretations of scores for their intended uses; and (4) safeguards against *inappropriate score interpretations* for intended uses.

Fairness

Standard 3.0

All steps in the testing process, including test design, validation, development, administration, and scoring procedures, should be designed in such a manner as to minimize construct-irrelevant variance and to promote valid score interpretations for the intended uses for all examinees in the intended population.

(p. 63)

Cluster 1: Test design, development, administration, and scoring procedures

Standard 3.1

Those responsible for test development, revision, and administration should design all steps of the testing process to promote valid score interpretations for intended score uses for the widest possible range of individuals and relevant subgroups in the intended population.

(p. 63)

Standard 3.2

Test developers are responsible for developing tests that measure the intended construct and for minimizing the potential for tests' being affected by construct-irrelevant characteristics, such as linguistic, communicative, cognitive, cultural physical, or other characteristics.

(p. 64)

Standard 3.3

Those responsible for test development should include relevant subgroups in validity, reliability/precision, and other preliminary studies used when constructing the test.

(p. 64)

Standard 3.4

Test takers should receive comparable treatment during the test administration and scoring process.

(p. 65)

Cluster 2: Validity of test score interpretations for intended uses for the intended examinee population

Standard 3.6

Where credible evidence indicates that test scores may differ in meaning for relevant subgroups in the intended examinee population, test developers and/or users are responsible for examining the evidence for validity of score interpretations for intended uses for individuals from those subgroups.

(p. 65)

Standard 3.8

When tests require the scoring of constructed responses, test developers and/or users should collect and report evidence of the validity of score interpretations for relevant subgroups in the intended population of test takers for the intended uses of test scores.

(p. 66)

Cluster 3: Accommodations to remove construct-irrelevant barriers and support valid interpretations of scores for their intended uses

Standard 3.9

Test developers and/or test users are responsible for developing and providing test accommodations, when appropriate and feasible, to remove construct-irrelevant barriers that otherwise would interfere with examinees' ability to demonstrate their standing on the target constructs.

(p. 67)

Standard 3.10

When test accommodations are permitted, test developers and/or test users are responsible for documenting standard provisions for using the accommodation and for monitoring the appropriate implementation of the accommodation.

(p. 67)

Standard 3.11

When a test is changed to remove barriers to the accessibility of the construct being measured, test developers and/or users are responsible for obtaining and documenting evidence of the validity of score interpretations for intended uses of the changed test, when sample sizes permit.

(p. 68)

Cluster 4: Safeguards against inappropriate score interpretations for intended uses

Standard 3.15

Test developers and publishers who claim that a test can be used with examinees from specific subgroups are responsible for providing the necessary information to support appropriate test score interpretations for their intended uses for individuals from these subgroups.

(p. 70)

Standard 3.16

When credible research indicates that test scores for some relevant subgroups are differentially affected by construct-irrelevant characteristics of the test or of the examinees, when legally permissible, test users should use the test only for those subgroups for which there is sufficient evidence of validity to support sole interpretations for the intended uses.

(p. 70)

Standard 9.14

Test users should inform individuals who may need accommodations in test administration (e.g., older adults, test takers with disabilities, or English language learners) about the availability of accommodations and, when required, should see that these accommodations are appropriately made available.

(p. 145)

These standards for absence of bias contribute centrally to the fairness of an assessment. These standards, along with principles of fairness, can be used to build an argument for absence of bias through claims and sub-claims.

Building an Argument for Absence of Bias

Principles

Keeping in mind the definitions, guidelines, and standards for fairness (absence of bias) discussed earlier, the general principles of fairness with specific claims for absence of bias are articulated next.

Principle 1: Fairness

Principle: An assessment *ought* to be fair to all test takers by being free of bias.

Claims, Warrants, and Backing

A general claim regarding absence of bias of an assessment and sub-claims could be operationalized into key warrants that can be articulated as illustrated in

EXTRACT 7.1 FAIRNESS ARGUMENT FOR ABSENCE OF BIAS

Principle: An assessment ought to be fair to all test takers by being free of bias.

General Claim: The university placement assessment is free of bias.

Sub-claim 1a: The university placement assessment is free of bias in terms of dialect, content, or topic across test taker groups.
Warrant 1a: Research on the university placement assessment will show that the assessment is free of bias in terms of dialect, content, or topic across test taker groups.

Sub-claim 1b: The university placement assessment is free of bias in terms of differential performance across different test taker groups of similar ability in terms of gender, age, race/ethnicity, and L1.
Warrant 1b: Research on the university placement assessment will show that the assessment is free of bias in terms of differential performance by different test taker groups of similar ability in terms of gender, age, race/ethnicity, and L1.

Sub-claim 1c: The university placement assessment is free of bias, as it has provided appropriate accommodations for test takers with disabilities.
Warrant 1c: Research on the university placement assessment will show that the assessment is free of bias, as it has provided appropriate accommodations for test takers with disabilities.

Sub-claim 1d: The university placement assessment is free of bias in terms of score interpretation, standard setting, and decision-making.
Warrant 1d: Research on the university placement will show that the assessment is free of bias in terms of score interpretation, standard setting, and decision-making.

Sub-claim 1e: The university placement assessment is free of bias in terms of cost and uniformity and free of fraud.
Warrant 1e: Research on the university placement assessment is free of bias in terms of cost and uniformity and free of fraud.

Also: see Standard 3.0, APA, AERA, NCME (2014)

Extract 7.1 and Figure 7.1. The examples used in this chapter all relate to university assessments.

> *Sub-claim 1a:* The university placement assessment is free of bias in terms of dialect, content, or topic across test taker groups.
>
> *Warrant 1a:* Research on the university placement assessment will show that the assessment is free of bias in terms of dialect, content, or topic across test taker groups.

All assessment agencies would like to claim that their assessments are free of all types of bias. The first type of bias-free assessment is one that does not

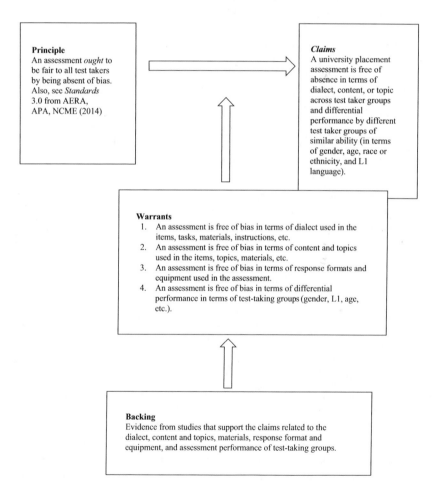

Principle
An assessment *ought* to be fair to all test takers by being absent of bias. Also, see *Standards* 3.0 from AERA, APA, NCME (2014)

Claims
A university placement assessment is free of absence in terms of dialect, content, or topic across test taker groups and differential performance by different test taker groups of similar ability (in terms of gender, age, race or ethnicity, and L1 language).

Warrants
1. An assessment is free of bias in terms of dialect used in the items, tasks, materials, instructions, etc.
2. An assessment is free of bias in terms of content and topics used in the items, topics, materials, etc.
3. An assessment is free of bias in terms of response formats and equipment used in the assessment.
4. An assessment is free of bias in terms of differential performance in terms of test-taking groups (gender, L1, age, etc.).

Backing
Evidence from studies that support the claims related to the dialect, content and topics, materials, response format and equipment, and assessment performance of test-taking groups.

FIGURE 7.1   Generic structure of Principle, Claims Warrants, and Backing for Principle 1, Fairness—Absence of bias

disadvantage test takers in terms of dialect, content, and topic. But in terms of dialects, this is easier said than done, especially when languages have many varieties or dialects (such as Arabic, Chinese, German, Hindi, Spanish, and Tamil) based on region, history, social class, and caste, where a different dialect may be used for the assessment materials (for reading or listening) and instruction in school from the one used at home or in the community. In most assessments, there is no formal statement in the assessment specifications of the dialect that is used, which leads to confusion on the part of the test taker or the rater (particularly with vocabulary and grammar).

In terms of content (the general subject matter) and topics, assessments could cause bias to different test-taking groups if there is a dominant content or topic area in the assessment materials for listening and reading. This is particularly critical in general language assessments at the university level where test takers may have different academic majors already (such as arts, business, humanities, science and engineering, etc.). The difficulty here is to balance content and topic areas across these fields so that no single group has an advantage over the other. Along with the content and topic, another related area of concern is the language of instructions and source material.

Research using coders or raters who identify different dialect use, content, and topic is necessary to examine whether the assessment materials might cause bias or disadvantage some test-taking groups.

> *Sub-claim 1b:* The university placement assessment is free of bias in terms of differential performance across different test taker groups of similar ability in terms of gender, age, race/ethnicity, and L1.
>
> *Warrant 1b:* Research on the university placement assessment will show that the assessment is free of bias in terms of differential performance by different test taker groups of similar ability in terms of gender, age, race/ethnicity, and L1.

Differential item or task functioning (DIF) is an analytical procedure that examines whether an item or task favors a test-taking group. For example, DIF examines whether an item or task is biased against male or female test takers who are from the same ability range (say, 90 to 100 points). The expectation is that test takers from the same ability range, although from different groups will have similar (or close to) performances for each item or task. When there is a statistically significant difference on an item or task, such an item is said to have differential item or task functioning (Ferne & Rupp, 2007; Kunnan, 2010; Zumbo, 2007). When an item is classified as having DIF, then such items are flagged for a thorough content analysis in order to determine whether such items are biased or not. Thus, statistical analysis is the first step of this two-step analysis, and content analysis is the second step.

DIF analyses can be used to examine bias in items when test-taking groups are from different gender, race, ethnicity, age, dialect, academic major, or any other group membership. Thus, if test takers from different backgrounds are likely to take an assessment, test performance data analysis with group membership variables for different dialects, content or topics, or performance could be used to examine performance for differential item or task functioning. Such analyses are best conducted when there is prior theory in support of such analyses. For example, if it is felt that by examining the materials (listening or reading) of an assessment that the content and topic areas are predominantly from science and engineering, it will be useful then to test whether other academic major test-taking groups (such as from arts, business, and humanities) will find items or tasks to have DIF based on test performance data. In fact, DIF analyses unmotivated by theory or prior findings are generally frowned upon, as these studies could just lead to fishing expeditions with no useful findings.

> *Sub-claim 1c:* The university placement assessment is free of bias, as it has provided appropriate accommodations for test takers with disabilities.
>
> *Warrant 1c:* Research on the university placement assessment will show that the assessment is free of bias as it has provided appropriate accommodations for test takers with disabilities.

The need to provide accommodations in assessments for test takers with disabilities has become an important component in assessment development in many countries. In the U.S., with the American with Disabilities Act of 1990, all assessments need to have accommodations for test takers with disabilities. One of the main difficulties is that according to the U.S. government, there are 60 or so different types of disabilities, and providing accommodations for all of them is definitely a challenge (see Keonig & Bachman, 2004 for details). The second challenge is matching the appropriate accommodation with the disability. And, finally, the defensibility of the accommodations seems to be in doubt, as there is insufficient research to support the different accommodations (Koenig & Bachman, 2004).

For example, the accommodation of extended time for the completion of an essay task is a popular accommodation. Therefore, if test takers without disabilities have 30 minutes to complete an essay task, test takers with a disability receive 45 minutes. But as Koenig and Bachman (2004) point out, there is insufficient research to support such an accommodation. This can lead to even more questions: Should there be no extra time or 20 or 30 minutes extra or even more? A more important question that arises is whether the accommodation changes the construct of the assessment task or whether the accommodation is creating construct-irrelevant variance?

Similarly, in the U.S., there is a movement among researchers in the area of English language learning who have proposed accommodations for English language learners who have to take subject-matter assessments (such as mathematics, science, and history and civics) in English. Similar difficulties probably exist in countries like the U.K., Canada, and Australia, where recent immigrants in the school system have to take assessments in English but their English language ability may be behind their mathematical and scientific skills. Such test takers' scores in mathematics and science are likely to be confounded with their English language ability.

In order to reduce or eliminate this confounding effect, Abedi (2009, 2014) proposed many measures such as language simplification in word problems in mathematics and science and glossing and translation of critical mathematical and scientific terms. Once again, there is insufficient empirical research as yet to support the appropriate accommodation and to provide assessment agencies the appropriate strategy for glossing or translation when multiple languages are involved.

Thus, although accommodations have been deemed essential to level the playing field between test takers with disabilities and English language learners, insufficient evidence has been gathered to support the requirement. Focused research on separate accommodations that are being considered for an assessment needs to be conducted so that evidence can be gathered in support of the warrant.

Sub-claim 1d: The university placement assessment is free of bias in terms of score interpretation, standard setting, and decision-making.

Warrant 1d: Research on the university placement will show that the assessment is free of bias in terms of score interpretation, standard setting, and decision-making.

Score interpretation, along with standard setting and decision-making, are collectively the final and arguably the most critical step in an assessment. After the performance is scored, scores have to be interpreted along with standard setting to be "outstanding, excellent, good, fair, and poor" or pass–fail grades. These in turn are used to make decisions such as "accepted for admission with a scholarship, accepted for admission, not accepted for admission" or "approved for employment or not approved for employment," or "eligible for immigration or citizenship." Therefore, focused research on standard-setting methods used are necessary to support cut scores for decision-making.

Sub-claim 1e: The university placement assessment is free of bias in terms of cost and uniformity and free of fraud.

Warrant 1e: Research on the university placement assessment will show that the assessment is free of bias in terms of cost and uniformity and free of fraud.

These are administrative aspects of an assessment. That an assessment should be affordable to test takers—not priced so high as to leave out significant portions of the possible test-taking population—is not a difficult concept. However, this aspect needs examination. Similarly, that an assessment should be administered locally or within a reasonable geographical distance from test takers is obvious. However, this, too, needs to be examined. Checklists or survey questionnaires should be able to gather sufficient evidence to support these warrants.

Uniform administration is critical for fair and consistent assessments across occasions, forms, and locations. Clear protocols for assessment administration can provide uniform administration without much difficulty. With regard to fraud and cheating, several different procedures need to be in place. In classroom assessments, teachers can devise means by which these can be prevented; in large-scale assessments, a great deal of effort has to be in place to prevent fraudsters and cheaters from exploiting technology to game the system. Psychometric means by examining test performance patterns to identify fraudsters and cheaters has been found to be useful (Geranpayeh, 2014).

Illustrative Studies

Studies that focus on assessment bias in terms of first language, gender, and age backgrounds are presented.

DIF in Terms of L1 and Gender: Kunnan (1990)

Claim: The ESLPE is free of bias.

Sub-claim: The ESLPE is free of bias in terms of L1 (first language) and gender of test taker groups.

Warrant: Research on the ESLPE will show that the assessment is free of bias in terms of L1 and gender of test taker groups.

Kunnan's (1990) study was concerned with the identification of DIF among four L1 groups and the two gender groups in the fall 1987 version of UCLA's ESLPE. The sample for the study was 844 non–L1-speaking students entering UCLA. The L1 language groups analyzed were Chinese (262), Spanish (81), Korean (76), and Japanese (59). In terms of gender, the sample was distributed as follows: male, 478 and female, 347. The test instrument, the ESLPE, consisted of 150 items in five 30-item subtests and one 20-minute composition. The five subtests in this test were listening comprehension, reading comprehension, grammar, vocabulary, and writing error detection—all multiple-choice items that were dichotomously scored. The one-parameter Rasch model from Item Response Theory that calibrates item difficulty estimates was used for this study. Results of the analysis indicated that 13 items in the L1 group and 23 items in the gender group displayed DIF.

L1 Language Analysis

The three items that favored the Japanese L1 group and the three items that favored the Chinese L1 group were grammar items, but different ones. These grammar items tested the appropriate use of grammar points, such as the definite article, preposition, or verb tense. These items may have been easy for these two L1 groups because of their instructional background and/or familiarity with discrete-point grammar testing in their home countries. Thus, the source for this type of DIF can be hypothesized to be *instructional background*, both in terms of test content (grammar-based teaching and testing) and test method (multiple-choice format). The four items that favored the Spanish L1 group were all vocabulary items. The words that were tested were hypothetical, implication, elaborate, and alcoholics. All these words have Spanish *cognates*, making the items potentially easy for this L1 group. Thus, the source for this type of DIF may be hypothesized to be cognates, a test-content facet based on test taker L1. The potential sources of DIF for two grammar items, one that favored the Japanese L1 group and one that favored the Chinese L1 group, and one vocabulary item that favored the Korean L1 group could not be identified.

Gender Analysis

The 20 items that favored the male group came from all sections of the test: 7 in listening, 4 in reading, 3 in grammar, 4 in vocabulary, and 2 in writing error detection. The 11 listening and reading items were based on the listening and reading passages and, therefore, the content of the passages could be a source of the DIF. These items were based on passages from business, culture/anthropology, and aerospace engineering passages. These subject areas seem to favor the male group. In addition, one of the vocabulary items tested, "simulates," may be used frequently in engineering/science classes. Out of 478 male students who took part in this study, 72 percent indicated that they were engineering/science majors compared with 24 percent of the 347 female students. The potential source of this type of DIF may have been test taker *academic major field*, a test-content facet. The potential source for DIF for three grammar, three vocabulary, and two writing error detection items could not be hypothesized. In addition, the source for DIF for three items that favored the female group, one each from listening, vocabulary, and writing error detection, could not be hypothesized.

Backing and Rebuttal

In terms of backing, in both analyses, out of the 150 items in the ESLPE, 36 items (24 percent) with no overlap between L1 and gender groups were identified as displaying DIF. Potential sources of DIF for 22 of these items (61 percent) were hypothesized, leaving 14 items (39 percent) for which there were no hypotheses. But identifying potential sources of DIF is only the first step in this kind of analysis. The next step, determining what to do with items that display DIF and how to compensate test takers for such "bias," typically follows one of three procedures: (a) sources causing DIF should be examined, hypothesized, and causally related, if possible; (b) items displaying DIF can be improved or discarded; and (c) items displaying DIF in a post hoc test analysis should be dropped from the test and not scored.

Figure 7.2 shows the relationships among the principles, claims, warrants, backing, and rebuttal regarding the claims of the ESLPE. As the findings of the study do not clear the ESLPE of bias, there is a rebuttal to the claim. Thus, the claim that the ESLPE is free of bias is not supported. The X mark in the claims box and flow of backing and warrants going to the claims from the principle shows that the claims are invalidated or cancelled for now. Therefore, a deferred

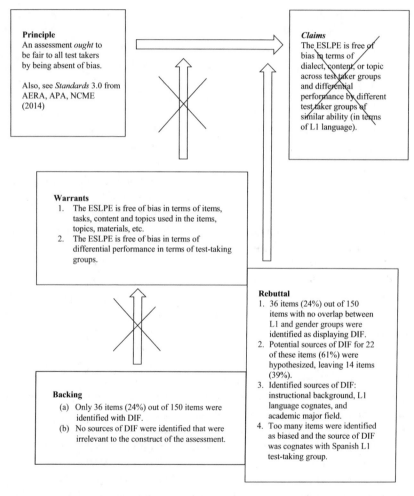

FIGURE 7.2 Principle, claims, warrants, and backing for Principle 1, Fairness, sub-claim 1—Absence of bias—with rebuttal (L1 and gender). Note the X marks on the sub-claim and on the arrow from the backing to warrant to the claim indicates that the claim cannot be supported.

judgment pending additional backing from further empirical studies is the most logical conclusion.

DIF in terms of age: Geranpayeh and Kunnan (2007)

Claim: The CAE is free of bias.

Sub-claim: The CAE is free of bias in terms of age of test taker groups.

Warrant: Research on the CAE will show that the assessment is free of bias in terms of age of test taker groups.

Geranpayeh and Kunnan's (2007) study examined the relationship between test performance and test takers' age. This is an important concern in the Cambridge Language Assessments' suite of examinations, as there has been a shift in the traditional test population, where test takers of many age groups are taking these cognitively challenging tests. Anecdotal historical observations had indicated that if there were going to be any DIF in these examinations, it was likely to affect mainly listening items. As there had been no empirical research in this area with the Certificate in Advanced English (CAE) examination, it was decided to investigate whether listening test items would exhibit DIF across age groups. The CAE listening paper contains 30 items in four parts. Each part contained a recorded text or texts and corresponding comprehension tasks. The texts in Parts 1, 3, and 4 were heard twice; the text in Part 2 was heard only once. The recordings contained a variety of accents corresponding to standard variants of English L1 speaker accent and to English non-L1 speaker accents that approximated to the norms of L1 speaker accents. Items were scored dichotomously.

The two research questions were: (1) Do CAE listening paper test items exhibit DIF toward test taker groups in terms of age? And, if so, to what extent? (2) Are CAE listening paper test items biased toward test taker groups in terms of age? And, if so, to what extent? To answer these questions, statistical analyses were performed first, items were then flagged, and content analyses were performed on these items, as well as on the items that were not flagged.

Data in this study are based on 4941 test takers who took the CAE examination in December 2002. Test takers' background information was collected through electronic Candidate Information Sheets completed before the test administration. These included information about each candidate's gender, age, first language, years of study in English, and previous exams taken. Test takers were divided into three age groups: 17 and younger (Group 1), 18 to 22 (Group 2), and 23 and older (Group 3).

The IRT-based DIF detection procedure implemented in BILOG-MG was used for the study. To satisfy the IRT assumption of unidimensionality, an exploratory factor analysis was conducted. A one-factor solution was obtained with an eigenvalue of 2.2 accounting for 55 percent of the total variance. The sample response data (n = 1000) was read into BILOG-MG for DIF analysis. Items that were identified as ones exhibiting DIF through the statistical analysis were subject to content analysis. These items were submitted to the subject officer responsible for the CAE listening paper, as well as five other content experts for further review. The content experts were asked to rate the suitability of the test items for each age group using a questionnaire with a 5-point scale. The experts rated each item on a scale: 1 for strong advantage, 2 for advantage, 3 for neither advantage nor disadvantage, 4 for disadvantage, and 5 for strong disadvantage.

Results of the analyses showed that 6 items out of 30 items exhibited DIF: Items 4, 11, 18, 20, 21 and 27. Of these six items, only Item 4 shows DIF in both group comparisons (Groups 1 and 2 and Groups 2 and 3). A discussion of the six items that exhibited DIF is presented next.

> *Item 4*: This item is in Part 1 (Environmental Adviser), and the sub-skill targeted (or primary dimension, if you like) is the ability to recall explicitly mentioned detail. The correct answer is "conservation group," but an analysis of the common wrong answers revealed that the three most frequent wrong answers are "conversation group," "consultation group," and "conciliation group." Was the younger group writing "conversation group" because it was familiar to them from conversation classes in school? Was the older group writing "consultation group" and "conciliation group," which are more sophisticated answers, equally incorrect? It is evident that all groups were having difficulty with this item and may have been trying to find an answer from their world experience (percent correct is 0.56).

> *Item 11*: This item is from Part 2 (Tractors), and the sub-skill or primary dimension targeted is the ability to recall explicitly mentioned detail. This item exhibits DIF in only one direction, between Groups 1 and 2. The average expert content rating for each group on this item was 3, which indicates the experts did not believe this item would advantage or disadvantage any age groups: "Jason's vintage tractor was found in a. . . behind his house," the correct answer being "shed." Item difficulty (0.44 percent correct) and item discrimination (0.37) statistics indicate the item to be quite difficult, but there was no reason to believe the item was biased toward any age group.

> *Item 18*: This item is from Part 3 (Tom Davies), and the sub-skill or primary dimension targeted is the ability to correctly identify the inference (from multiple-choice options) from implicitly mentioned ideas. This item exhibits DIF in only one direction, between Groups 2 and 3. The expert content rating on this item indicates no advantage/disadvantage for the aforementioned two groups. The experts, however, indicated a slight disadvantage for the first age group, which was not supported by DIF analysis. Item difficulty (0.50 percent correct) and item discrimination (0.16) statistics indicate the item to be quite difficult, and the low item discrimination value could indicate that this could confound the DIF estimates on this particular item.

Item 20: This item is from Part 3 (Tom Davies), and the sub-skill or primary dimension targeted is the ability to correctly identify the inference (from multiple-choice options) from explicitly mentioned ideas. This item exhibits DIF in only one direction, between Groups 1 and 2. The average expert content rating for each group on this item was 3, which indicates the experts did not believe this item advantaged or disadvantaged any age group. Item difficulty (0.75 percent correct) and item discrimination (0.40) statistics indicate the item to be relatively easy and discriminating quite well. Therefore, there was no reason to believe that the item was biased toward any age group.

Item 21: This item is also from Part 3 (Tom Davies), and the sub-skill or primary dimension targeted is the ability to correctly identify the inference (from multiple-choice options) from implicitly mentioned ideas. This item exhibits DIF in only one direction, between Groups 2 and 3. The expert content rating on this item indicates no advantage or disadvantage for these two groups. On the other hand, the experts indicated a slight disadvantage for Group 1, which was not supported by the DIF analysis. Item difficulty (0.60 percent correct) and item discrimination (0.34) statistics indicate the item to be quite easy and discriminating quite well. Therefore, there was no reason to believe that the item was biased toward any age group.

Item 27: This item is from Part 4, Task 1 (Communication), and the sub-skill or primary dimension targeted is the ability to correctly identify the main idea of five short monologues in a statement-matching response format. This item exhibits DIF in only one direction, between Groups 2 and 3. The average expert content rating for each group on this item was 3, which indicates that the experts did not believe this item would advantage or disadvantage any age groups. Item difficulty (0.61 percent correct) and item discrimination (0.42) statistics indicate the item to be relatively easy and discriminating quite well. Therefore, there was no reason to believe that the item was biased toward any age group.

In terms of identifying the source of DIF, content expert ratings of these items only showed a 1-point rating difference. Thus, it is possible that the items were not clearly biased toward the age groups under investigation. It was also hypothesized earlier that the source of DIF in Item 4 could be related to the impact of test takers' difficulty in responding to Item 3—neighborhood-related DIF.

Another source of test takers' score variability across age may also arise from differences in test taker processes: for example, in Items 1, 4, 5, 11, and 21, the ability to recall information or the ability to use memory strategies may be critical, and different age groups might use these processes differently. Further, in Item 27, test takers are expected to listen to five monologues, and once again test taker responses' variability across age may be due to the differences in the ability to recall information or the ability to use memory strategies across age groups.

Another possible explanation is the multidimensional nature of CAE listening items. Geranpayeh's (2005a, 2005b) studies on the CAE examination have showed that CAE listening items have moderate to high correlations with items that test reading, writing, and speaking skills in addition to having high correlation with items that test grammatical ability. Thus, it is possible that CAE listening items measure multiple dimensions to some extent. The large DIF values observed on some of the items are probably due to measuring those additional dimensions differently across the reference and the focal groups.

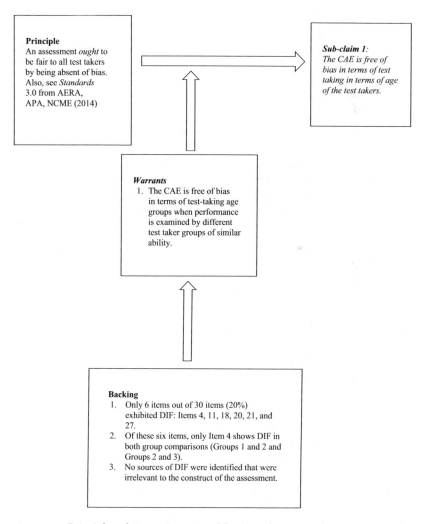

Principle
An assessment *ought* to be fair to all test takers by being absent of bias. Also, see *Standards* 3.0 from AERA, APA, NCME (2014)

Sub-claim 1:
The CAE is free of bias in terms of test taking in terms of age of the test takers.

Warrants
1. The CAE is free of bias in terms of test-taking age groups when performance is examined by different test taker groups of similar ability.

Backing
1. Only 6 items out of 30 items (20%) exhibited DIF: Items 4, 11, 18, 20, 21, and 27.
2. Of these six items, only Item 4 shows DIF in both group comparisons (Groups 1 and 2 and Groups 2 and 3).
3. No sources of DIF were identified that were irrelevant to the construct of the assessment.

FIGURE 7.3 Principles, claims, warrants, and backing for Principle 1, Fairness, sub-claim 1—Absence of bias (age).

Backing

Figure 7.3 shows the relationships among the principles, claims, warrants, and backing regarding the claim of the CAE. It also shows that there is sufficient evidence that the assessment is not biased in terms of age. Thus, the claim that the CAE is free of bias in terms of age is supported.

Structural Relationships for L1 Groups: Kunnan (1994)

Claim: The assessments in the study are free of bias.

Sub-claim: The assessments in the study are free of bias in terms of the internal factor structure in terms of L1 (first language) test taker groups.

Warrant: Research on the assessments in the study will show that the assessments are free of bias in terms of the internal factor structure of L1 test taker groups.

Kunnan (1994) explored a different approach to examining L1 groups within construct validation research. As mentioned earlier, language assessment researchers have typically dealt with the L1 issue as part of DIF studies. But this study explored the L1 issue from a broader perspective, as there is a need to establish generalizability boundaries that accurately demarcate the populations to which the empirical data can be generalized. This line of research is necessary, as the homogeneity assumption is unrealistic when applied to most data sets of large-scale language assessments. So the design here was to conduct construct validation research that can capture relationships among constructs for multiple test-taking groups.

The general research question investigated was the effect test taker characteristics such as formal instruction, informal exposure, English-speaking country exposure/instruction, and monitoring have on the four EFL tests for two L1 groups. Data from the Cambridge-TOEFL comparability study (Bachman, Davidson, Ryan, & Choi, 1991), which included 1448 subjects from eight sites in eight countries, were used: Bangkok, Cairo, Osaka, Hong Kong, Madrid, Sao Paulo, Toulouse, and Zurich. Two different L1 groups were created from this data to form the Non-Indo European (NIE) L1 group (Thai, Arabic, Japanese, Chinese) and the Indo-European (IE) L1 group (Spanish, Portuguese, French, German).

The instruments used were (1) a 45-item Likert scale background questionnaire, which collected responses regarding some of the test taker characteristics, such as previous instruction or exposure to English, and the use of monitoring; and (2) EFL test batteries: the First Certificate in English (FCE), administered by the University of Cambridge Local Examinations Syndicate; the TOEFL; the SPEAK, administered by the Educational Testing Service; and the Test of English Writing, a TWE-like test developed for the Cambridge-TOEFL comparability study (Bachman et al., 1991). Separate multiple-group structural modeling was used instead of the simultaneous multiple-group structural modeling (and the MIMIC and the multilevel models) because the main interest in this study was to investigate the different structural relationships for the NIE and IE groups, not comparisons between the two L1 groups for similar models, which the simultaneous multiple-group modeling would have provided.

Two models were tested: in Model 1, instruction and monitoring were modeled as independent factors and test performance as a dependent factor; in Model 2, instruction was modeled as an independent factor, monitoring as an intervening factor, and test performance as a dependent factor. Model comparison between the two structural models indicated that although both models were statistically (based on individual parameter estimates and goodness-of-fit indices) and substantively acceptable, structural Model 2 was the preferred model. This was based on the consideration that though the χ^2 difference between the two models was 21.28 and highly significant (p = 0.001), the second model, based on Gardner's prior research in SLA, provided a clearer interpretation that formal and informal instruction influenced self-monitoring and self-monitoring in turn influenced test performance. However, the findings indicated that there were very few differences between the relationships among the constructs, and these differences were not substantive for the NIE and IE groups. Table 7.2 shows the goodness-of-fit indices for two models that were tested for both L1 groups.

Backing

Figure 7.4 shows the relationships among the principles, claims, warrants, and backing and rebuttal regarding the claims of the TOEFL and FCE. It also shows

TABLE 7.2 Goodness-of-fit indices for Models 1 and 2 for both L1 groups

Index	Model 1		Model 2	
	NIE	*IE*	*NIE*	*IE*
χ^2	577.66	767.12	556.38	779.64
df	258	258	257	259
p	0.001	0.001	0.001	0.001
χ^2/df	2.24	2.97	2.17	3.01
SB χ^2	568.07	754.38	398.77	558.78
BBNFI	0.89	0.88	0.90	0.88
BBNNFI	0.93	0.90	0.93	0.90
CFI	0.94	0.92	0.94	0.92

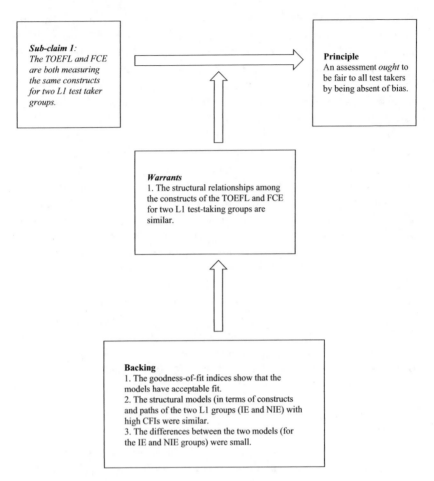

FIGURE 7.4 Principle, claims, warrants, and backing for Principle 1, Fairness, sub-claim 1—Structural relationships between L1 test-taking groups

that there is sufficient evidence that the assessment is not structurally different for the two NIE and IE groups. Thus, the claim that the TOEFL and FCE are assessing the same constructs (that is, there is no invariance) is supported.

Conclusion

In this chapter, the concept of absence of bias was presented and discussed as part of Principle 1, Fairness: Absence of bias. Three sources of construct-irrelevant variance (cognitive, affective, and physical) that are the main causes of bias were discussed. Specifically, cognitive-irrelevant variance sources include language difficulties due to dialect, grammatical structure, and vocabulary; affective-irrelevant variance sources include content and topics that are sensitive/taboo and that affect test takers; and physical-irrelevant variance sources include the use of visuals, media, and any equipment that is unfamiliar to test takers.

Specifically, in terms of DIF research, Zumbo (2007) indicated that post hoc or ad hoc research on DIF examining test performance with available data without hypotheses could result in incomplete and inconclusive findings. He exhorted researchers to use contextual variables such as instructional and home factors along with test taker characteristics in DIF research.

The illustrative studies presented the three generations of DIF research: the L1 and gender study (Kunnan, 1990) was in the tradition of the first generation. The study examined test performance of two L1 and gender groups in order to identify items that were biased. The second study (Geranpayeh & Kunnan, 2007) in the second generation examined test performance data for DIF in terms of age with the IRT method. The last study (Kunnan, 1994) in the third generation examined test performance of two L1 groups on two tests, but using a structural modeling approach with contextual factors in addition to the L1 factor. These research studies showed that absence of bias is a critical part of assessment and assessment practice. The next chapter focuses on beneficial consequences.

Note

1 Accommodations are also used for test takers with disabilities such as dyslexia and ADHD, as well as hearing impairment, speech impediments, etc. (see Keoning & Bachman, 2004). But the present discussion focuses only on accommodations with ELLs.

References

Abedi, J. (2009). Computer testing as a form of accommodation for English language learners. *Educational Assessment, 14*, 195–211.

Abedi, J. (2014). The use of computer technology in designing appropriate test accommodations for English language learners. *Applied Measurement in Education, 27*, 261–272.

Abedi, J., Courtney, M., & Leon, S. (2003). *Effectiveness and validity of accommodations for English language learners in large-scale assessments: (CSE Tech. Rep. No. 608).* Los Angeles University of California, National Center for Research on Evaluation, Standards, and Student Testing.

Abedi, J., Courtney, M., Leon, S., Kao, J., & Azzam, T. (2006). *English language learners and math achievement: A study of Opportunity to Learn and language accommodation: (Report No. 702).* Retrieved from The National Center for Research on Evaluation, Standards, and Student Testing (CRESST). Retrieved from: http://cresst.org/wp-content/uploads/R702.pdf

Abedi, J., & Lord, C. (2001). The language fact or in mathematics tests. *Applied Measurement in Education, 14*, 219–234.

Alderman, D. L., & Holland, P. W. (1981). Item performance across native language groups on the Test of English as a Foreign Language. *ETS Research Report Series, 1981*(1).

Alderson, J. C., & Urquhart, A. H. (1985). The effect of students' academic discipline on their performance on ESP reading tests. *Language Testing, 2*, 192–204.

Alderson, J.C., & Wall, D. (1993). Does Washback Exist? *Applied Linguistics, 14*, 115–129.

Americans Educational Research Association, American Psychological Association, the National Council on Measurement in Education. (1999). *Standards for educational and psychological testing.* Washington, DC: Author.

American Educational Research Association, American Psychological Association, the National Council on Measurement in Education. (2014). *Standards for educational and psychological testing.* Washington, DC: Author.

Americans with Disabilities Act of 1990, 42 U.S.C.A. § 12101 et seq. (West 1993): Educational Testing Service. (1987). *ETS standards for quality and fairness.* Princeton, NJ: Educational Testing Service.

Angoff, W. H. (1989). *Context bias in The Test of English as a Foreign Language.* Princeton, NJ: Educational Testing Service.

Aryadoust, V., Goh, C. C., & Kim, L. O. (2011). An investigation of differential item functioning in the MELAB listening test. *Language Assessment Quarterly, 8*, 361–385.

Bachman, L. F., Davidson, F., Ryan, K., & Choi, I.-C. (1991). *An investigation into the comparability of two tests of English as a foreign language: The Cambridge-TOEFL comparability study: Final report.* Cambridge, UK: Cambridge University Press.

Banerjee, J., & Papageorgiou, S. (2016). What's in a topic? Exploring the interaction between test-taker age and item content in high-stakes testing. *International Journal of Listening, 30*, 8-24.

Brown, J. D. (1999). The relative importance of persons, items, subtests and languages to TOEFL test variance. *Language Testing, 16*, 217–238.

Chen, Z., & Henning, G. (1985). Linguistic and cultural bias in language proficiency tests. *Language Testing, 2*, 155–63.

Educational Testing Service, Princeton. (1980). *ETS test sensitivity review process.* Princeton, NJ: Author.

Educational Testing Service, Princeton. (1987). *Standards for quality and fairness.* Princeton, NJ: Author.

Educational Testing Service, Princeton. (2009). *ETS Guidelines for fairness review of assessments.* Princeton, NJ: Author.

Geranpayeh, A. (2005a). Building the construct model for the CAE examination (Cambridge ESOL Internal Research & Validation Rep. No. 698). Cambridge, UK.

Geranpayeh, A. (2005b, November). Language proficiency revisited: Demystifying the CAE construct. Paper presented at the 12th University of Cambridge Language Testing Forum, Cambridge, UK.

Geranpayeh, A. (2014). Detecting plagiarism and cheating. In A.J. Kunnan (Ed.), *The companion to language assessment* (pp. 980–993). Boston, MA: Wiley.

Geranpayeh, A., & Kunnan, A. J. (2007). Differential Item Functioning in terms of age in the Certificate in Advanced English Examination. *Language Assessment Quarterly, 4*, 190–222.

Ginther, A. and J. Stevens. (1998). Investigating the differential test performance of native language groups on an Advanced Placement Examination in Spanish. In A. J. Kunnan (Ed.), *Validation in language assessment* (pp. 169-194). Mahwah, NJ: L. Erlbaum.

Hale, G. (1988). Student major field and text content: Interactive effects on reading comprehension in the TOEFL. *Language Testing, 5*, 49–61.

Hambleton, R., & Rodgers, J. (1995). Item bias review. *Practical Assessment, Research, and Evaluation, 4*, 1–3.

Harding, L. (2012). Accent, listening assessment and the potential for a shared-L1 advantage: A DIF perspective. *Language Testing, 29,* 163–180.

Holland, P. W., & Wainer, H. (Eds.). (1993). *Differential item functioning.* Hillsdale, NJ: Lawrence Erlbaum Associates.

Jensen, A. (1980). *Bias in mental testing.* New York: The Free Press.

Kim, E., & Jang, E. (2009). Differential functioning of reading subskills on the OSSLT for L1 and ELL students: A multidimensionality model-based DBF/DIF approach. *Language Learning, 59,* 825–865.

Kim, M. (2001). Detecting DIF across the different language groups in a speaking test. *Language Testing, 18,* 89–114.

Koenig, J. A., & Bachman, L. F. (Eds.). (2004). *Keeping score for all: The effects of inclusion and accommodation policies on large-scale educational assessments.* Washington, DC: National Academies Press.

Kunnan, A. J. (1990). DIF in native language and gender groups in an ESL placement test. *TESOL Quarterly, 24,* 741–746.

Kunnan, A. J. (1992). An investigation of a criterion-referenced test using G-theory, and factor and cluster analyses. *Language Testing, 9,* 30–49.

Kunnan, A. J. (1994). Modelling relationships among some test-taker characteristics and performance on EFL tests: An approach to construct validation. *Language Testing, 11,* 225–250.

Kunnan, A. J. (1995). *Test taker characteristics and test performance: A structural modeling approach.* Cambridge, UK: Cambridge University Press.

Kunnan, A. J. (2010). Test fairness and Toulmin's argument structure. *Language Testing, 27,* 183–189.

Kunnan, A. J., & Sasaki, M. (1989). *Item bias in UCLA's ESL Placement examination.* Paper read at the Ninth Second Language Research Forum, Los Angeles.

Lowenberg, P. (2000, October). Non-native varieties and issues of fairness in testing English as a world language. In Kunnan, A. J. (Ed.), *Fairness and validation in language assessment: Selected papers from the 19th Language Testing Research Colloquium, Orlando, Florida* (pp. 43-60). Cambridge, UK: Cambridge University Press.

Norton, B., & Stein, P. (1998). Why the "Monkeys Passage" bombed: Tests, genres, and teaching. In A. J. Kunnan (Ed.), *Validation in language assessment* (pp. 231–249). Cambridge, UK: Cambridge University Press.

Ockey, G. J. (2007). Investigating the validity of math word problems for English language learners with DIF. *Language Assessment Quarterly, 4,* 149–164.

Oltman, P. K., Stricker, L. J., & Barrows, T. S. (1988). *Native language, English proficiency, and the structure of the Test of English as a Foreign Language.* Research Report. Princeton, NJ: Educational Testing Service.

Pae, T. I. (2012). Causes of gender DIF on an EFL language test: A multiple-data analysis over nine years. *Language Testing, 29,* 533–554.

Pae, T. I. (2004). DIF for examinees with different academic backgrounds. *Language testing, 21,* 53–73.

Pennock-Roman, M., & Rivera, C. (2011). Mean effects of test accommodations for ELLs and non-ELLs: A meta-analysis of experimental studies. *Educational Measurement: Issues and Practice, 30,* 10–28.

Ramsey, P. (1993). Sensitivity review: The ETS experience as a case study. In P. Holland & H. Wainer (Eds.), *Differential item functioning* (pp. 367–388). Hillsdale, NJ: Lawrence Erlbaum.

Roever, C. (2007). DIF in the assessment of second language pragmatics. *Language Assessment Quarterly, 4,* 165–189.

Ryan, K., & Bachman, L. (1992). DIF on two tests of EFL proficiency. *Language Testing, 9,* 12–29.

Sasaki, M. (1991). A comparison of two methods for detecting differential I item functioning in an ESL placement test. *Language Testing, 8,* 95–111.

Shohamy, E. (1984). Does the testing method make a difference? The case of reading comprehension. *Language Testing, 1,* 147–170.

Shohamy, E., & Inbar, O. (1991). Validation of listening comprehension tests: The effect of text and question type. *Language Testing, 8,* 23–40.

Spurling, R. (1987). The fair use of English language admissions. *The Modern Language Journal, 71,* 410–421.

Swinton, S. S., & Powers, D. E. (1980). Factor analysis of the Test of English as a Foreign Language for several language groups. *ETS Research Report Series, 1980*(2).

Takala, S., & Kaftandjieva, F. (2000). Test fairness: A DIF analysis of an L2 vocabulary test. *Language Testing, 17,* 323–340.

Zeidner, M. (1986). Are scholastic aptitude tests in Israel biased towards Arab college student candidates? *Higher Education, 15,* 507–522.

Zeidner, M. (1987). Essay versus multiple-choice type classroom exams: The student's perspective. *The Journal of Educational Research, 80,* 352–358.

Zumbo, B. D. (2007). Three generations of DIF analyses: Considering where it has been, where it is now, and where it is going. *Language Assessment Quarterly, 4,* 223–233.

8

WASHBACK AND CONSEQUENCES

Introduction

The consequences of performing well or not on an assessment are always upper-most in the minds of test takers (and their families and well-wishers). This is because performing well in high-stakes assessments could mean increased career or life opportunities, and at the opposite end of the spectrum these benefits could be denied to test takers who do not perform well. Even in low-stakes assessments, where no career or life decisions depend on the performance, some test takers take these assessments seriously, and for them how well they perform is always important.

School, college, and university administrators expect test takers to perform well, and if they do not, they would like to hold their teachers directly responsible for the poor performances. In some contexts, teachers' salaries, bonuses, reappoint-ments, promotions, and other benefits are affected by test takers' performance.

Washback

Whereas the consequences of an assessment in the educational context at the micro level involve every test taker of an assessment, at the macro level, conse-quences involve the teacher, the school, the teaching, the learning, the syllabus and textbook writers, and the community. This effect is termed the "washback" of an assessment. Alderson and Wall (1993) listed 15 possible washback hypotheses; they are collapsed into the following:

(1)   A test will influence teaching and learning.
(2)   A test will influence what and how teachers teach.

(3) A test will influence what and how learners learn.
(4) A test will influence the rate and sequence of teaching and learning.
(5) A test will influence the degree and depth of teaching and learning.
(6) A test will influence attitudes to the content, method, etc., of teaching and learning.
(7) Tests that have important consequences will have washback, and those that do not have important consequences will have no washback.
(8) Tests will have washback on all learners and teachers.
(9) Tests will have washback effects for some learners and some teachers, but not for others.

These hypotheses have been investigated by many researchers. Alderson and Hamp-Lyons (1996) led the way with an examination of these washback hypotheses in TOEFL preparation classrooms in an American university. Similarly, a number of empirical studies conducted in a variety of contexts have helped reveal the complex relationship between washback, specifically, assessment and teaching and learning (for example, Cheng & Watanabe, 2004; Wall, 2005).

Specifically, Qi (2005) examined why the National Matriculation English Test (NMET) in China failed to bring about the intended washback effects of promoting changes in English language teaching in schools. Qualitative data were collected from interviews and questionnaires from four groups of stakeholders: 8 NMET developers, 6 English inspectors, 388 teachers, and 986 students. Qi found that NMET's failure to achieve its intended washback was mainly due to the conflicting functions that the test serves, namely, the selection function and the function of promoting change. This conflict makes the NMET "a powerful trigger for teaching to the test, but an ineffective agent for changing teaching and learning in the way intended by its constructors and the policymakers" (p. 142).

O'Loughlin (2011), in his investigation into the interpretation and use of IELTS scores for admission purposes at an Australian university, found that IELTS scores were not used to guide English language learning except for undergraduate students sometimes admitted with an overall band score of less than 6.5. He explored how the IELTS score was used in the selection of international ESL students within one faculty in an Australian university and the knowledge and beliefs that administrative and academic staff had about the test. Data gathered included relevant university policy and procedures documents, as well as statistics related to English entrance, a questionnaire administered to 20 staff and follow-up interviews with 12 selected staff. With regard to the way IELTS scores were used in admission, the study found that first, there was neither a principled basis for originally establishing IELTS minimum entry scores nor further tracking of student success to validate entry requirements. Second, applicants' IELTS scores were not considered in relation to other relevant individual factors as recommended in the guidelines listed in the *IELTS Handbook* (2007), including age, motivation, educational and cultural background, first language, and language learning history. Both findings indicated that the interpretation and use of IELTS test scores in this context were invalid. O'Loughlin thus proposed that a major change needs to be made in admission policy and procedure in Australian universities, which would allow test scores to be interpreted in relation to other relevant information about applicants. Meanwhile, all university stakeholders, including university policy makers, admission staff, and academic staff, need to be better educated in score interpretation and use and the other accepted measures of proficiency. Thus, research on the impact of the assessment on the wider stakeholders will show whether the assessment is beneficial or not.

In the context of immigration and citizenship, consequences of performing well or not on language assessments are serious, as test takers' careers, and travel and stay plans could be altered. Language assessments in this context are used to enforce immigration and citizenship policy that are often not based on explicitly stated purposes and uses, and, in some cases, there are hidden agendas that are discriminatory and detrimental.

Consequences

The consequences of an assessment based on how test takers perform could also be linked to the quality of the assessment. Cronbach (1988) argued decades ago that negative consequences counted against the validity of a test's use. He stated:

> [T]ests that impinge on the rights and life chances of individuals are inherently disputable... validators have an obligation to review whether a practice has appropriate consequences for individuals and institutions, and especially to argue against adverse consequences.
>
> *(p. 6)*

Messick (1989) was the first theorist to promote the concept of consequential validity as one of his six distinguishable aspects of construct validity. He stated:

> The consequential aspect appraises the value implications of score interpretation as a basis for action as well as the actual and potential consequences of test use, especially in regard to sources of invalidity related to issues of bias, fairness and distributive justice.
>
> *(p. 293)*

This statement implies that both intended and unintended consequences of an assessment, its value implications in interpreting scores, and bias and fairness are all matters that should be examined. Kane (2016) characterized this debate as three approaches: an interpretation-only model, a consequences-as-indicators model, and an interpretation-and-use model. In the first approach, assessment developers would only be responsible for the interpretation of assessment scores and would be able to ignore the effects of unintended consequences of an assessment program. In the second approach, championed by Messick (1989), assessment developers would be required to consider both intended and unintended consequences, as these would be evaluated as part of a validation program. If there were negative consequences like construct irrelevant variance, it would count against the validity of the assessment program. In the third approach, score interpretations and score use, although seen as separate aspects of an assessment program, would both be evaluated.

Kane (2016) summed up the differences this way:

> Most testing programmes are defined in terms of intended score interpretations and intended uses. Under the consequences-as-indicators model, the evaluation of consequences helps to validate score interpretations. Under the interpretation-and use model, the evaluation of consequences plays a *crucial role* in validating score uses, and in validating testing programmes that include score uses.
>
> *(p. 208 my emphasis)*

Using an interpretation-and-use model means that assessments ought to be evaluated in terms of whether they can bring about *beneficial consequences* to test takers and the communities in which they are used. If assessments are unable to bring beneficial consequences, there would be no purpose in using the assessment. This chapter will use the third approach to discuss arguments regarding consequences of assessments in the context of immigration and citizenship. The claims and sub-claims are illustrated with warrants and backing, with brief descriptions from a citizenship assessment.

Assessments for Immigration and Citizenship

Background

Immigration in the 21st century has continued unabated, much like in the previous century, with generally two kinds of immigrants: voluntary and involuntary immigrants. *Voluntary* immigrants are people who voluntarily leave their home countries; they are generally students going abroad to study, workers seeking new opportunities, families planning reunification, and tourists exploring new adventures. These immigrants could plan to remain in the receiving countries temporarily. *Involuntary* immigrants, in contrast, are people who are forced to leave their home countries due to political or religious persecution, political or social instability due to war and conflicts, high unemployment, extreme poverty, etc. Such immigrants could plan to stay on in their new countries for a long time, often seeking and obtaining immigrant and/or naturalized citizenship status. In many countries such immigrants are referred to as economic immigrants.

Short-term immigrants also may need to demonstrate relevant abilities, which may include language abilities related to their study or employment before they are issued visas to enter or stay in the receiving country. In some receiving countries, there are requirements such as a minimum level of language ability in the standard variety of the dominant language of the country that have to be met. In contrast, people planning long-term stays will need to apply for immigration and/or citizenship in their receiving countries. These applicants for immigration or citizenship are required to take language tests, history and civics tests, and/or social integration courses before they can be granted their new status.

Modern nation-states, including liberal democracies, have debated state-mandated national language requirements on the one hand, as part of political and social integration policies and, on the other hand, have made attempts to maintain minority or indigenous languages of minority communities as part of multilingual and multicultural rights. In terms of language rights, most countries strongly embrace the idea of a public monolingualism of the dominant language, whereas a few countries promote a limited public multilingualism with a limited set of individual rights.

Early U.S. Language and Immigration Policy

Although these notions of immigrants and citizens have to be rethought because of the era we live in, immigrant behavior and suitability of immigrants to be granted citizenship have been debated for decades in receiving countries. Pickus (2005) pointed out that in the late 18th century and early 19th century in the U.S., there was disagreement regarding how to turn new immigrants into the proper kinds of citizens. The main questions were: What kind of requirements for officeholders or immigrants wishing to be naturalized would best ensure their loyalty and their ability to understand America's civic principles and participate in its public life? Was the simple fact that the immigrant chose to come to the U.S. sufficient, or should there be a required amount of time before naturalization, variously set between 3 and 14 years? Or would newcomers never be trusted fully and be barred from holding elective office? (p. 15).

The history of the U.S. in terms of English versus non-English language policy shows how American institutions were wary of immigrants and their languages. The early decades after American independence were dominated by assimilationist thinking with ideas such as making English the sole official language, limiting access to voting and civil rights to non-English speakers, and opposing any form of bilingual education. Ricento and Wright (2008) reported that during this time indigenous Native American languages and cultures were stigmatized, and colonies and later states passed "compulsory ignorance" laws that made it a crime to teach slaves to read or write. In terms of language education, by 1923, 22 states had laws prohibiting the teaching of foreign languages in primary schools in a country that was made up of large numbers of first-generation immigrants. Courts intervened and found these laws unconstitutional: the two most important cases were *Meyer v. Nebraska* (1923) in which the U.S. Supreme Court decision ruled that a previous Nebraska law that forbade teaching in any language other than English to be unconstitutional and *Farrington v. Tokushige* (1927) in which the U.S. Supreme Court ruled that Hawai'i's effort to abolish private Japanese, Korean, and Chinese language schools was unconstitutional. Later in the 1950s, many states imposed English as the sole language of instruction in schools and passed laws banning the teaching of other languages.

In the 1930s, there was a push toward English language programs for foreign-born adults as part of the English First movement. These efforts were also promoted by American employers such as Ford, U.S. Steel, and Pennsylvania Railroad. According to Crawford (1992), employers believed that low proficiency in English led workers to socialist propaganda and prevented them from believing in free enterprise. Pavlenko (2002) observed that the main purpose was to solidify "the link between English and patriotism in the public consciousness so well that twenty years later Philadelphia's *Evening News* still argued that all aliens are to be taught the minimum of English necessary to guarantee a belief in democracy" (p. 180). Extract 8.1 presents the views of two U.S. presidents who support the use of English.

EXTRACT 8.1   U.S. PRESIDENTS WOODROW WILSON AND THEODORE ROOSEVELT ON THEIR SUPPORT FOR ENGLISH (1919)

President Wilson:
You cannot become thorough Americans if you think of yourselves in groups. America does not consist of groups. A man who thinks of himself as belonging to a particular national group in America has not yet become an American.

President Roosevelt:

We have room for but one language here, and that is the English language, for we intend to see that the crucible turns our people out as Americans, of American nationality, and not as dwellers in a polyglot boarding house; and we have room for but one sole loyalty, and that is the loyalty to the American people.

(cited in Pavlenko, 2002, pp. 183–184)

In the 1960s, the U.S. shifted its thinking regarding immigration. Then Senator John Kennedy acerbically commented that previous immigration policies would better reflect Emma Lazarus's words amended in the following way:

> Give me your tired, your poor, your huddled masses yearning to breathe free—as long as they come from Northern Europe, are not too tired or too poor or slightly ill, never stole a loaf of bread, never joined any questionable organization.
>
> *(Kennedy, 1964, p. 124)*

There have been many liberal and conservative shifts in policy and procedures in the last five decades, but what has become established is English language assessment to enforce citizenship statutes (see Kunnan, 2009, for details). A full description of the U.S. Naturalization Test is discussed in the illustrative study later in the chapter.

Australia's Dictation Test

Australia has a long history of using language testing to control immigration. Davies (1997) reported that during the infamous "White Australia policy," the government used a dictation test starting in the early decades of the 20th century. The *Immigration Restriction Act 1901* implemented a race- and color-based approach through what is perhaps Australia's most infamous language policy. Section 3 (a) of the act prohibited the immigration of:

> Any person who when asked to do so by an officer fails to write out at dictation and sign in the presence of an officer a passage of fifty words in length in an European language directed by the officer.

This law was used up until 1958 to restrict the migration of "undesirable" people, including anyone who was visibly non-White. This was achieved by the immigration official choosing a language that they expected would be unknown to the would-be migrant. What is particularly striking when looking at the law is that there is no explicit mention of the discriminatory way in which it would be implemented. This is even clearer when compared with the laws that preceded it, such as the *Coloured Races Restriction Bills* (passed in various parts of Australia) and the *Chinese Act 1881* (Victoria). Debates in Parliament in the lead-up to the act's creation indicate that the test would not apply to "qualified European immigrants" and that officers were to intentionally choose a language that the unwanted immigrants would not know (Crock & Berg, 2011). Yet there was clearly a desire to present the legislation itself in a much more neutral form than previous statutes, balancing the need for diplomacy with Asia against ongoing White-centrism (Mason, 2014).

The test was designed was a 50-word paragraph dictation test in a number of European languages and administered with intent to discriminate against non-Whites and undesirables. Two examples of how individuals were targeted are the cases of Egon Kisch and Mabel Freer. Jewish activist Egon Kisch from Czechoslovakia, who was exiled from Germany for opposing Nazism, arrived in Australia in 1934. The Australian government went to extraordinary lengths to try to exclude Kisch, including using the dictation test. As he was fluent in a number of European languages, he passed the dictation test in them, but failed when he was tested in Scottish Gaelic. But later a court ruling found that Scottish Gaelic was not within the fair meaning of the law and overturned Kisch's convictions for being an illegal immigrant. He was allowed to remain in Australia. Similarly, in 1936, the government planned to keep out Mabel Freer, a White British woman born in India. She failed the dictation test in Italian twice, but as the press and legal matters proceeded, the government was not able to provide convincing reasons for her exclusion and eventually she was admitted into the country. But examining the number of people who passed the test will demonstrate the harshness of the policy and the use of the test: between 1902 and 1903, 46 people passed the test out of 805 applicants; between 1904 and 1909, only 6 passed out of 554 applicants; and no one was able to pass the dictation test after 1909. The test was not

---

EXTRACT 8.2   SAMPLE DICTATION TEST PASSAGES, AUSTRALIAN DICTATION TEST, 1932

From 1st to 15th July 1932. (No. 32/13.)

The tiger is sleeker, and so lithe and graceful that he does not show to the same appalling advantage as his cousin, the lion, with the roar that shakes the earth. Both are cats, cousins of our amiable purring friend of the hearth-rug, but the tiger is the king of the family.

From 16th to 31st July 1932. (No. 32/14.)

Ice and snow over the Poles, which are not farther from the sun than we are, but the sun's rays reach them slantwise, and are stopped by such a thickness of air that not enough of them reaches the surface of the earth at the Poles to keep them warm.

From: http://guides.naa.gov.au/more-people-imperative/gallery/image011.aspx
Retrieved on June 10, 2015.

used after the 1930s and was formally abolished in 1973 when a less restrictive immigration policy was introduced. Extract 8.2 presents two different dictation passages from 1932.

This Australian Dictation Test clearly violated the general fairness principle for not observing the concept of fairness to all test takers. Specifically, it violated subprinciple 3: An assessment *ought* to be free of bias against all test takers, in particular by avoiding the assessment of construct-irrelevant matters. Clearly, requiring test takers to respond to tasks in languages in which they were not literate was an example of a construct-irrelevant task. And making decisions on the performance on these tasks was inappropriate except that it served the racist Australian immigration policy of those years. Thus, in terms of whether such a test was beneficial to the Australian community, it is clear it could not have been except in the perverse sense of the government's racist immigration policy.

The Dictation Test ceased to be legal when changes were made in Australia's immigration policy. The Dictation Test can be faulted on many grounds, but a few comments will suffice for now. First, the very idea of a language test in a language other than the immigrant's own or one that he or she knows shows what the intention of the policy was—to keep out certain immigrants. Second, as it was in operation for more than 30 years, it was obviously a perfect instrument to keep the White Australia policy working. Third, the test ensured a way for the government to give an educational reason for denying entry to the undesirable immigrants, although the process was clearly racist and it enabled the government to ensure a White Australia. Finally, no technical merits of the Dictation Test should trump the main purpose of the test—to keep out undesirable immigrants. Thus, we have for scrutiny and discussion a perfect example of an unfair test and an unjust institution.

In the 21st century, a formal testing regimen for people wishing to gain citizenship was launched in Australia. This new citizenship test is administered in English by computer and takes the form of 20 multiple-choice questions on Australian institutions, customs, history, and values. There is no separate test of English language skills, but English language ability is necessary to read the questions and select the correct answers.

The new test is expected to assess basic English language ability, an adequate knowledge of Australia and of the responsibilities and privileges of citizenship, and an understanding of the nature of their application. The 20 questions are specifically regarding Australia and its people; Australia's democratic beliefs, rights, and liberties; and government and the law in Australia. In order to pass the test, applicants need to have 75 percent of the questions correct. Extract 8.3 presents sample questions from the Australian Citizenship Test.

Piller and McNamara (2007) carried out a number of analyses to assess the linguistic difficulty of the resource book *Becoming an Australian Citizen*. First, a comparison between the language of the booklet and widely used definitions of "basic English," such as the first two levels of the CEFR, revealed that the booklet's

---

EXTRACT 8.3 SAMPLE AUSTRALIAN CITIZENSHIP TEST, 2015

1. What do we remember on ANZAC Day?
A. The landing of the Australian and New Zealand Army Corps in Gallipoli, Turkey.
B. The landing of the First Fleet at Sydney Cove.
C. The arrival of the first free settlers from Great Britain.

2. What are the colours of the Australian Aboriginal flag?
A. Black, red, and yellow.
B. Blue, white, and green.
C. Green, white, and black.

3. Which of these statements about government in Australia is correct?
A. The government does not allow some religions.
B. Government in Australia is secular.
C. Religious laws are passed by parliament.

From: www.border.gov.au/Citizenship/Documents/practice-questions.pdf
Retrieved on September 24, 2016.

---

language is well above the so-called "basic" level. Second, a lexical analysis using the web-based lexical profiler Web VP showed that about two-thirds of the content words in the booklet are beyond the level of the top 1000 most frequent words in English and that only 16.23 percent of the words in the booklet are of Anglo-Saxon origin. Both findings suggested the relatively abstract and complex nature of the material. Furthermore, the lexical density of the booklet language reaches 57 percent, which is at the very upper end of the range for written texts. These findings led the researchers to conclude that "the resource booklet *Becoming an Australian Citizen* is certainly out of the reach of a basic user of English and would present difficulties for many native speakers of English with limited education and/or limited familiarity with texts of this type" (p. 1).

The Netherlands' Integration Policy

The Netherlands is generally perceived as a liberal democracy with social policies resulting in a multilingual, multicultural society. But this perception would have to be modified with the recent social attitudes and public policies toward would-be immigrants, immigrants, and naturalized citizens. Newcomers to the Netherlands now have to pass three stages of testing in order to become citizens: admission to the country, civic integration after arrival, and naturalization to citizenship. According to Extra and Spotti (2009),

> the testing regimes for adult non-native speakers of Dutch and the recent abolition of languages of instruction other than Dutch in the primary schools should be evaluated against an ideological background of demanded cultural and linguistic homogenization at the national level.
>
> *(p. 125)*

The Law on Integration Abroad passed in 2006 described what applicants for admission to the Netherlands need to do—they have to take a computerized phone test of the Dutch language called the *Toets Gesproken Nederlands* (TGN), using Versant's computer-scoring technology showing knowledge of Dutch politics, work, education, health care, history, and living. This type of requirement is the first in the modern world, as it clearly presents barriers to family reunification (particularly for women in Morocco and Turkey) and has been criticized on the grounds of human rights. Extra and Spotti (2009) also cited a Human Rights Watch 2008 report that considered this testing regimen discriminatory "because it explicitly applies to particular 'non-Western' countries and because it violates the qualified human right to marry and start a family" (p. 133). This is because the program exempts citizens from European Union countries, Switzerland, Canada, Australia, New Zealand, Japan, and the United States, while simultaneously placing a big burden on North African immigrants.

In 2009, a collection of 12 case studies edited by Extra and Spotti (2009) on language testing and citizenship was published under the title "Language Testing, Migration and Citizenship: Cross-National Perspectives on Integration Regimes." Extra and Spotti (2009) outlined, analyzed, and evaluated these testing regimens by taking into account both the history and phenomenology of these regimens. For example, their evaluation of the first part of the admission test, which is supposed to measure test takers' knowledge of Dutch society, revealed that it is actually a hidden language test, because all questions are in Dutch and all answers also have to be provided in Dutch. With regard to the second part of the admission test, which is a computerized phone test of listening and speaking skills at the CEFR A1 minus level, external judgments offered by a group of four experts in linguistics, testing, and speech technology were cited. Concerning the quality of the test, the experts concluded that "there was not enough evidence that the proposed phone test would be valid and reliable" (p. 132).

In recent years, the Dutch Parliament has extended the time period for naturalization (citizenship) from five to seven years of residency, increased the salary requirements for highly skilled migrants as of 2014 (to Euro 4018 gross per month without the 8 percent holiday allowance or Euro 4372 with the holiday allowance), and in 2015, the TGN was removed and a new speaking test was put in its place. Extract 8.4 describes the various current components of the Dutch

---

EXTRACT 8.4 DUTCH *INBURGERING* TEST

Knowledge of Dutch Society
The theory part of the Inburgeringsexamen tests your Knowledge of Dutch Society. A minimum of 60% is needed to pass this part of the programme.

The Speaking Test
A short video using a few sentences of spoken Dutch will be played. Two questions need to be answered.

Reading, Listening and Writing
The reading and listening tests are multiple-choice tests which are taken on a computer. The writing test is done with pen and paper; tasks include writing short notes, e-mails, fill in forms and complete unfinished sentences.

Portfolio Oriëntatie Nederlands Arbeidsmarkt
In addition to the 5 tests above, applicants need to create a portfolio of their orientation on the Dutch job market. Once this task is completed, the applicants need to go and talk about the portfolio.

From: http://en.inburgeren.nl/examen-doen.jsp
Retrieved on September 24, 2016.

---

inburgering test. An integration course is available prior to taking the test in which applicants can learn about living and working in the Netherlands. Once the applicants have learned enough, they can take the integration exam.

Standards

The APA, AERA, and NCME *Standards* (2014) under the category of the rights and responsibilities of test takers (Chapter 8) and test users (Chapter 9) are relevant here.

Standard 9.0

Test users are responsible for knowing the validity evidence in support of the intended interpretations of scores on tests that they use, from test selection through the use of scores, as well as common *positive and negative consequences of test use*. Test users also have a legal and ethical responsibility to protect the security of test content and the privacy of test takers and should provide pertinent and timely information to test takers and other test users with whom they share test scores.

(p. 142; emphasis added)

Standard 11.1

Prior to development and implementation of an employment or credentialing test, a clear statement of the intended interpretations of test scores for specified uses should be made. The subsequent validation effort should be designed to determine how well this has been achieved for all relevant subgroups.

(p. 178)

Standard 11.2

Evidence of validity based on test content requires a thorough and explicit definition of the content domain of interest.

(p. 178)

Standard 12.8

When test results contribute substantially to decisions about student promotion or graduation, evidence should be provided that students have had an *opportunity to learn* the content and skills measured by the test.

(p. 197, emphasis added)

Standard 13.4

Evidence of validity, reliability, and fairness for each purpose for which a test is used in a program evaluation, policy study, or accountability system should be collected and made available.

(p. 210)

These standards are relevant not only for assessment developers and score users, but also for school and college contexts, as well as in contexts where legislators and policy makers intend to use assessments as instruments to further public policy.

Building an Argument

Principles

Keeping in mind the definitions, guidelines, and standards for justice discussed earlier, the general principles of justice with specific claims for justice are articulated next.

Principle 2: Justice

Principle: An assessment ought to be just.
Claim 1: An assessment and its assessment practice ought to be just.

Claims, Warrants, and Backing

This general claim regarding beneficial assessment of an assessment and sub-claims could be operationalized into key sub-claims and warrants that can be articulated as illustrated in Extract 8.5 and Figure 8.1.

Sub-claim 1a: Administrative remedies to challenge decisions such as rescoring or re-evaluation are available.
Warrant 1a: Research on administrative remedies to challenge decisions such as rescoring or re-evaluation will show that such remedies are available.

Assessment systems in many countries have administrative remedies that help test takers challenge their received scores in school or college contexts.

EXTRACT 8.5   THE PRINCIPLE OF JUSTICE

Principle 2: An assessment and its decision-making advance justice.
Claim 1: An assessment's decision-making advances justice.

Sub-claim 1a: Administrative remedies to challenge decisions such as rescoring or re-evaluation are available.
Warrant 1a: Research on administrative remedies to challenge decisions such as rescoring or re-evaluation will show that such remedies are available.

Sub-claim 1b: Provision for legal challenges related to decision-making is available.
Warrant 1b: Research on legal challenges related to decision-making will show that the remedies are available.

Sub-claim 1c: Decision-making of the assessment corrects existing injustice or advances justice.
Warrant 1c: Research on decision-making will show that the assessment promotes positive values and advances justice.

Also: *Standards 9.0, 11.0,* and *13.0* from AERA, APA, and NCME (2014)

These remedies could include manual rechecking of scores, retotaling of scores, and rescoring of responses to offer retaking the assessment at a later date. But often these procedures are unclear, or ambiguous, or they are cumbersome (as test takers are expected to file such requests in a big city) or too expensive. Further, the perception in many communities is that such remedies would not produce a new verdict but would restate the original scores. Of course, in many countries, these remedies are not available as assessments are considered infallible because assessments are developed by experts or an expert non-profit or government agency. In such countries, even if assessments are invalid, unreliable, biased, or have administrative problems, there are no remedies. In the immigration and citizenship contexts, there is much less transparency than in the school and college contexts. This may be because school and college assessments have to be accountable to citizens due to local, state, and national regulations regarding accountability, whereas assessments for immigration and citizenship are not accountable to immigrants (as they have very few rights in these matters).

> *Sub-claim 1b:* Provision for legal challenges related to decision-making is available.
>
> *Warrant 1b:* Research on legal challenges related to decision-making will show that remedies are available.

Legal challenges are a necessary component of remedies that make up the principle of justice. In the U.S., Title VII of the Civil Rights Act of 1964 and subsequent legislation provided remedies for persons who feel they are discriminated against due to their gender, race/ethnicity, native language, national origin, and so on. Almost a century earlier, the 14th Amendment to the U.S. Constitution adopted in 1868 addressed citizenship rights and equal protection of the laws. Thus, the U.S. provides a range of possibilities when it comes to legally challenging assessments that do not offer equal protection.

A few examples of litigation in the U.S. related to societal equity and assessments include *Hobson v. Hansen (1967)*, *Larry P. v. Riles (1971, 1984)*, and *PASE v. Hannon (1980)*. In all three cases, the plaintiffs charged that African American children were being discriminated against as disproportionate numbers of such children were placed into lower-track programs based on test scores (in the first case), placed into a mildly retarded program (in the second case), and into an educable handicapped program (in the last case). The courts found for the plaintiffs in all three cases. In another case, *Debra P. v. Turlington* (1981), the grounds for legal challenge was curricular, after African American students who took a minimum competency test had approximately 10 times the failure rate of White students. The court found for the plaintiff, stating that "if the test covers material not taught to the students, it is unfair and violates the

Equal Protection and Due Process clauses of the U.S. Constitution" (Debra P., at 402). In *Griggs v. Duke Power* (1971), the grounds for challenge was the requirement of a passing test score in addition to a high school diploma for promotion on the job after African Americans working at the company were denied promotion. The court found for the plaintiff, stating that employment tests have to be job-related: "What Congress has commanded is that any tests used must measure the person for the job and not the person in the abstract" (Griggs, at 436). In *Albermarle Paper Co. v. Moody* (1975), a test was found invalid as it was not designed to the standards laid down by the AERA, particularly referring to the technical quality of employers' validity and reliability studies. In *Golden Rule Insurance Co. v. Mathias* (1984), an out-of-court settlement was agreed upon between the insurance company, on the one hand, and the Illinois Department of Insurance and Educational Testing Service, Princeton (the test developer), on the other.

In *Breimhorst v. Educational Testing Service* (2001), Breimhorst sued ETS as he took the GMAT under nonstandard conditions with the accommodation of extended time. But his score report was flagged to indicate that the scores were obtained under nonstandard conditions. Prior to the case, test takers with disabilities could receive extended time, but their score reports would be accompanied with an asterisk or flag. As part of the court settlement, however, ETS agreed to stop flagging test takers who received extra time because of disabilities. In the context of immigration and citizenship assessments in the U.S., it is generally not possible to seek legal remedies, as laws protecting individuals may only apply to permanent residents and citizens. Many refugee review tribunals are set up to provide redress to asylum seekers who have to submit to the LADO (Language Assessment for the Determination of Origin) procedure (see Eades, 2009, for details regarding Australian asylum and refugee process).

> *Sub-claim 1c:* Decision-making of the assessment corrects existing injustice or advances justice.
> *Warrant 1c:* Research on decision-making will show that the assessment promotes positive values and advances justice.

One of the most valuable qualities of an assessment is the extent or degree to which an assessment is beneficial to the immediate and wider stakeholders and communities. In addition, an assessment ought to be able to promote positive values in a community, and not to have a detrimental effect on test takers or a test taking group. Further, an assessment ought to be able to promote or advance justice. Research on an assessment practice will be able to show whether the assessment is promoting positive values or advancing justice.

An Illustrative Study

The U.S. Naturalization Test: Kunnan (2009b, 2012)

Background

After World War II, the Immigration and Nationality Act of 1952 enshrined both the English language and the history and government requirements for citizenship; they were also known as the educational requirements. The act itself was controversial in many aspects as it was conservative to some and more restrictive to others and was vetoed by President Truman, but his veto was overridden by a vote of 278 to 113 in the House and 57 to 26 in the Senate.

Section 312 of the act, titled "Requirements as to understanding the English language, history, principles of form of government of the United States," required applicants for citizenship to demonstrate their ability to *speak, write, and read English and to demonstrate their knowledge of U.S. history, principles, and form of government*. In the words of DelValle (2003), "in passing the English literacy provision, Congressmen clearly linked the inability to speak or understand English to political suspicion" (p. 93). Specifically, the Immigration and Nationality Act stated:

No person except as otherwise provided in this title shall hereafter be naturalized as a citizen of the United States upon his own petition who cannot demonstrate—

(1) an understanding of the English language, including an ability to read, write, and speak words in ordinary usage in the English language: *Provided*, That this requirement shall not apply to any person physically unable to comply with therewith, if otherwise qualified to be naturalized, or to any person who, on the effective date of this Act, is over fifty years of age and has been living in the United States for periods totally at least twenty years: *Provided further*, That the requirements of this section relating to ability to read and write shall be met if the applicant can read or write simple words and phrases to the end that a reasonable test of his literacy shall be made and that no extraordinary or unreasonable condition shall be imposed upon the applicant; and

(2) a knowledge and understanding of the fundamentals of the history, and of the principles and form of government, of the U.S.

(INA, §312, 8 U.S.C. 1423)

The government enforced these requirements for naturalization in different ways over time. Starting in 1952, the requirement was informally enforced by immigration examiners and local judges. The idea of a standardized test was only raised when aliens seeking citizenship through the Immigration Reform and Control Act of 1986 were required to meet educational requirements. It was first proposed in the mid-1980s, although a test was not required to satisfy the Section 312 statute. At first, in 1991 the Immigration and Naturalization Service (INS) contracted with six private testing services to administer the standardized test. By 1996, these organizations operated about 1000 testing sites through sub-contractors. This arrangement was stopped and contracts canceled after an episode of the *20/20* TV program exposed testing fraud. The test then reverted to the control of the INS, and it has been part of the naturalization process ever since.

The Old Test

The old naturalization test had three sections in the English language part: (1) Speaking: Informal interaction took place between the examiner and the applicant regarding the naturalization paperwork (N-400 form, etc.) or other topics; (2) Reading: The applicant was to read one sentence; (3) Writing: Applicants were expected to write one sentence from about 100 sentences provided as dictated by the examiner. The applicant was given three chances. The history and government (civics) part was composed of 10 to 12 open-ended questions on U.S. history and civics selected at random from a hundred in the *Federal Textbooks on Citizenship*. Six correct answers were required to pass the test. Del Valle (2003, p. 113) reported one study regarding pass rates:

> A 1998 study commissioned by INS found that 34% of all denials (based on 7,843 petitions) were because of a failure on the language and civic test. . . the number may even be higher since applicants who fail the test initially can retake the test and are considered "continued." 25% of those continued are on account of failure on one of the tests.

The Redesigned Test

Given the general dissatisfaction with the old naturalization test, the test was ripe for redesign. As early as 2002, a redesign plan was underway, with the first contract issued by the new U.S. Citizenship and Immigration Services office (USCIS, which replaced INS) to a private company. Soon, the project was taken away from the private company and handed to the Board of Testing and Assessment (BOTA) at the National Research Council. The BOTA recommended a multi-tiered advisory structure and a technical advisory panel to oversee the project and to create a plan for test development. Instead, in 2005 the USCIS announced changes: The redesign was shifted from USCIS to the Office of Citizenship (OoC), the USCIS contract with BOTA was terminated, and another private company was given the contract with the new target date of January 2007 for completing the project. In December 2006, the USCIS announced that it had worked with community-based organizations

EXTRACT 8.6   THE U.S. NATURALIZATION TEST, ENGLISH LANGUAGE TEST, SAMPLE DICTATION ITEMS, 2009, 2016

Write the following sentence. (2009)
Here are some examples:

Today is a beautiful day.
Oath of allegiance.
I work hard.
I drive a blue car.
Martha Washington was the first first lady of the U.S.
Cited in Kunnan (2009a)

———

Reading Vocabulary List (2016)

PEOPLE
Abraham Lincoln
George Washington

CIVICS
American flag
Bill of Rights
Capital
Citizen
City

From: www.uscis.gov/sites/default/files/USCIS/Office%20of%20Citizenship/Citizenship%20Resource%20Center%20Site/Publications/M-1122.pdf
Retrieved June 8, 2015.

and other stakeholders to help ensure that the redesigned naturalization test and the testing procedures were developed and implemented in a fair and consistent manner. USCIS also concluded that the current format would be continued for the English language test. Thus, the format would consist of the following: (1) Writing: Applicants will have three chances to read and write a sentence in English based on a vocabulary list (rather than actual sentences as in the old test). (2) Reading and writing sentences will cover U.S. history and civics, and applicants will be asked to read a sentence and then write the answer dictated to them. (3) Applicants' answers to questions normally asked about their application (N-400) during the interview will form the speaking test. (4) One hundred new study questions on U.S. history and government were made available; the applicants would have to answer 6 out of 10 questions to pass this requirement. The USCIS also released vocabulary lists for reading and writing and speaking tasks with the N-400 application.

Extract 8.6 shows two sets of sample items. The first is a set of sentences meant for writing from the old test. The second is a reading vocabulary list from the redesigned test meant for the reading test from the USCIS website. The way it is supposed to work is that the examiner would use the list to form sentences for writing.

There are also newly issued scoring guidelines for the test. It provides a general description of how the U.S. naturalization test is evaluated and scored by USCIS officers in speaking, reading, writing, and civics.[1] Here are the guidelines for speaking, reading and writing:

Speaking: An applicant's verbal skills are determined by the applicant's answers to questions normally asked by USCIS officers during the naturalization eligibility interview. USCIS officers are required to repeat and rephrase questions until the officer is satisfied that the applicant either fully understands the question or does not understand English. If the applicant generally understands and can respond meaningfully to questions relevant to the determination of eligibility, the applicant has demonstrated the ability to speak English.

Reading: To sufficiently demonstrate the ability to read in English, applicants must read one sentence out of three sentences in a manner suggesting to the USCIS officer that the applicant appears to understand the meaning of the sentence. Once the applicant reads one of three sentences correctly, USCIS procedures require that the USCIS officer will stop administering the reading test. Applicants shall not be failed because of their accent when speaking English. A general description of how the reading test is scored follows:

Pass:

- Reads one sentence without extended pauses
- Reads all content words but may omit short words that do not interfere with meaning
- May make pronunciation or intonation errors that do not interfere with meaning

Fail:

- Does not read the sentence
- Omits a content word or substitutes another word for a content word

- Pauses for extended periods of time while reading the sentence
- Makes pronunciation or intonation errors that interfere with meaning

Writing: To sufficiently demonstrate the ability to write in English, the applicant must write one sentence out of three sentences in a manner that would be understandable as written to the USCIS officer. An applicant must not abbreviate any dictated word in the written sentence. Once the applicant writes one of three sentences correctly, USCIS procedures require that the USCIS officer will stop administering the writing test. An applicant shall not be failed because of spelling, capitalization, or punctuation errors unless the errors would prevent understanding the meaning of the sentence. A general description of how the writing portion is scored follows:

Pass:

- Has the same general meaning as the dictated sentence
- May contain some grammatical, spelling, punctuation, or capitalization errors that do not interfere with meaning
- May omit short words that do not interfere with meaning
- Numbers may be spelled out or written as digits

Fail:

- Writes nothing or only one or two isolated words
- Is completely illegible
- Writes a different sentence or words
- Written sentence does not communicate the meaning of the dictated sentence
- Writes an abbreviation for a dictated word

According to regulations, applicants who fail the English literacy and/or civics test during their first examination will be rescheduled to appear for a second opportunity to take the test (8 CFR 312.5).

TABLE 8.1 Pass rates for the redesigned test and the old test (in %)

Pass Rates	Redesigned Test	Old Test	
	FY 2010	*FY 2008*	*FY 2003–04*
Overall test	95.8	93.8	87.1
English	97.0	94.1	90.0
Civics	97.5	93.3	94.2

Source: U.S. Citizenship and Immigration Services' Records Study on Pass/Fail Rates for Naturalization Applicants (ICF Inc., 2011)

TABLE 8.2 Pass rates for the overall test by key demographic groups

	FY 2010 Total N % passed		FY 2008 Total N % passed		FY 2003–04 Total N % passed	
Gender						
Male	1576	96.2	941	94.4	1252	88.7
Female	1883	95.4	1105	93.4	1418	86.0
Age						
18–24	392	97.7	238	96.6	339	95.9
25–39	1663	97.6	931	96.1	1144	91.9
40–49	865	96.0	543	93.2	630	90.0
50–64	442	89.4	270	88.5	427	74.5
65 plus	95	83.2	64	78.1	147	53.1
Nationality						
Africa	327	95.1	176	97.2	136	87.5
Asia	1404	96.3	827	93.8	1032	88.0
Europe	484	97.3	275	94.2	392	93.6
Caribbean	322	92.9	176	93.2	237	81.0
Central America	462	93.7	351	92.0	477	82.6
South America	349	96.8	183	93.4	238	90.3
North America	77	98.7	41	100.0	33	97.0
Oceania	26	92.3	17	88.2	6	100.0

Source: U.S. Citizenship and Immigration Services' Records Study on Pass/Fail Rates for Naturalization Applicants (ICF Inc., 2011)

Analyzing the Consequences

Principles

Keeping in mind the definitions, guidelines, and standards for justice discussed earlier, the general principles of justice with specific claims regarding the U.S. Naturalization Test (USNT) are articulated next.

Principle 2: Justice

Principle: An assessment ought to be just.

Claim: The U.S. Naturalization Test's decision-making is beneficial to the immediate and wider community and larger society.

Sub-claim 1a: The USNT's decision-making is beneficial to immediate stakeholders (e.g., test takers, teachers, and administrators).

Warrant 1a: Research on the USNT's decision-making is beneficial to immediate stakeholders (e.g., test takers, teachers, and administrators).

Backing for USNT's decision-making to immediate stakeholders

Research on whether the USNT's decision-making is beneficial to immediate stakeholders (e.g., test takers, teachers, and administrators) shows negative evidence. A review of the test materials showed that there were a number of problems with the redesigned test, including the way it is organized: (1) Examiners could use different sentences for reading and writing. (2) Examiners could use different content for listening and speaking; some could use history and civics test questions (although these questions could be answered in the applicant's first language), and some could use questions about daily life, current events, and sports to talk to the applicants informally. (3) The level of difficulty of the sentences for the dictation test (for reading and writing) could vary in topic, length, and complexity. Sentences created by one examiner could be more complex than by another examiner. (4) Applicants do not know what constitutes a clear pass or a fail in the dictation test and what constitutes a pass or a fail in the reading or speaking test, as there are no samples of correct or incorrect responses.

In terms of the test's administration, there is very little transparency regarding the examiner's choice of test items, the test taker's correct or incorrect responses, and the overall result at the individual level. As no data of pass and failure rates are publicly available in terms of immigration office or by test takers' gender, race and ethnicity, nationality, or first language, patterns of bias, if any, cannot be uncovered. And, of course, there is no diagnostic feedback to the test taker or teachers. Thus, the redesigned test, by all accounts, is unable to meet the standards or qualities of reliability, validity, and fairness (AERA, APA, and NCME, 2014 *Standards*). This means there is insufficient positive evidence to support the claims under the principle of justice.

In addition, in terms of intended and unintended consequences of the test, the level of English language needed to pass the USNT is not high enough to ensure that citizens would switch to English in their communities after the test instead of their first languages. Besides, all individuals residing in the U.S. can participate in civic activities and community work without both the required English language skills and knowledge of U.S. history and government (although these skills and knowledge may help). Further, the test authorities do not offer any diagnostic feedback to any of the immediate stakeholders (test takers or teachers from community colleges who teach courses on the USNT). All the test taker receives is a letter of pass or continuation (meaning, fail).

The pass rates reported from a study conducted by ICF International (2011) and submitted to the USCIS showed that pass rates have improved for both the English and history and civics components in the redesigned test compared to the old test from a records study of about 3800 cases for FY 2010 when compared to FY 2008 and FY 2003–2004. Table 8.1 shows these statistics, and Table 8.2 shows the pass rates for the key demographic groups. So from a pass rate point of view, the USNT can be said not to have too much of a negative effect on citizenship applicants, but at the same time, with about 700,000 applicants every year, even a 4 percent fail rate means that 28,000 were not successful the first time.

All of these pieces of evidence do not support the USNT claim of being beneficial to immediate stakeholders. Therefore, in terms of whether USNT's decision-making is beneficial to immediate stakeholders (e.g., test takers, teachers, and administrators), the backing evidence is generally negative, and in some instances the evidence is insufficient to come to a positive conclusion. In fact, a series of English language courses offered in community colleges might be beneficial to applicants instead of the USNT.

> *Sub-claim 1b:* The USNT's decision-making is beneficial to the wider stakeholders (e.g., school district, community, province/state, country).
>
> *Warrant 1b:* Research on the USNT's decision-making is beneficial to the wider stakeholders (e.g., school district, community, province/state, country).

Backing for USNT's wider stakeholders

Research on the USNT showed that the test as it is conceptualized cannot serve the wider purpose of serving the larger community by bringing about civic nationalism or social integration through the indirect measures of English language ability and knowledge of U.S. history and government, as these are skills and knowledge and not measures of community participation and activism.

First, for most applicants from non–English-speaking countries, English is a new second language, and sophisticated responses that they may have regarding U.S. history and government may not be easy to express in English. An empirical study conducted in California (Min, 2010) showed that applicants for citizenship of Korean origin in Los Angeles did not show any difference in civic nationalism before taking the test and after passing the test. This raises the concern that the test's purpose may not be ever met.

Second, native-born citizens are not asked to demonstrate their ability in the English language or U.S. history and government before they receive their driver's license or passport, as such requirements are not needed for U.S.-born citizens. Therefore, the naturalization test requirement could even be in violation of laws against racial and ethnic discrimination, although courts are reluctant to review citizenship requirements as Article 1, Section 8 of the U.S. Constitution leaves the power to establish rules regarding naturalization to Congress. Even if we accept the 1952 Act and the English and U.S. history and government requirement as it stands, there is no constitutional requirement that this should be satisfied through a test. This leaves the door open for alternative ways of satisfying this requirement.

In terms of general public opinion, the test has been seen as meaningless and seen to hinder citizenship applicants. Pickus (1998, p. 25a) concluded that "questions deal with rights and freedoms but none speaks of its obligations . . . civic knowledge does not make one a good citizen—native-born Americans do not have to take any such test." Etzioni (2007, p. 355) summed it up with this: The "test hinders those who do not speak English and favors immigrants from English-speaking countries and persons who can afford extensive English education prior to their arrival, or once they are in the U.S."

Therefore, in terms of whether USNT's decision-making is beneficial to the wider community (e.g., e.g., school district, community, province/state, country), the backing evidence is negative.

Rebuttal of Sub-claims

There are many grounds for rebuttal of the sub-claims (which then is also a rebuttal of the general claim). First, until the USNT meets the *Standards* (APA,

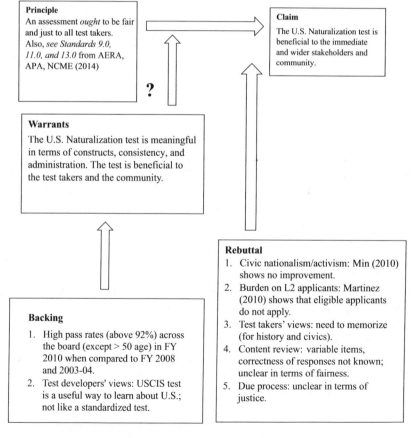

FIGURE 8.1 Principle, claims, warrants, and backing for Principle 2, Justice—Consequences. Note the question mark from the warrants to the claim.

AERA, and NCME, 2014) in the most important categories such as reliability, validity, fairness, access, and accommodations, the principle of fairness and the associated claims cannot be supported with appropriate and sufficient backing. A rebuttal claim that the USNT does not have reliable scores, valid score interpretations, biased assessments can be made. Research to support the rebuttal claims needs to be conducted. Second, the civic nationalism argument is also not supported in Min's (2010) study, which did not find a difference in terms of civic participation with applicants of Korean origin before and after taking the USNT. Martinez's (2010) study further showed that the test is a burden on L2 U.S. residents who are eligible to apply to become citizens, as they have to memorize answers to the history and civics questions. Finally, the due process that is necessary of a high-stakes test—in terms of providing diagnostic feedback, clearer criteria for correct responses with sample passing and failing performances of reading and writing, and transparency with the pass–fail data—is not available. Thus, the claim that the USNT's decision-making is beneficial to the immediate and wider community and larger society is not supported and therefore can be rebutted. Research studies are needed to support the rebuttal argument. Figure 8.1 shows the warrants, backing, and rebuttal for these studies.

Conclusion

This chapter discusses the consequences of the high-stakes language assessments in the arena of immigration and citizenship. The consequences at both the micro and macro levels in the immigration and citizenship arena, as well as for selection and admission to schools, colleges, universities, and employment at the workplace, need to be examined regularly. Such examinations will inform us of the extent to which a particular assessment is meeting the principles of fairness and justice. The examples of the U.S. Immigration policy, the infamous Australian Dictation Test, and the social integration policy in the Netherlands provide background information about the kinds of policies that resulted in discriminatory and/or inappropriate practices. The illustrative study with the U.S. Naturalization Test shows that there are problems in terms of meaningfulness and consistency of scores, in addition to whether it is beneficial to the test takers and the community. Therefore, a question that can be asked is whether enforcing the Immigration and Nationality Act, §312 with the USNT is the best way to go about it. With an English language assessment part that requires applicants to read and write one out of three sentences each and speak to an officer in English for a minute or two, one wonders how it is beneficial to the test taker and the wider community.

In the next chapter, the discussion will move to how fairness and justice can be advanced among assessment professionals and agencies.

Note

1 This web link shows the USCIS scoring guidelines: Retrieved on September 22, 2016, from: www.uscis.gov/sites/default/files/USCIS/Office%20of%20Citizenship/Citizenship%20Resource%20Center%20Site/Publications/PDFs/Test_Scoring_Guidelines.pdf.

References

Alderson, J. C., & Hamp-Lyons, L. (1996). TOEFL preparation courses: A study of washback. *Language Testing, 13*, 280–297.

American Educational Research Association, American Psychological Association & National Council on Measurement in Education. (2014). *Standards for educational and psychological testing.* Washington, DC: AERA.

Cheng, L., & Watanabe, Y. (2004). *Washback in language testing.* Mahwah, NJ: Lawrence Erlbaum.

Crawford, J. (1992). *Language loyalties: A source book on the Official English controversy.* Chicago, IL: University of Chicago Press.

Crock, M., & Berg, L. A. (2011). *Immigration, refugees and forced migration: Law, policy and practice in Australia.* Australia: University of Technology Sydney, Federation Press.

Cronbach, L. J. (1988). Five perspectives on validity argument. In W. Howard & H. I. Braun (Eds.), *Test validity* (pp. 1–14). Hillsdale, NJ: Lawrence Erlbaum.

Davies, A. (1997). Demands of being professional in language testing. *Language Testing, 14*, 328–339.

Del Valle, S. (2003). *Language rights and the law in the United States.* Clevedon, UK: Multilingual Matters.

Eades, D. (2009). Testing the claims of asylum seekers: The role of language analysis. *Language Assessment Quarterly, 6*, 30–40.

Etzioni, A. (2007). Citizenship tests: A comparative, communitarian perspective. *The Political Quarterly, 78*, 353–363.

Extra, G., & Spotti, M. (2009). Testing regimes for newcomers to the Netherlands. In G. Hogan-Brun, C. Mar-Molinero & P. Stevenson (Eds.), *Language testing, migration and citizenship* (pp. 125–147). Amsterdam, The Netherlands: John Benjamins.

ICF International. (2011). *U.S. Citizenship and Immigration Services' records study on pass/fail rates for naturalization applicants: Report: [RFQ/Project No. HSSCCG-09-Q-00228].* Washington, DC.

The Immigration and Nationality Act of 1952, Pub. L. No. 82–414, § 66 Stat. 163.

The Immigration and Nationality Act. (1952). *Requirements as to understanding the English language, history, principles of form of government of the United States Act, INA,* §312, 8 U.S.C. § 1423.

The Immigration Reform and Control Act (IRCA). (1986). Pub. L. No. 99–603, § 100 Stat. 3445.

The Immigration Restriction Act. (1901). *An Act to place certain restrictions on Immigration and to provide for the removal from the Commonwealth of prohibited Immigrants (1901, December 23).* Australia: Parliament of Australia.

Kane, M. T. (2016). Validity as the evaluation of the claims based on test scores. *Assessment in Education, 23*, 309–311.

Kennedy, J. F. (1964). *A nation of immigrants.* New York, NY: Harper & Row.

Kunnan, A. J. (2009a). Politics and legislation in citizenship testing in the U.S. *Annual Review of Applied Linguistics, 29,* 37–48.

Kunnan, A. J. (2009b). The U.S. Naturalization Test. *Language Assessment Quarterly, 6*, 89–97.

Kunnan, A. J. (2012). Language assessment for immigration and citizenship. In G. Fulcher & F. Davidson (Eds.), *The handbook of language testing* (pp. 152–166). New York, NY: Routledge.

Martinez, J. (2010). *Why are eligible Latinos not becoming U.S. citizens?* Seminar paper, TESL 567b, California State University, Los Angeles.

Mason, R. (2014). Incorporating injustice: Immigrant vulnerability and Latin Americans in multicultural Australia. *Journal of Intercultural Studies, 35*, 549–562.

Messick, S. (1994). Standards-based score interpretation: Establishing valid grounds for valid inferences. *ETS Research Report Series, 2*, 291–305.

Min, K. (2010). *Is the U.S. Naturalization Test meaningful in achieving its purposes of "civic Nationalism," "social integration," and "political allegiance" with citizens of Korean origin?* Seminar paper, TESL 567b, California State University, Los Angeles.

O'Loughlin, K. (2011). The interpretation and use of proficiency test scores in university selection: How valid and ethical are they? *Language Assessment Quarterly, 8*, 146–160.

Pavlenko, A. (2002). Poststructuralist approaches to the study of social factors in second language learning and use. In V. Cook (Ed.), *Portraits of the L2 user* (pp. 277–302). Clevedon, UK: Multilingual Matters.

Pickus, N. (1998). *Immigration and citizenship in the 21st century*. Lanham, MD: Rowman & Littlefield.

Pickus, N. (2005). *True faith and allegiance: Immigration and civic nationalism*. Princeton, NJ: Princeton University Press.

Piller, I., & McNamara, T. (2007). *Assessment of the language level of the August 2007 draft of the resource booklet: Becoming an Australian citizen*. Retrieved from: www.languageonthe move.com

Qi, L. (2005). Stakeholders' conflicting aims undermine the washback functions of a high-stakes test. *Language Testing, 22*, 142–173.

Ricento, T. K., & Wright, E. (2008). Language policy and education in the United States. *Encyclopedia of Language and Education, 1*, 285–300.

Title VII of the Civil Rights Act, Vol. 42 § section 2000e. (1964).

U.S. Citizenship and Immigration Services' records study on pass/fail rates for Naturalization applicants. (2011). RFQ/Project No. HSSCCG-09-Q-00228. Retrieved from: www.uscis. gov/sites/default/files/USCIS/files/Records_Study_for_the_Naturalization_Test.pdf

Wall, D. (2005). *The impact of high-stakes examinations on classroom teaching: A case study using insights from testing and innovation theory [Studies in Language Testing, Vo. 22]*. Cambridge, UK: Cambridge University Press.

Court cases

Albemarle Paper Co. v. Moody, 422 U.S. 405 (1975).

Breimhorst v. Educational Testing Service, No. C-99–3387 (N.D. Cal. 2001).

Debra P. v. Turlington, 644 F.2d 397 (5th Cir. 1981), 730 F.2d 1405 (11th Cir. 1984).

Farrington v. Tokushige, 273 U.S. 284 (1927).

Golden Rule Life Insurance Co. v. Mathias, 408 N.E.2d 310 (Ill. App. Ct. 1980).

Griggs v. Duke Power Co, 401 US 424 (1971).

Hobson v. Hansen, 252 F. Supp. 4 (D.D.C. 1966).

Larry P. v. Riles, 402 U.S. 1, 31 (1971).

Larry P. v. Riles, 793 F.2d 969 (9th Cir. 1984).

Meyer v. Nebraska, 262 U.S. 390 (1923).

Parents in Action on Special Ed. (Pase) v. Hannon, 506 F. Supp. 831 (N.D. Ill. 1980).

9

ADVANCING FAIRNESS AND JUSTICE

Introduction

The previous four chapters illustrated how to build an argumentative model for each of the sub-principles of fairness and justice and related claims: Opportunity-to-Learn, meaningfulness, absence of bias, and washback and consequences. In each of the chapters, after the sub-principles were presented, relevant standards (APA, AERA, NCME, 2014 *Standards*) were listed. Then, illustrative research studies were discussed with claims, warrants, and backing evidence. Evidence in support of the claims was presented and diagrammed, but in some cases, there was insufficient evidence and therefore rebuttals of the claims were offered.

In this chapter, the focus is shifted to how the principles of fairness and justice can be advanced among a variety of assessment stakeholders, from the design to the consequences stages. One such group would be school or college teachers or university professors who are responsible for developing and scoring and assigning grades for their school, college, or university courses. Another group of individuals responsible for assessments would be assessment professionals working for university, non-profit, and commercial agencies responsible for the entire gamut of the assessment process: designing, writing, assembling, administering, scoring, reporting, and making decisions based on the scores. An important third group would be test takers in all contexts who are the centerpiece of the assessment enterprise and hopefully the beneficiaries of assessments. Finally, there is the group that is arguably the most powerful of the whole lot: institutional administrators, government officials, and policy makers.

Therefore, ways to bring appropriate thinking and operations in support for the principles of fairness and justice need to be charted. I am proposing two ways of doing this. The first way is to include *ethical decision-making* in the pre-service and in-service training programs for school, college teachers, and university professors and on-the-job training for assessment professionals and institutional administrators, government officials, and policy makers. The focus of such training programs should include the area of consequences of assessments. Test takers, too, need to be made aware of ethical thinking that can bring about responsible behavior related to assessments. One clear way of making ethical thinking and moral justifications come alive is to translate ethical theories, principles, codes, and standards into plain language that can be understood easily (see Nagy, 2000 for an excellent example). A related way is to introduce hypothetical scenarios or case studies from the different contexts of language assessments. These scenarios could provide examples of exemplary awareness, as well as a woeful lack of knowledge of ethical thinking and moral justifications. The scenarios could then be analyzed from an ethical standpoint in order to provide guidance for appropriate behavior.[1]

The second way to advance the principles of fairness and justice is to *refocus traditional curricula* in language assessment for pre-service and in-service training programs with courses in applied ethics and responsible assessment development and score use. Such curricula would include the history of language assessment, highlighting how discriminatory practices in the past and the present have crept into the field. This would include cases where language assessments have been used to enforce public policy in immigration, citizenship, and asylum. These illustrations would help stakeholders be aware of the detrimental effects of language assessments generally used to mask hidden agendas and discriminatory practices. The chapter elaborates on these two approaches.

Ethical Decision-Making

A popular way of understanding ethical decision-making and moral justification is to understand the three prominent contemporary methods of ethics: *outcomes based* (utilitarianism and consequentialism), *duty based* (deontology), and *virtue based* (persons as moral agents) (see Baron, Pettit, and Slote, 1997).[2] In the first method, simply put, philosophers Bentham and Mill outlined that utility and consequences are all that matter in ethical decision-making. For example, the value of an assessment would lie in its worth or value in terms of whether a large majority were happy (or very few were unhappy) with the assessment. In the second method, championed by Kant, Rawls, and Sen, what is paramount in ethical decision-making is the duty or responsibility that one party ought to have to the other. For example, an assessment agency would consider its duty to produce a high-quality assessment for all test takers most critical without factoring in how many test takers were happy (or unhappy) or whether the assessment was a commercial success. In the last method, championed by Plato and Aristotle and contemporary philosophers Anscombe and MacIntyre, virtues espoused by the assessment agency as a moral agent would be critical. For example, assessment agencies would be expected to have virtuous character with ideal and aspirational motives.

One way of translating these ethical methods into real-world situations is to consider hypothetical scenarios as thought experiments. An excellent thought experiment called the trolley problem brings consequentialists (outcome-based thinkers) into conflict with deontologists (duty-based thinkers) in a unique way. The trolley problem was devised by philosopher Philippa Foot (1967) as a thought experiment, but there are many interesting variations today (see the work of Judith Thomson, 1976 and in the Tanner lectures by Frances Kamm, 2016).

The Trolley Problem Scenarios

In its original form, the first scenario goes as follows (Figure 9.1): A trolley is hurtling down a track after its brakes have failed. Farther down the track, there are five workers who are unable to leave the track. The trolley is headed toward them and is going to run over all five of them. But you are a bystander and you are near a switch that can steer the trolley onto a side track. On the side track, there is one worker. If you steer the trolley onto the side track, one innocent worker would die but five workers on the main track would be saved. What ought you to do? Steer the trolley onto the side track and cause the death of one worker? Or do nothing even though this would mean that five workers would die?

What ethical decision would you make, and how would you morally justify your action? Would you use outcomes-based or consequentialist thinking to make your decision and morally justify your action? If you do, you would justify your decision that one person's death would be preferable to five, as it is for the greater good, and, therefore, your action to flip the switch, although causing the death of an innocent person, would be justifiable. On the other hand, if you were to use duty-based or deontologist thinking, you would argue that it is one's duty to save all persons' lives, and therefore you ought not to cause the death of an innocent person.[3]

Kaman Chang
University of Macau

FIGURE 9.1 The trolley scenario: bystander with switch

In a second scenario, instead of the switch, you are standing near a fat man on a bridge above the trolley track (Figure 9.2). The trolley is once again hurtling down the track and is going to kill five workers. But if you push the fat man over the bridge onto the track, it will certainly stop the trolley and save the five workers but will cause the death of the fat man. What ought you to do? Push the fat man over the bridge and onto the trolley's track so that you can save the five workers, although this would certainly cause the death of the fat man? Or do nothing even though this would mean that five workers would die?[4]

Once again, what ethical decision would you make, and how would you morally justify your action? Would you use outcomes-based or consequentialist thinking to make your decision and morally justify your action? If you do, you would justify your decision that pushing the fat man onto the track would be permissible in order to save five workers, causing death to one person instead of five. Therefore, it could be seen as a case of *killing five versus killing one*. On the other hand, if you were to use duty-based or deontologist thinking, you would argue that it is one's duty to save all persons' lives and therefore you ought not to cause the death of an innocent person, whether it is an innocent person on the sidetrack or an innocent fat man on the bridge.

In a third scenario, imagine you are a transplant surgeon in a hospital who has five patients, each in need of a different vital organ. They will die without the transplants, but no organs are available. But just then a healthy person walks into the hospital for a routine checkup. When another doctor does the checkup, she discovers that the patient's organs are compatible with all five of his dying patients. What ought you to do or not do? Would you take the vital organs from the healthy person and conduct the organ transplant surgeries, thus saving the five patients although the healthy person would die?

What ethical decision would you make, and how would you morally justify your action? Would you use outcomes-based or consequentialist thinking to make your decision and morally justify your action? If you do, you would justify your

Kaman Chang
University of Macau

FIGURE 9.2 The trolley scenario: the fat man on the bridge

decision that harvesting vital organs from one healthy person to save five dying patients, although the healthy person would die, is morally justifiable. For the duty-based or deontologist thinker, as all lives are to be respected and because it is one's duty to save all persons, you ought not to cause the death of an innocent healthy patient even though it may save five others.

Now that we have seen these three scenarios, how do we make decisions and morally justify them? Can the scenarios be summarized into Principle 1: Killing Five versus Killing One? Or Principle 2: Permissible Harm (Kamm, 2016)? Or Principle 3: Negative Duty versus Positive Duty? If we use Principle 1, we are squarely in the consequentialist way of thinking and moral justification—that killing one would be preferable to killing five. But what about the transplant case then? Isn't that scenario also a case of killing one (healthy person) versus killing five (dying patients)? But is the doctor's act morally impermissible? Why is that so?

If we think our decision-making ought to follow Principle 2, we might argue that causing the death of an innocent person on the sidetrack is permissible harm to him because it will result in saving five persons, which is a greater good. But what about throwing the fat man over the bridge onto the trolley? Is this not a case of permissible harm as well? Why not?

Of course, in considering applications of ethical decision-making and moral justifications in real-world contexts, it is possible that the three methods of ethics may need to be made up of mixed ethical systems. Such mixed systems are more likely to be the reality when ethical decisions have to be made.

Language Assessment Scenarios

Following the trolley problem scenarios, hypothetical scenarios and real-world examples and reflections from language assessment are presented in order to better illustrate issues that surround fairness and justice. These scenarios exclude concrete realistic details so that we can focus on a limited number of issues. Let us now consider scenarios from different assessment contexts that illustrate some real-world challenges related to fairness and justice. These challenges need to be resolved by assessment developers, administrators, score users such as teachers, test takers, and decision makers. Some of the scenarios are related to the principle of fairness, whereas others are related to the principle of justice. The scenarios span the full range of assessment development and use—from design and tasks to administration and public justification. Reflections are offered after some scenarios.

Assessment Development

Scenario 1: Pretesting of Assessment Tasks

Imagine Kid Twist, who joined a large professional language assessment organization (university or commercial) that develops assessments for high-stakes contexts.

After he had worked at the organization for three months, he began to be concerned about many of the agency's practices. Kid took note of them: First, they did not pre-test or trial their test tasks; instead, they used the non–pre-tested tasks in a real administration and did not delete the scores from those tasks when they computed the scores for the test takers. In other words, test takers received scores that included tasks that were not pretested. Kid approached his supervisor, Stuart Bell, who was head of assessment development. He was at first disinterested in Kid's concern, but later admitted that pre-testing tasks would cost too much money for the organization, and if they conducted a pre-test, the assessment would also cost the test takers much more.

Scenario 2: Checks for Bias

Kid Twist also found that the organization did not conduct any review or investigation to examine whether the assessment was fair to all test takers in terms of content, dialect, test delivery, or test performance. Kid brought this matter up with his supervisor too. Stuart, the supervisor, said that although these are important matters, the organization did not have staff with expertise to conduct such investigations. Stuart also reminded him that, once again, these investigations would cost the organization a lot of money and the final result would be that the assessment would cost the test takers more.

Scenario 3: Defective Tasks 1

Sally Tomato wrote a test for her undergraduate class. As a conscientious instructor, she showed her test to her colleague for comments. Her colleague pointed out that 10 test items out of 50 needed revisions. But Sally decided to go ahead and administer the test without revisions. She reasoned as follows: (1) In order to revise the items, she would have to spend another 2 hours to change or revise the graphs and charts, which would cost money; (2) only 20 percent of the items were defective; (3) only 10 students out of 60 would lose a few points; and (4) it would not make a difference to the ranking of the students.

Scenario 4: Defective Tasks 2

Imagine Holly Lightly, the administrator of an assessment, had two forms of a paper and pencil assessment—Forms A and B. The forms belonged to a high-stakes university admissions assessment. It was known previously through pre-testing that there were a few defective tasks in the two forms: 10 tasks in Form A and 5 tasks in Form B out of a total of 100 tasks in each. But the administrator went ahead and used both forms, as a cost–benefit analysis conducted earlier showed that only 10 percent of the test takers who took Form A and 5 percent of the test takers who took Form B were misclassified as failed due to the defective tasks. Holly felt these figures were within the usual margin of error. She wrote in her report that the cost of replacing the defective tasks (designing and writing new tasks, pre-testing them, assembling them into the forms, and printing the new assessments) would be much higher than that of errors in classification, although she did not assign a monetary value to the misclassified test takers' lost opportunities due to the errors.

Reflection

If we consider the different philosophical methods, each may take a view that supports the actions and decisions of the players in our scenarios. The main questions here are: Did Kid do the right thing by bringing to the matter to Stuart's attention? Was Stuart doing the right thing by not investigating the assessment for its fairness? Are such investigations required in an assessment that is a high-stakes assessment? Are Stuart's reasons for not conducting these investigations defensible? Is there a violation of an accepted code of ethics and practice? Would this be an example of an unfair assessment? The utilitarian could take the view that the cost–benefit analysis provided the basis for the Sally's and Holly's decision and that such decisions have to be made in order to run a profitable business. The utilitarian could also concede that Holly should have preferred Form B to Form A as it had more utility. The contractarian could argue that Holly did not act morally, as she did not uphold the rights of all test takers to a fair assessment by holding defective assessments. These arguments could lead us to some important questions: What about Kid's, Sally's, and Holly's decisions? Can they be justified? Should they have been more duty conscious rather than worrying about the extra cost for revisions of test items? These scenarios are related to the principle of fairness and in particular sub-principle 2 (meaningfulness) and sub-principle 3 (absence of bias).

Scoring and Score Interpretation

Scenario 5: Compensation for Misclassification

Imagine further that Holly was convinced of her error and agreed to pay compensation to the test takers who were misclassified as failed. She offered a free retake of the assessment at a later date (as per the contract issued by the agency), but the results would be available only after the completion of the university admissions cycle. The test takers were not satisfied with the remedy offered: Some test takers wanted more compensation, whereas others planned to file a lawsuit in court against the assessment agency.

Reflection

The main question here would be about the nature of compensation offered as per the contract. Should a different compensation or more compensation save Holly? In the future, should more checks be in place to reduce or eliminate such errors in misclassification? Obviously, better assessment practices in the agency could have avoided such negligence and Holly would not have faced a lawsuit.

Scenario 6: Scoring Difficulties

Ni Nyoman Yohana, a history instructor, designed a final assignment for her 12th grade class. She provided a short essay on "Is Bali overtaken by too much tourism?" Students were to read the essay and write a short essay of their own, taking a position on the topic. Yohana read the essays and gave grades to all. But the next day, she re-read the essays and gave new grades. When she compared the two sets of grades, she found that there were differences. For example, "A" grade students in the first grade list were not "A" grade students in the second list. Yohana reasoned she would go ahead with the second set of grades as no one else knew about the problem.

Reflection

The main questions are: Did Yohana do the right thing in not considering rescoring by giving the essays to another teacher in the school? Should she have checked whether her scoring criteria were appropriate? Should she have brought this to the attention of her school principal? Are her actions defensible? Is there a violation of an accepted code of ethics and practice? Would this be an example of an unfair assessment? This action raises additional questions regarding the right thing to do. The utilitarian could claim that the consequences of the assessment were mostly successful, as most test takers were assessed appropriately, thus satisfying the principle of maximizing utility and the maxim of "greatest good for the greatest number of people." Further, as the assessment did not provide sufficient utility for these test takers who were erroneously misclassified, they were offered compensation as per the contract. The contractarian could argue that the administrator did not carry out her duty and therefore should be tried for dereliction or breach of duty, as she did not uphold the rights of all test takers to a fair assessment. The argument could then be made that the administrator and her agency should face a tort, product liability, or a similar lawsuit that would be available in a just institution. These simplified arguments from different perspectives show how difficult it is to do the right thing. Both scenarios are related to the principle of fairness and in particular sub-principle 2 (meaningfulness) and sub-principle 4 (administration), and the principle of justice, in particular sub-principle 2 (beneficial consequences) and sub-principle 3 (advancing justice).

Accommodation

Scenario 7: Selecting an Assessment

Imagine Alpana Chitra, an elementary school teacher in the U.S. in a 5th grade class. She has 10 ESL students, 5 students with disabilities, and 10 other students in her class. The students were administered a mathematics test. The test had items that required calculation from formulae and items that required calculation based on real-world scenarios written in English. After Alpana scored her students' performances, she discovered that many ESL students performed well on the first type of items but not on the items based on scenarios, and students with disabilities performed poorly on both types of test items. Alpana noticed these differences and brought this to the attention of the principal. The principal, although aware of the legal requirement in the U.S. regarding accommodations in assessments for test takers with disabilities, did not contact the test developer, as she said it would make the test more expensive for the school.

Reflection

The questions that arise are: Did Alpana know that accommodations for students with disabilities are required by law? Did she know that accommodations for ESL students in test subjects like mathematics are desirable? In addition to the legal requirements, did the principal feel that she had a moral obligation or duty to provide accommodations? Was it appropriate to not take up the matter with the test developer because it may have cost the school more for accommodations? This scenario poses problems for the principle of fairness and in particular sub-principle 4 (access).

Assessment Selection

Scenario 8: Selecting an Assessment

Now imagine, Catrina Blair, a head teacher, was authorized by the school principal to choose an assessment for a Grade 8 reading class in English. The teachers had to choose from three assessments that were commercially available. Test A was developed by a well-established company known for its quality products; the test was traditional and was broadly suitable in terms of content, it was normed for the national population, and it cost $500 for a class of 40. Test B was developed by a small local company; it was highly suitable in terms of content, it was normed for the local population and checked for fairness, it was proven to offer accurate results and useful diagnostic information, and it cost $800 for a class set of 40. Test C was an innovative test developed by teachers from another local school; it had not been analyzed yet but was available for free for the class.

Reflection

The main question is: On what grounds should Catrina choose from these assessments? Should her decision be based on cost? If her decision was to be made on this ground, the choice would be Test C even though the assessment had not been analyzed; the argument could be that the assessment was not high stakes in Grade 8. Another consideration would be consequences and fairness—whether the assessment would have consequences that were beneficial to the students and the community. If the decision was to be made on these grounds, the choice would be Test B. This would appeal to the consequentialist doctrine. Yet another consideration would be the quality of the organization developing the assessment. If these were the grounds, then it would be Test A. You will see that the choice is not straightforward and teachers have to weigh several factors such as quality, cost, and so on in order to make their choice. This scenario is related to the principle of fairness, in particular sub-principle 2 (meaningfulness), and the principle of justice, in particular sub-principle 1 (beneficial consequences).

Administration

Scenario 9: Differential Pricing

Imagine you received a questionnaire from a well-known assessment developer and publisher who is planning on introducing differential pricing to test takers for different services. Which of these would you find acceptable? The proposal is higher test-taker fees for new services. Thus, there would be two levels of pricing: regular pricing for regular assessment and premium pricing for additional services. Table 9.1 presents possible different services.

Reflection

The main questions are: For which of these services would we consider differential pricing appropriate? On what grounds would we accept or not accept differential pricing? Is there an obligation on the part of the assessment developer

TABLE 9.1 Differential pricing for different services

Services	Regular pricing	Premium pricing
Thorough validity, reliability, and fairness studies		
Individual diagnostic feedback		
Experienced raters		
Faster turn-around time for results		
Front row seating for large-group listening tests		
Better room facilities (air conditioning, heating, etc.)		
Assistance from grammar and spell checks for writing		
Upgraded technological equipment (color monitor, larger size monitors, etc.)		
Accommodations for test takers with disabilities		
Human raters and automated machine scoring		

Note: Write in Y for Yes and N for No for each of the services listed.

to offer some of these services without differential pricing? Would the differential pricing for some of these services violate the principles of fairness and justice? In summary, differential pricing for these different services poses problems for the principle of fairness and the principle of justice.

Public Justification

Scenario 10: Assessment Quality

Imagine a high-stakes high school exit examination that was conducted by a ministry of education. The examination had been in use for many years, and students worked hard during the months prior to the examination. After the examination, some students got together and exchanged thoughts on the examination. They concluded that some of the tasks and topics were new to them. When the results were announced, it turned out these students had received low grades. Apart from feeling upset, the students could do nothing else (there was no review or appeal process in place), but their parents went to the ministry and complained that something was wrong with the examination. The ministry officials said that there could not be anything wrong with the examination questions, as they were written by expert senior teachers who had been doing this for decades. When the ministry officials were pressed to show that the examination was an appropriate assessment procedure, they defended their examination by saying there were no prior complaints and therefore no analysis of the examination was necessary.

Scenario 11: Public Reasoning

Imagine now that the parents of the students who received low grades protested the ministry's approach and demanded that they provide a public justification of the assessment. The ministry replied with a firm NO, as it had never responded to such a request before and did not consider it necessary to do so. Once again, the test takers were denied basic freedoms such as the basic right to be treated with respect and dignity and to have fair assessments and assessment practices. They could also argue that public reasoning (in public forums) would be the only way to ensure that the assessment is fair and the institution is just. Both these scenarios are related to the principle of fairness and the principle of justice.

Reflection

The main question here is whether the ministry had the motivation and expertise to provide the best possible examination. There were numerous problems with the examination from an equal rights perspective (a Rawlsian concern): Did some of the students not have the Opportunity-to-learn all the material? Did their school or teacher perhaps not cover all the topics? Did the ministry's regulations not have any provision for review or appeals? Further, were no analyses of the examination tasks conducted, although they were written by experts? Were there no research studies that examined the quality of the assessments and the test performance? Was the examination valid, reliable, and fair? Was the examination providing a beneficial service to the community? Did the ministry owe the student community public justification (a Rawlsian requisite)? Finally, was the ministry acting responsibly? In general, Rawlsian theorists would particularly be up in arms with the ministry's lack of provision for basic rights to the students and its dereliction of duty to the students and community.

Expanding the Curriculum

As mentioned earlier, a second way of advancing fairness and justice is by refocusing the training curriculum. Whether assessment development is conducted by individual teachers or a committee of teachers, many aspects need careful consideration. Different levels of expertise may be required based on whether the assessment that is being developed is a large-scale assessment with high or low stakes. In thinking about the components that make up optimum assessment knowledge needed for assessment development and research, there seems to be three approaches.[5]

The Traditional Engineering-Oriented Curriculum

This approach includes:

(1) An overview of *skills and components* to be assessed (listening, speaking, reading writing; pronunciation, grammar, vocabulary; pragmatics, integrated skills, etc.)
(2) *Techniques for test development*, creation, and scoring (item writing and revision, using different response formats, writing rubrics for scoring, designing score reporting formats, etc.)
(3) *Skills for improving, editing, and assembling* of items and tests (planning revision cycles, writing protocols for item banking, etc.)
(4) *Research themes*: reliability (internal consistency, inter-rater), content, construct and predictive validity, and item and test bias (differential item/test functioning analysis)
(5) *Research methods*: quantitative (classical true score theory, item response theory) and qualitative (introspective analysis, conversational analysis) approaches for research (procedures for item and test difficulty, discrimination, bias, analyzing cognitive and affective processes in test taking, etc.)
(6) *Training with software*: SPSS, ITEMAN, and SAS for descriptive and inferential statistics; FACETS and WINSTEPS for analyzing ratings; MULTILOG for bias analysis, etc.

(7) *Technical and score user manuals* (writing parts of a technical manual that includes a description of the test; administrative, scoring, and reporting details; accommodations for test takers with disabilities; a report of research studies that support the claims of the test; samples of tests, scoring rubrics, and score reports; and pricing of different services—standard prices, rush score reporting, human scoring, detailed score report, and diagnostic feedback, etc.).

The Innovative-Design Curriculum

This approach includes:

(1) *Innovative design* in items and tests and scoring and reporting (integrated tasks such as listening–writing, reading–speaking, tasks that match professional work such as assessing the English language ability of aviation professionals, etc.)
(2) *Use of new technologies* (tasks that involve audio–video, multi-media, multi-modal, automated scoring of writing and speaking, tests on tablets, etc.)
(3) *New needs and uses* (immigration, citizenship, asylum, forensic purposes, etc.)
(4) *Research themes*: authenticity, instructiveness, cognitive diagnostic feedback, dynamic assessment, etc.
(5) *Research methods*: new analyses using structural equation modeling, hierarchical linear modeling, multi-level modeling, conversational analysis, etc.
(6) *Training with advanced software*: AMOS, EQS, Mplus for modeling, etc.

The Ethical-Critique Curriculum

This approach ought to include:

(1) *Understanding of the history* of language assessment (from the Chinese Civil Service Examinations, *Le Baccalaureate*, and *Abitur* to popular modern language assessments such as the TOEFL, iBT, FCE, CAE, CPE, IELTS, SAT, etc.)
(2) *Understanding the political motivations and legal bases* for assessments (the U.S. Naturalization Test, similar tests in the U.K., Australia, Germany, South Korea, etc.)
(3) *Understanding the social and cultural assumptions* of assessments (knowing the semiotic domain and having embodied experiences)
(4) *Understanding the philosophical underpinnings* of assessments (utilitarian, social contract/deontological, pragmatist, and humanist approaches)
(5) *Working with hypothetical scenarios* or case studies of assessments that need judgments using moral or ethical philosophy.
(6) *Using ethical principles* to evaluate assessments (parochial versus global ethics, etc.)
(7) *Writing defenses and critiques* of assessments and assessment practice (assessment reviews).

To a language assessment professional, it may be obvious that the focus of most training programs (certificate, BA, MA, or PhD) would be on the first approach, although a few programs would address the second approach. And, unfortunately, aspects of the third approach are ignored or not offered regularly. This could be due to a number of reasons: The first approach lays the foundation of training and therefore has to be included in all programs. The focus of particular programs could be based on the expertise of the faculty of the program (which is generally in the first strand). The second approach has to do with innovation in design, tasks, and research and is based on new purposes, contexts, and technologies. The third approach is the newest and requires the most time to develop, as it is interdisciplinary with subjects in humanities and social sciences. These strengths and weaknesses of language assessment curricula are also reflected in published works (in journals and books) and in conference themes and presentations. A good example is the Brown and Bailey (2008) survey report of language testing courses.

Fulcher (2012, p. 125) offered an expanded working definition of language assessment literacy:

> The knowledge, skills and abilities required to design, develop, maintain or evaluate, large-scale standardized and/or classroom based tests, familiarity with test processes, and awareness of principles and concepts that guide and underpin practice, including ethics and codes of practice. The ability to place knowledge, skills, processes, principles and concepts within wider historical, social, political and philosophical frameworks in order [to] understand why practices have arisen as they have, and to evaluate the role and impact of testing on society, institutions, and individuals.

In Figure 9.3, Fulcher showed the different layers of knowledge working together: knowledge of skills and abilities (termed practices); processes, principles, and concepts (termed principles); and historical, social, political, and philosophical frameworks (termed contexts). Although this framework does not completely overlap with the curricula presented earlier, it is clear that the traditional engineering curriculum can be matched with the practices and the ethical–critique curriculum can be matched with the contexts.

The challenge for language assessment training programs then would be to offer a comprehensive approach incorporating the most important components of the three curricula of Fulcher's layers based on needs and orientation of the programs. It is hoped, however, that all programs will include elements of the ethical-critique curricula or a historical, social, political, and philosophical context so that students and professionals are aware of the context of their work, as well as their responsibilities (for example, like health care professionals such as medical doctors, pharmacists, and hospital nurses and engineers and computer scientists are increasingly asked to do).

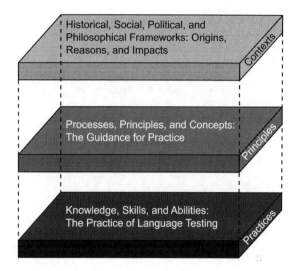

FIGURE 9.3   Language assessment literacy: an expanded definition

Source: Published in: Glenn Fulcher; *Language Assessment Quarterly* 2012, 9, 113–132. Copyright © 2012, Taylor & Francis, Ltd.

Conclusion

In conclusion, two ways of advancing fairness and justice have been proposed and discussed. I suggested that the first way of advancing fairness and justice in language assessment is by training for ethical thinking with a series of hypothetical scenarios that cover the entire range of assessment activities, from design to research. I also suggested that another way of advancing fairness and justice in the field is to offer curricula that cover ethical-critique matters along with the more traditional engineering-oriented and innovative-design curricula approaches.

The next chapter will provide a summary of the book's leading themes and offer some ideas regarding fairness and justice for consideration.

Notes

1   See Eyde, Robertson, and Krug (2010) for a set of 85 case studies for the training of psychologists. These case studies are from various testing process categories: professional development (training, responsibility, and ethics), test selection, test administration, test interpretation, and reporting test results.
2   This list of three normative methods of ethics ignores many others like feminist ethics, care-based ethics, and meta-ethics and regional perspectives as Asian or African ethics.
3   Another variation of the scenario is this: The trolley is hurtling down track A, and if nothing is done the five workers on the track would be killed. If the bystander pushes a switch, the trolley would go down track B and that would kill the one worker. If the bystander pushes a double switch, the trolley would go down track C and would kill the bystander.

4 The fat man scenario has many variations: Instead of a fat man would you push a thin or tall man onto the track? Or would you push an ill fat man onto the track? What if he was a healthy fat man? Or what if the fat man was a famous pop star or a popular athlete? What if the fat man was replaced with a fat woman? What if she was pretty or a brilliant scientist? Or, for that matter, if it was a fat cow or buffalo? Would it make a difference in your ethical decision-making and moral justification? These variations should not make a difference unless you see things from a narrow utilitarian perspective.

5 Brown and Bailey (2008) document the state of language testing courses in 2007 through a questionnaire study. They report on course characteristics, including topics (such as test consistency and validity), statistical concepts (such as mean, median, mode, standard deviation, variance), and required books. The study showed that most of the courses focus on traditional components and offer few newer areas of interest, including alternative assessment.

References

American Educational Research Association, American Psychological Association, the National Council on Measurement in Education. (2014). *Standards for educational and psychological testing.* Washington, DC: Author.

Baron, M. W., Pettit, P., & Slote, M. (1997). *Three methods of ethics.* Malden, MA: Wiley-Blackwell.

Brown, J. D., & Bailey, K. M. (2008). Language testing courses: What are they in 2007? *Language Testing, 25,* 349–383.

Eyde, L. D., Robertson, G. J., & Krug, S. E. (2010). *Responsible test use: Case studies for assessing human behavior (2nd Edn.).* Washington, DC: American Psychological Association.

Foot, P. (1978). *The problem of abortion and the doctrine of the double effect in virtues and vices.* Oxford: Basil Blackwell.

Fulcher, G. (2012). Assessment literacy for the language classroom. *Language Assessment Quarterly, 9,* 113–132.

Kamm, F. M. (2016). *The trolley problem mysteries.* Oxford, UK: Oxford University Press.

Nagy, T. F. (2000). *Ethics in plain English: An illustrative casebook for psychologists (2nd Edn.).* Washington, DC: American Psychological Association.

Thomson, J. J. (1976). Killing, letting die, and the trolley problem. *The Monist, 59,* 204-217.

10
APPLICATIONS AND IMPLICATIONS

Introduction

The primary purpose of this book is to address two fundamental questions relevant to language assessment: (1) What's the right thing to do to bring about fair assessments and just institutions and (2) What's the right thing to do to remove manifest unfairness and injustice?

When these questions are operationalized and applied to particular language assessments, specific questions that could be asked about the assessment and the institution that administers the assessment are: Is the assessment fair to all test takers? Is the assessment practice fair? Is the assessment beneficial to the community? Is the assessment advancing fairness and justice? Is the institution administering and using the assessment a just institution? In addition, what are the rights and responsibilities of test takers and test users? What are the obligations of researchers and policy makers? And, what do the implications of this application mean for assessment agencies, stakeholders, oversight bodies, and legal systems? Finally, what are the limits to fairness and justice?

Summary of Chapters

These questions imply that all language assessments may not be fair and that institutions that administer language assessments may not be just. In Chapter 1, I described language assessments from the different contexts of civil service, literacy and immigration, and school-based assessments and offered brief evaluations. Based on these, it is obvious that language assessments need to be evaluated in terms of fairness and justice.

First, although assessments may be part of imperial or government policy, as with the Chinese Civil Service, the British Civil Service, or the U.S. literacy tests both for voting rights and immigration, there were definite problems with fairness with such assessments and assessment practice. Second, assessments and assessment practices that were unfair were typically not challenged by test takers or by the community because of the general feeling that assessments are infallible, as they are written or administered by experts, professors, or teachers. Another reason that unfair assessments and assessment practices could not be challenged, as there were no clear remedies in many countries.

Chapter 2 discusses two approaches to assessment evaluations: standards-based (based on the AERA, APA, and NCME, 2014 *Standards*) and argument-based approaches. These approaches have not been very successful. The main deficiencies in the two approaches and the evaluations based on the approaches are: There is little intellectual foundation for the evaluations, fairness is included as one aspect of the evaluation sometimes, test performance data are rarely available, no independent research findings are available, and evaluations are brief and not comprehensive. The key questions then are how can we change this? What ought to be done? If the public needs to be informed of assessments from the point of view of fairness and justice, what kind of framework should we have in place?

Chapter 3 provides a principled basis for fairness and justice by drawing on theoretical work from moral philosophers John Rawls and Amartya Sen. They offer ways in which their thought experiments, called the original position/veil of ignorance and the impartial spectator, respectively, can contribute to the intellectual background. This intellectual background provides the basis for the formulation of principles of fairness and justice. Using these methods, two principles and sub-principles of fairness and justice for language assessment are formulated. The chapter also put forth the idea that there should be public justification or reasoning of assessments. This would mean that whether an assessment is fair or not and whether an institution is just or not should be a matter of public discourse for which public justification or reasoning is necessary. This is a critical part of justifying assessments and institutions.

The *Standards* and the argumentation model proposed by Toulmin are both put to work with the principles of fairness and justice in Chapter 4. The chapter discusses how to evaluate arguments and concludes with issues related to the application of fairness and justice in terms of language assessment. A worked example of building an argument about the U.S. Naturalization Test based on the principles and sub-principles of fairness and justice was provided. Warrants and backing for each sub-claim were articulated.

Chapters 5 to 8 explore various sub-claims, warrants, and backing (and rebuttals in some cases) and their use in the argumentation model. Specifically, discusses Chapter 5 discusses the concept of *Opportunity-to-Learn* (OTL) as part of Principle 1,

Fairness. Four types of OTL are examined from the point of view of the school context: (1) OTL in terms of *content coverage, teacher competence, and instructional strategies and resources*; (2) OTL in terms of providing adequate time for *notice and preparation*, where new assessments are being developed and launched in provinces or states; (3) OTL in terms of providing sufficient *practice time with new technologies* prior to the assessment, termed Opportunity-for-Success; and (4) OTL providing *adequate opportunity in the relevant literacy and semiotic domains, social practices, and embodied experiences*. The illustrative studies highlight ways in which OTL can be examined and the kinds of information that assessment developers, reviewers, and evaluators could use in their work. First, the Herman et al. (2000) study examined the concept of OTL in the context of school-level instruction and assessment in the U.S. in terms of three variables: curriculum content, instructional strategies, and instructional resources. Second, two additional studies investigated the diagnostic feedback of two automated essay evaluation systems (*MyAccess*, Hoang & Kunnan, 2016 and *WriteToLearn*; Liu & Kunnan, 2016) and found that there is divergent evidence in terms of whether they are offering adequate and appropriate feedback to student essay writers.

The concept of *Meaningfulness* (validity) is discussed as part of Principle 1, Fairness, in Chapter 6. There are many different aspects of meaningfulness from which evidence can be gathered for this principle: (1) in *terms of the blueprint and specifications written* prior to assessment development; (2) in *terms of the cognitive processes test takers use to complete the assessment;* (3) *constructs that assess the knowledge or ability meant to be assessed;* and (4) *consequences of an assessment for test takers, stakeholders, and the community*. The illustrative study by Johnstone et al. (2007) showed the results of a large-scale survey of the blueprints and specifications related to reading assessments in all the states in the U.S. It included examining assessment blueprints or test specifications in terms of the purposes and constructs of assessments. The Kunnan studies (1992, 1994) examined the consistency or dependability and the internal factor structure of the assessment.

Chapter 7 discusses the concept of *absence of bias* as part of Principle 1, Fairness. Three sources of construct-irrelevant variance (cognitive, affective, and physical) that are the main causes of bias are discussed: (1) *cognitive-irrelevant variance* sources include language difficulties due to dialect, grammatical structure, and vocabulary; (2) *affective-irrelevant variance* sources include content and topics that are sensitive/taboo and affect test takers; and (3) *physical-irrelevant variance* sources include the use of visuals, media, and any equipment that is unfamiliar to test takers. The illustrative studies presented three generations of DIF research: Kunnan (1990), a first-generation study, examined the test performance of two *L1 and gender groups* in order to identify items that were biased. Geranpayeh and Kunnan (2007), a second-generation study, examined test performance data for *DIF in terms of age* with the IRT method. Kunnan (1994), a third-generation study, examined *test performance of two L1 groups* on two tests but using a structural modeling approach with contextual factors in addition to the L1 factor. These research studies show that absence of bias is a critical part of assessment and assessment practice.

The consequences of the high-stakes language assessments in the arena of immigration and citizenship are discussed in Chapter 8. The examples of the U.S. immigration policy, the infamous Australian Dictation Test, and the social integration policy in the Netherlands provide background information about the kinds of policies that have resulted in discriminatory and/or inappropriate practices. The illustrative study (Kunnan, 2010) with the U.S. Naturalization Test showed that there are problems in terms of meaningfulness, consistency of scores, and biased items, in addition to whether it is beneficial to the test takers and the community. Further, the study found that the USNT is not clearly beneficial to the immediate stakeholders, the wider stakeholders, and the larger community.

Chapter 9 focuses on how to advance the concepts of fairness and justice with discussion of two areas: (1) *ethical thinking* with hypothetical scenarios from the trolley problem and language assessment scenarios covering all aspects of development, research, administration, and consequences; and (2) expanding the *curricula in language assessment* training (in pre-service, in-service, and university-level courses) to include the ethical-critique approach to traditional engineering-oriented and innovative-design approaches to training.

In the next sections, the discussion will be on how to apply ethical thinking and how to apply assessment standards in the area of language assessment.

Applying Ethical Thinking

A few of the critical ideas from ethics presented in previous chapters are revisited here from the perspective of applying them to evaluating language assessments.

Rawls' Original Position and Veil of Ignorance and Sen's Impartial Spectator

Rawls (1971) and Sen (2010) offer ways in which the original position/veil of ignorance (OP/VoI) and the impartial spectator (IS), respectively, can be used in deliberations regarding public policy. One way would be to apply them in language assessment development. The way the OP/VoI ideas would work is that if committee members on a development team are oblivious of their own backgrounds (such as age, gender, education qualifications, socioeconomic status, first language, etc.) and they do not have any knowledge of their vested interests (such as giving a particular group some benefits) The expectation is that they would succeed in developing assessments that are fair with just assessment institutions. The members would deliberate on the design of an assessment and operationalization of the blueprint, writing specifications, items, tasks, scoring guidelines, selecting or writing source material for reading and listening tasks, etc., without any intention to favor or discriminate against any group(s). But as the conditions for the OP/VoI are stringent and not easy to replicate, it may not be usable in all assessment development contexts.

The IS, on the other hand, is a more common procedure. The IS can be seen as an "outsider," "external," or "independent" reviewer. For example, the IS idea can be used in reviews of assessments where an individual examiner could be tasked with examining an assessment and assessment institution. The impartiality that is needed of the examiner is achievable, as in the case of reviewers in the blind review process of manuscripts submitted to journals. However, the IS also may not always be able to be impartial, particularly when an examiner is invited or commissioned by an assessment developer to examine one of their assessments.

Therefore, although there are merits in both thought experiments, they are methods that may not work in their purest forms. Appropriate variants such as having members on an assessment review team who know nothing about the context where an assessment is to be launched or a team of impartial spectators instead of just one impartial spectator needs to be devised in order to evaluate assessments and assessment institutions.

Public Justification and Reasoning

The most important idea that can be put forward in terms of promoting and advancing fairness and justice is public justification and public reasoning. For fairness and justice to work in an assessment context, public justification or public reasoning should be part of the process of engaging all the stakeholders. Rawls (1971) argued that it was necessary to justify policy judgments to fellow citizens so that public consensus could be reached. He also suggested the use of the methodology of "reflective equilibrium" to help in the public justification process. In this methodology, initial ideas, beliefs, or theories are subjected to reason, reflection, and revision until the ideas, beliefs, or theories reach a state of equilibrium in public justification. For example, public justifications of assessments through public forums such as conferences, papers, debates, and so on are examples of this approach.

Sen (2010) went a step further and argued that public reasoning of government policy was essential to convince the public of a policy. Using this approach would mean that public reasoning is provided for the various aspects of an assessment and that some adjustments may be necessary based on the views of the community. For example, it is possible that when public reasoning is provided for a particular assessment (say, a computer-based assessment), the community may bring up concerns regarding the computer familiarity of test takers. This would mean that the assessment agency would need to conduct a survey of computer familiarity of likely test takers and then to delay the use of computers if likely test takers are found not to have the necessary computer familiarity and/or to provide opportunities for computer familiarity prior to assessment.

Of course, in both public justification and public reasoning, it is assumed that the governments and the civic bodies that have put assessments in place through public policy regulations (in school, college, university, workplace, immigration, and citizenship contexts) are not authoritarian and are willing to hear community members' concerns, if any. In authoritarian states where public consultation, justification, or reasoning are not available, assessments could result in being unfair and institutions unjust.

Non-parochial, Global Justice

Sen (2010) argued that it is not sufficient to use principles to design and establish fair assessments and just institutions, but that efforts should be made to remove manifest injustice that exists in the world today. He also argued that a non-parochial, global justice view would be best suited to review unjust institutions and that such institutions need to be evaluated by enforcing categorical imperatives with obligations and *ought-to* general principles. Such a non-parochial, global justice, Sen argued, would remove manifest unfairness and injustice in different parts of the world that exist because of unacceptable local practices. In the assessment context, this would mean assessments would have to be deemed to be fair and institutions just worldwide; the cultural/local context argument that "we do things our way" would not hold. Positions on a wide range of topics such as slavery of Blacks, Native American civil rights in the U.S., the internment of Japanese during World War II in the U.S.; the Nazi extermination of Jews; Turkish genocide in Armenia; the Japanese massacre in Nanjing; Soviet-era war crimes; Apartheid in South Africa; China's treatment of human rights lawyers and ethnic and religious minorities; treatment of women in Saudi Arabia and of lower caste and religious minorities in India; the Hutu genocide of Tutsi in Rwanda; and so on, have seen global justice arguments contesting local government practices.

However, in terms of the assessment context, the idea of global justice is a large undertaking, as there is no global institution authorized to evaluate and issue sanctions, if necessary, against unfair assessments and/or unjust institutions across national boundaries. The only international organization, the UNESCO, addresses education issues; the only ones that are relevant for us is access to education, inclusion and equity, gender equality. But, the Incheon declaration titled "Education 2030" does not mention assessments or assessment practices.

Another popular argument against global justice would be that assessments, like many other public matters (such as governance, institutions, etc.), cannot be viewed as universal institutions. They need to be considered contextually, as they are based on different languages and contexts that need to follow local, regional, or national lines of governance. Still, when unfair assessments are deployed by unjust institutions anywhere in the world, it would be parochial and insular not to take up arms against repressive policies and practices no matter where they occur. Thus, the big question to ask here is whether we can have a group such as "Language

Assessment Without Borders" like "Doctors without Borders/Médecines Sans Frontières," (an international humanitarian, non-governmental organization best known for its projects in war-torn regions and developing countries afflicted by diseases that has an overall global mission while being sensitive to local practices). The "Language Assessment without Borders" group could review, evaluate, and advise agencies around the world on the merits and deficiencies of language assessments irrespective of language or geographical context.

It would be wise to remember here Martin Luther King's Letter from a Birmingham Jail: "Injustice anywhere is a threat to justice everywhere. We are caught in an inescapable network of mutuality, tied in a single garment of destiny. Whatever affects one directly, affects all indirectly."

Applying Assessment *Standards*

The main question here is how assessment standards (such as the AERA, APA, and NCME, 2014 *Standards*) can be applied in the area of language assessment to bring about fairness and justice. In the education sector, assessment agencies responsible for language assessments (along with other subject areas) are run as separate organizations, but normally within the ministry of education or affiliation with such a department. Well-known government assessment agencies such as The National Education Examinations Authority in China, the Hong Kong Examinations and Assessment Authority, the Singapore Examinations and Assessment Board, the Central Board of Secondary Education in India, and the CITO in the Netherlands provide assessments for their respective education departments. These agencies may have their own standards in designing and developing their assessments, but they do not present any documents on their own websites. In fact, there is very little public justification or public reasoning of their assessments. In comparison, OfQual, the U.K. government agency that oversees examinations and assessments in schools in England and helps maintain standards and regulate qualifications, offers through their website[1] research reports and discussions of their examinations and assessments.

Non-profit and commercial organizations play a big role in high-stakes language assessments worldwide as well. Well-known assessment agencies such as Educational Testing Service in the U.S., Cambridge English Language Assessments in the UK, Pearson in the UK, and the British Council design and develop large-scale English language assessments for worldwide use. These agencies demonstrate an understanding of standards and research, and their websites show this awareness. Universities and not-for-profit units affiliated with universities also conduct language assessments for use in their universities, but awareness and use of standards vary greatly. The Association of Language Testers of Europe (ALTE), a non-profit organization of language assessment member groups, goes a step further and conducts a self-audit of the language assessments of its members. They offer member groups assistance in meeting assessment standards.

Rights and Responsibilities

The *Standards* (AERA, APA, and NCME, 2014) outline the rights and responsibilities of both test takers and test users from the point of view of fairness to individual test takers. The *Standards* for test takers are separated into four thematic clusters:

(1) Test takers' rights to information prior to testing
(2) Test takers' rights to access their test results and to be protected from unauthorized use of test results
(3) Test takers' rights to fair and accurate score reports
(4) Test takers' responsibilities for behavior throughout the test administration process

Under Cluster 1, test takers are expected to have the right to receive information prior to assessment. This would include information about the content and purpose of the assessment, the materials to be taken to the assessment site, how the results are to be used, task types and response formats, availability of accommodations, choice of assessments, if any, and informed consent, except when the assessment is mandated by educational or employment agencies.

Under Cluster 2, test takers are expected to have confidentiality protection rights related to the release of their scores and accompanying identifying information and how assessment agencies will guard against improper access and disclosure of information, as well as improper storage, transmission, and use of data. Under Cluster 3, test takers are expected to have the right to receive fair and accurate score reports that describe performances, provide grades or scores, and provide descriptive labels or levels of performance. Under Cluster 4, test takers are expected to be responsible for their behavior at the assessment site, including not indulging in any cheating, fraud, deceit, or plagiarism.

The 2014 *Standards* also address *the rights and responsibilities of test users*. Test users are persons or institutions who select assessments and supervise administrations, as well as those who have a responsibility for interpretation and use of results. The *Standards* are separated into three thematic clusters:

(1) Validity of interpretations
(2) Dissemination of information
(3) Test security and protection of copyrights

Under Cluster 1, test score users are expected to examine the validity evidence in support of the intended interpretation of scores and also have the legal and ethical responsibility to protect the security of test content and privacy of test takers. They are also expected to be alert to the possibility of scoring errors and misinterpretation of scores. Under Cluster 2, the right to receive adequate information about an assessment is noted. This right should be available to all persons who are interested in an assessment that include test takers, parents, guardians, educators, courts, other professionals, and the community. This right includes release of score records and appropriate feedback, as well as opportunities to retake an assessment, make an appeal for rescoring, and/or seek remedy through arbitration or a court. Under Cluster 3, test users have the responsibility to protect the security of assessments and intellectual property rights of materials used in an assessment.

Current Practices

With these rights and responsibilities in mind, an examination of current practices of a few well-known English language assessments was conducted. Table 10.1 presents the findings as of November 2016. In the first two columns, the table presents the name of the language assessment and the country of the agency that developed the assessment. This is followed by six indicators that are shown to be present or not present on their respective websites (indicated by a Y for presence of the indictor or N for not present). Many of the assessment agencies have Ys in terms of providing information about their assessments, but fail with some of the other indicators. Most agencies have handbooks in print form or on dedicated websites, and a few have research reports that help justify their assessments.

Table 10.2 presents the documentation of research of a few English language assessments from a few universities in Canada, China, Hong Kong, Japan, New Zealand, Taiwan, U.K., and the U.S. as of November 2016. Once again, many of the assessment agencies have Ys indicating that they provide general information on their assessments but fail with many of the other indicators. In comparison to Table 10.1, there are fewer Ys indicating the presence of research documentation for English language assessments in Table 10.2. The differences show that university agencies collect less research data to justify their own assessments. The websites also do not hold assessment handbooks or equivalent material for test takers, except for the excellent handbook developed for DELNA. Most websites do not hold any research publications relevant for the justification of their assessments. This is unfortunate, as many of these assessments are designed, developed, and administered by departments where there are faculty members who are knowledgeable about standards in assessment.

Oversight Bodies

Most assessments and assessment agencies (including government and non-profit agencies) worldwide are not governed by rules and regulations of any national or state regulatory boards or oversight bodies (excluding control by ministries of education). This means these assessment agencies and their assessments do not need to be certified as valid, reliable, or fair to operate in public, but they enter the marketplace, make claims regarding their assessments, and take a major role in determining the careers and life opportunities of millions of test takers. The

TABLE 10.1 Documentation of research of a few English language assessments*

Name of language assessment	Country of developer	Information provided	OTL	Meaningfulness (validity)	Absence of bias	Access	Consequences
Certificate of Academic English (CAE)	UK	Y	Y	Y	Y	N	Y
Canadian Assessment of English Language (CAEL)	Canada	Y	N	Y	N	N	Y
College English Test (CET)	China	Y	Y	Y	N	N	N
Duolingo English Test (DET)	USA	Y	Y	N	N	N	N
First Certificate in English (FCE)	UK	Y	Y	Y	N	N	Y
General English Proficiency Test (GEPT)	Taiwan	Y	Y	Y	Y	N	N
International English Language Testing System (IELTS)	UK, Australia	Y	Y	Y	N	N	Y
Pearson Test of English (PTE)	UK	Y	N	N	N	Y	N
STEP EIKEN Test in Practical English	Japan	Y	Y	Y	N	N	N
Test of English as a Foreign Language (iBTOEFL)	USA	Y	Y	Y	Y	Y	Y
Test of English for International Communication (TOEIC)	USA	Y	Y	Y	Y	N	Y
Test for English Majors (TEM)	China	Y	Y	N	N	N	N
Versant (VER)	USA	Y	Y	Y	N	N	N
U.S. Naturalization Test (USNT)	USA	Y	Y	N	N	N	N

Notes: * Documentation collected from the assessment agencies' websites as of November 30, 2016.
Y indicates the presence of information; N indicates information is not available on the websites.

TABLE 10.2 Documentation of research of a few English language assessments in universities*

Name of language assessment	University	Information provided	OTL	Meaningfulness (validity)	Absence of bias	Access	Consequences
DELNA	Univ. of Auckland	Y	Y	Y	Y	N	N
DELTA	Hong Kong Polytechnic Univ.	Y	Y	N	N	N	N
DUOLINGO English Test (DET)	Carnegie Mellon Univ.	Y	Y	N	N	N	N
ESL Placement Examination (ESLPE)[2]	UCLA	Y	N	N	N	N	N
English Placement Test (EPT)	Illinois, Urbana–Champaign	Y	Y	Y	N	N	N
English Placement Test (EPT)	Iowa State Univ.	Y	Y	N	N	N	N
English Proficiency Test (EPT)	Georgia State Univ.	Y	Y	N	N	N	N
English Language Diagnosis and Assessment (ELDNA)	Univ. of Toronto	Y	N	N	N	N	N
Michigan English Language Assessment Battery (MELAB)	CaMLA	Y	Y	Y	Y	N	N

Notes: * Documentation collected from the assessment agencies' websites as of November 30, 2016.
Y indicates the presence of information; N indicates information is not available on the websites.

burden therefore is on the assessment agencies themselves to self-monitor and self-review their assessments and assessment practices.

Although the setting up of a regulatory authority may not be ideal in all cases, meeting assessment standards (such as the AERA, APA, and NCME, 2014 *Standards*) through self-evaluation and reflection could be one way of assuring stakeholders of the quality of assessments. Another way forward would be to have national or international organizations take the role of accrediting agencies authorized to evaluate assessments based on specific qualities of assessments. The Association of Language Teachers of Europe (ALTE), although not an oversight body, provides such audit, guidance and support to its members and member groups in terms of every aspect of language assessment: development, administration, and research. Similar associations (like the British Council) provide informal guidance to its members on various topics relevant to language assessment through workshops and conferences.

Examination Boards

Oversight of assessments by examination boards is another way of ensuring that fairness and justice in assessments prevail. Here is an example of intervention by an examination board that resulted in transparency in assessment. In 1980, in the U.S., after considerable pressure from consumer and civil rights groups, the trustees of the College Entrance Examination Board voted to provide test takers throughout the U.S. with copies of their Scholastic Aptitude Tests (now known as the SAT), as well as with their answer sheets and a list of correct answers. This change was a result of two court cases in which the test had errors and Educational Testing Service was forced to raise the scores of thousands of test takers. This right to test takers granted by the board is an excellent example of an agency's willingness to be transparent in the assessment process.

Formal and Informal Groups

In lieu of official oversight bodies, formal and informal groups of professional linguists have put forth resolutions against unprofessional practices that are unfair and unjust. To illustrate, a group of linguists produced *Guidelines for the Use of Language Analysis in Relation to Questions of National Origin in Refugee Cases June 2004 Language and National Origin Group*.[3] This was in response to the unfair process and poor quality of language analysis (typically through an interview) conducted by a number of European and Australian governments as part of the process to determine whether an asylum seeker's case is genuine.

Another example is the informal opt-out movement of parents, teachers, and teacher associations in protest against school tests in New York State. These protests led to the subsequent retreat by Governor Cuomo from Common Core Standards and related assessments (see Taylor, 2015).[4] By the end of 2016, many states in the U.S. began to resist the Common Core Standards.[5]

Report of the Council of Great Schools in the U.S., 2015

In 2015, a report from the Council of Great Schools in the U.S. (Hart, Casserly, Uzzell, Palacios, Corcoran, and Spurgeon, 2015, pp. 9–10)[6] set into motion thinking related to a reduction in mandatory assessments in schools. The main findings were:

- In the 2014–2015 school year, 401 unique tests were administered across subjects in the 66 Great City School systems. Students in the 66 districts were required to take an average of 112.3 tests between pre-K and Grade 12. The students in the 66 urban school districts sat for tests more than 6570 times. Some of these tests were administered to fulfill federal requirements under No Child Left Behind (NCLB) waivers or Race to the Top, whereas many others originated at the state and local levels.
- The average student in these districts typically took about eight standardized tests per year, for example, two NCLB tests (reading and math) and three formative exams in two subjects per year. The average amount of testing time devoted to mandated tests among 8th grade students was approximately 4.22 days, or 2.34 percent of school time (the 8th grade had the highest testing time).

Two months later, the U.S. Congress replaced NCLB with a comprehensive overhaul of the federal Elementary and Secondary Education Act, called the "Every Student Succeeds Act" (ESSA).[7] The rewrite ended the test-and-punish mandates of NCLB.

Legal Remedies

When oversight bodies fail or do not exist, legal remedies ought to be available to test takers (and assessment agencies) so that if violations of professional, ethical, or legal norms occur, test takers (and agencies) can either go to an arbitration body as a first measure or go to the courts as a last resort. Some of the cases filed successfully in the U.S. and the U.K. were discussed in the previous chapter. In the U.S., these cases have removed manifest unfairness in assessments and assessment practices by harnessing equal protection and due process clauses in the 14th Amendment of the U.S. Constitution, although every new assessment needs to be checked for compliance with these clauses. If similar avenues are not available in other countries, it will be all the more critical for assessment agencies to be aware of how to develop and administer a fair assessment with a just institution.

The Supreme Court of India Ruling on Evaluated Answer Books

In a landmark case that has implications for assessment agencies and professionals worldwide, the Supreme Court of India addressed the issue of whether a test taker has the right to inspect his or her evaluated answer book. This case is described in detail here so that we can understand the unique issues well.

In the Civil Appeal No. 6454 of 2011,[8] the Supreme Court considered whether test takers (the respondents) should be given back their examination answer books for inspection and re-evaluation. The case involved the first respondent (among many) who sat for the Central Board of Secondary Examination (CBSE), which is a large-scale end-of-Grade 12 course examination. He was disappointed by his low marks because in his opinion he had done well and the answer books were not properly evaluated, and the improper evaluation resulted in his low marks. Therefore, he applied to CBSE for inspection and re-evaluation of his answer book based on India's Right to Information (RTI) Act of 2005. CBSE rejected his request for the following main reasons:

(1) The information sought was exempted under Section 8(1)(e) of RTI since CBSE shared fiduciary relationship with its evaluators and maintain[s] confidentiality of both manner and method of evaluation.
(2) The Examination Bye-laws of the Board provided that no candidate shall claim or is entitled to re-evaluation of his answers or disclosure or inspection of answer book(s) or other documents.
(3) The larger public interest does not warrant the disclosure of such information sought.

Unhappy with this decision, the first respondent filed Writ Petition No. 18189 (W)/2008 in the Calcutta High Court and sought the following reliefs:

(a) For a declaration that CBSE's action in excluding the provision of reevaluation of the answer book was illegal, unreasonable and violative of the provisions of the Constitution of India
(b) For a direction to CBSE to appoint an independent examiner for reevaluating his answer book and issue of a fresh marks card on the basis of reevaluation
(c) For quashing the earlier letter from CBSE and for a directive to CBSE to produce his answer book so that they could be properly reviewed and a fresh marks card can be issued after reevaluation

CBSE resisted the petition and responded with the following points: (1) that verification is restricted to checking whether all the answers have been evaluated, that there has been no mistake in the totaling of marks for each question, and that the marks have been transferred correctly onto the title page of the answer book and to the award list and (2) that no test taker shall claim, or be entitled to, revaluation of his or her answers or disclosure or inspection of the answer book.

Further, CBSE also countered that it had 1.3 million test takers from about 9000 affiliated schools across the country in Grade 10 and 12 examinations and that this generated about 6.0 to 6.5 million answer books and that if it was asked to reevaluate answer books or offer inspection, it would create confusion and chaos, subjecting its examinations to delay and disarray. They also submitted to the Court that their examination papers are set by teachers with at least 20 years of teaching experience with proven integrity with a moderation team that ensured correctness, consistency of different sets of questions, and appropriate level of difficulty. In addition, they submitted that the evaluation system is well organized with test takers' identities concealed, along with those of the schools and examination centers, followed by a marking that is uniform in order to ensure fairness; that marking and totaling are done very carefully and triple-checked; and that results are standardized in an impersonalized way.

But a Division Bench of the Calcutta High Court heard the writ petition in a judgment in 2009. The High Court held that the evaluated answer books of a test taker writing a public examination conducted by statutory body like CBSE are a "document, manuscript record, and opinion" falling within provisions of the RTI Act and should be interpreted in a manner that would lead toward dissemination of information rather than withholding the information, and in view of the right to information, the examining body was bound to provide inspection of evaluated answer books to the test taker. Therefore, it directed CBSE to grant inspection of the answer book to the test taker. It did not direct CBSE to perform a re-evaluation of the answer book, as this was considered to be outside the purview of the RTI Act.

CBSE then appealed to the Supreme Court of India. The Supreme Court considered the following key questions:

(1) Whether a test taker's right to information under the RTI Act includes a right to inspect his evaluated answer book in a public examination or taking certified copies

(2) Whether an examining body holds the evaluated answer book "in a fiduciary relationship" and consequently has no obligation to inspect the evaluated answer books under Section 8 (1)(e) of RTI Act

(3) Whether the test taker is entitled to inspection of the evaluated answer book or to seek certified copies thereof and whether such right is subject to any limitations, conditions, or safeguards

On Question 1, the Court ruled that the definition of "information" in Section 2(f) of the RTI Act refers to any material in any form that includes records, documents, opinions, and papers among several other enumerated items. The Court stated that when a test taker participates in an examination and writes his answers in an answer book and submits it to the examining body for evaluation and declaration of the result, the answer book is a document or record. When the answer book is evaluated by an examiner appointed by the examining body, the evaluated answer book becomes a record containing the "opinion" of the examiner. Therefore, the evaluated answer book is also "information" under the RTI Act.

On Question 2, the Court ruled that an examining body does not hold the evaluated answer books in a fiduciary relationship and therefore cannot be exempt; the examining body therefore will have to permit inspection of the answer books sought by the test takers.

On Question 3, the Court ruled as a safeguard that the pages of the answer book that contain the identity of examiners, coordinators, or scrutinizers should be removed, covered, or otherwise severed from the non-exempted part of the answer book and also ruled as a condition that the answer book needs to be available for only the three-month period after the examination as per existing CBSE rules.

In summary, the Supreme Court affirmed the Calcutta High Court's earlier ruling directing CBSE to permit test takers to allow inspection of their answer books, subject to the safeguards and conditions mentioned.

This ruling could have reverberations for assessment agencies around the world if laws similar to the RTI Act in India exist in other countries. Test takers in such countries with low scores could file cases for inspection of their answer books and receive a court's support. Notwithstanding some safeguards and conditions, the release of answer books in general would help make the assessment process more transparent and ensure fair assessments and just institutions. In cases of any errors in the evaluation, the assessment agency would have the opportunity to set this right.

Revisiting Toulmin's Argumentation Model and a Research Agenda

After all the previous discussions regarding underlying ethical theories and the application of standards, it would be useful to revisit how Toulmin's argumentation model can provide a path to articulating and supporting an assessment agency's claims.

Going from Principles to Claims (and Sub-claims)

Based on a firm foundation of ethics, assessment developers need to outline their principles and sub-principles in terms of fairness and justice. Once the principles and sub-principles are in place, they can be operationalized into claims and sub-claims. These claims and sub-claims can then be evaluated using the Toulmin argumentation model with warrants, backing, and rebuttal, if necessary. Here's an illustration of how claims and sub-claims can be made regarding fairness and justice. My assessment is a fictional assessment (use your own name).

Claim 1 is directed to the fairness of the assessment with four sub-claims:
Sub-claim 1—The assessment provides adequate Opportunity-to-learn the knowledge, abilities, and skills prior to the assessment for all test takers.

Sub-claim 2—The assessment is consistent and meaningful in terms of the score interpretation for all test takers.

Sub-claim 3—The assessment is free of bias and avoids construct irrelevance for all test takers.

Sub-claim 4—The assessment provides appropriate access in terms of financial, geographical, and technological aspects for all test takers and appropriate accommodations for test takers with disabilities; it provides appropriate administration in terms of providing equal opportunity for all test takers to demonstrate their knowledge, abilities, or skills; and its standard-setting procedures are equitable for all test takers.

Claim 2 is directed to the justice of assessment institutions with two sub-claims:

Sub-claim 1—The assessment has beneficial consequences to the assessment community.

Sub-claim 2—The assessment promotes positive values and advances justice through public reasoning.Extract 10.1   Claims of an Assessment

Claim 1: Fairness

My assessment is fair to all test takers; that is, it treats all test takers with equal respect.

Sub-claim 1: The assessment provides adequate opportunity to acquire the knowledge, abilities, or skills to be assessed for all test takers.

Sub-claim 2: The assessment is consistent and meaningful in terms of its test score interpretation for all test takers.

Sub-claim 3: The assessment is free of bias against all test takers, in particular by avoiding the assessment of construct-irrelevant matters.

Sub-claim 4: The assessment provides appropriate access, administration, and standard-setting procedures so that decision-making is equitable for all test takers.

Claim 2: Justice

My assessment institution is just; it brings about benefits in society, promotes positive values, and advances justice through public reasoning.

Sub-claim 1: The assessment has beneficial consequences to the test-taking community.

Sub-claim 2: The assessment promotes positive values and advances justice through public reasoning.

Planning Research Studies for the Backing

At this point, a few points that were presented in Chapter 4 might be worth repeating here:

(1) Principles and claims have to be *clear and unambiguous*.
(2) Warrants and backing should be *relevant* to the claim being supported.
(3) Backing should be based on *sufficient* size in terms of test taker samples, assessment materials, conditions, administration and scoring, reporting, and decision-making procedures.
(4) Backing should provide *positive* evidence (not negative evidence, as the absence of something does not mean that something is present).
(5) Backing should lead to *convergent* findings (not divergent), especially in the case of multiple warrants; divergent findings could lead to delayed judgments.
(6) Backing should be based on *primary analysis of test performance data* and not based on test manuals and technical reports.
(7) In rebuttals, backing should *defeat or undercut* the claim.

Collecting the Backing

Once an assessment agency's claims for an assessment are made known (explicitly or implicitly), warrants need to be articulated and research studies organized for each claim (or sub-claim) so that sufficient backing can be supplied to support the claims. If sufficient and necessary backing has been collected, the case can be made that the claim (or sub-claim) is supported. But it could also be case that support for a claim (or sub-claim) may not be available. If this is the case, then a rebuttal claim could be articulated and then support for the rebuttal claim could be explored.

Arriving at the Decision

Once the backing is collected for each of the claims (and sub-claims), decisions have to be made regarding whether all the claims have been supported or not. If all the claims have been supported with positive and convergent findings, then the following conditions need to be noted:

(1) *Reasoned full acceptance (RFA)* of the claim when there is relevant, sufficient, positive, and convergent evidence to support the claim.
(2) *Reasoned partial acceptance (RPA)* of the claim when there is only partially relevant, sufficient, positive, and/or convergent evidence to support the claim. In this situation, some of the assessment's claims may be accepted, whereas others are rejected or deferred.

If all the claims have not been supported with positive and convergent findings, then the following conditions need to be noted:

(3) *Reasoned rejection (RR)* of the claim when there is not enough relevant, sufficient, positive, and/or convergent evidence (or there are divergent findings) to support the claim. In this situation, there could be rebuttals or counterclaims to the original claims.

(4) *Deferred judgment (DJ)* of the claim when there is not enough or clear relevant, sufficient positive and convergent evidence (or there are divergent findings) to support or reject the claim. In this situation, more evidence is necessary to make a judgment on this claim.

Whatever the decision, assessment designers and developers and commissioned and independent researchers need to post and publicize their findings from these analyses so that there is public justification or public reasoning for the assessments. This is critical, as often such research findings and overall decisions do not leave the offices or libraries of assessment development agencies and therefore remain unknown to the community where the assessment is used or planned to be used.

A Research Agenda

Pulling together the ideas presented thus far in all the chapters, a research agenda for the evaluation of language assessments is presented in the sequence of a typical assessment development cycle. Table 10.3 presents the main areas and sub-areas that can be focused on, with research areas for each. These areas and sub-areas can be articulated as claims and sub-claims that need warrants and backing or rebuttal and backing. The possible list of research areas provides details for the development of specific warrants and backing; it is likely this list may be different based on the claims an assessment agency might make. The order of presentation reflects the linear sequence of assessment development, from receiving the mandate to developing an assessment to the overall evaluation of the assessment. It somewhat distorts the actual process of assessment development in general, but it is used here to show the research areas with more clarity.[9]

Revisiting Fairness and Justice

Fairness as a Requirement of Justice

What I have argued throughout the book is that fairness of an assessment is a fundamental quality necessary for the fair participation and treatment of different groups of test takers in terms of age, gender, education, income, language,

TABLE 10.3 A research agenda for evaluating language assessments through the assessment cycle

Main areas	Sub-areas	Research areas
1. Assessment mandate	a. Purpose and scope; relationship to instruction;	Analyses regarding assessment preparation; Opportunity-to-learn; intended washback; of benefits of the assessment
	b. Benefit to test takers	
2. Assessment design	a. Cognitive sources of irrelevant-variance	Analyses of test takers' cognitive process while taking the assessment; irrelevant processes
	b. Content sources of irrelevant-variance	Analyses of specialized knowledge; customs, values, traditions, socialization
	c. Affective sources of construct-irrelevant variance	Analyses of controversial, upsetting or inflammatory language/content in the assessment
	d. Physical sources of construct-irrelevant variance	Analyses of audio and visual materials in the assessment; of needs of test takers with disabilities
3. Assessment development	a. Item/task conceptualization and writing	Analyses of match between specifications and items/tasks
	b. Item/task analyses and reviews, banking, and assembly	Analyses of item/task difficulty, discrimination, speededness; form equivalence
4. Translated/adapted assessments in dual languages	a. Comparability of translated /adapted or dual-language	Analyses of equivalence (construct-bias, method-bias, item-bias); equating and linking
	b. Equating and linking	
5. Assessment administration	a. Site facilities (room, furniture, equipment, etc.)	Analyses of technology and equipment, computers, and monitors
	b. Site operations (check-in, directions, monitoring test takers, check-out, storage or return of materials)	Analyses of administration staff; procedures for check-in (biometric data, assistive technologies, hearing aids, etc.); of security and fraud check; procedures for dealing with irregularities

TABLE 10.3 (Continued)

Main areas	Sub-areas	Research areas
	c. Test takers with disabilities	Analyses of accommodations: extended time, frequent breaks, large font size, etc.
	d. L2 test takers taking math and science assessments in L1	Analyses of accommodations: from glossaries to dual-language presentations
6. Assessment scoring, interpretation, and decision-making	a. Human and automated scoring	Analyses of consistency among raters; of rating systems; comparability of feedback; differential item/task functioning; standard setting
	b. Washback and instruction	Analyses of intended and unintended washback of the assessment on teaching and learning
	c. Consequences	Analyses of standard setting; pass–fail rates; differential effects on test taker groups; public policy
7. Overall evaluation	a. Benefit to immediate stakeholders	Analyses of pros and cons of the assessment to the community
	b. Benefit to the community	

nationality, etc. And justice is the quality needed of an institution that administers a fair assessment. These two concepts can work together with corresponding principles for an assessment agency that designs, develops, and administers a fair assessment and wants to be a just institution. But as discussed in Chapter 3, the first principle, the principle of fairness, has to exist prior to the second, the principle of justice, because if the first principle is not satisfied, then the second principle cannot be satisfied. In other words, if the presumption that treating every test taker with equal respect in an assessment is not satisfied, then the assessment will not succeed in being beneficial to the community and bringing justice to the community. The principle of fairness underscores the need for assessment agencies to treat all test takers with equal respect and therefore to give them an appropriate level of opportunity to succeed in the assessment. Once assessments are fair to test takers, institutions that administer the assessments can be just.

Standardized Assessments and Teacher-made Assessments

Often in discussions, there is an argument made that teacher–made, low–stakes assessments for classroom use do not have to comply with standards and qualities or fairness and justice and that these concepts are only necessary for the high-stakes standardized assessments that are offered at a national or international level. This is a totally wrong approach to take. For example, consider a Grade 5 school teacher who designs an assessment poorly, or writes items and tasks that under-represent the construct, or chooses content that is outside the experience of students, or grades written essays inconsistently, or makes pass–fail decisions with biased standards? How would we like to be this teacher's student? How would we like to be a parent or guardian of a child in this teacher's classroom? It is more than likely that no student in such a classroom will forget an unfair teacher who developed, administered, and scored unfair assessments. Additionally, students in the classroom who received low scores due to unfair assessment practices could become unmotivated, and this could be the start of a downhill path to failure. Thus, fairness and justice cannot be dispensed with totally in teacher–made, low-stakes classroom assessments, but a careful look at Table 10.3 will show areas that are not as relevant and therefore can be ignored.

On the other hand, it is true that high-stakes, standardized, large-scale assessments—as in school exit and college entrance examinations—need heightened scrutiny in many areas of fairness and justice. But often, high-stakes assessments are not standardized and large scale, as in the case of immigration and citizenship assessments. In these high-stakes assessments, too, scrutiny is necessary.

Application in Other Languages

Although this book focuses mainly on English language assessment, Toulmin's argumentation model and the procedures that accompany it, can be used for evaluation of assessments in any language. This is important, as many of the new thinking and innovative practices in the field do not go beyond language assessments in English, a few European languages and even fewer Asian languages. Thus, language assessments in different languages, including language assessments that are translated from one language into another around the world, remain to be examined in order to determine whether the claims of those assessments are supported. Research studies with such language assessments are also likely to show us any new types of claims that assessment agencies see as salient. For example, articles on assessments in languages from around the world have made us aware of morphological and orthographical problems with the cloze test in Malayalam (Sadanandan, 2014), diglossic and dialectal difficulties in Tamil (Sankar, 2014), language variety in French (Ryan, 2014), and the role of Sheng in assessing Swahili (Thompson, 2014).

The Road to Fairness and Justice

Although the concepts of fairness and justice may have been understood to be critically necessary, the highway to arriving at a fair assessment with a just institution may be filled with obstacles. Table 10.3 shows us a list that is long already and may seem daunting. For example, in some cases, test takers may have fundamental problems with opportunity-to-learn prior to test taking where teaching, learning, and assessing are not aligned with each other. This may result in an assessment with an under-representation or irrelevant representation of the construct. In other cases, only a single rater may be available to read all written responses, or no pilot testing or trialing of items or tasks is conducted due to security concerns, or content bias or performance bias analyses may not be routinely performed. Or anonymity of test takers is not maintained, and test takers are known to all raters who could be biased. This list of possible problems can go on, but even if there may be many things wrong in some assessments, we have to work hard to remove the unfairness and injustice one step at a time even though the road may be long.

Limits to Fairness

There have always been concerns among language assessment professionals about whether there are limits to fairness and what these limits might be. A number of researchers presented papers addressing the theme of "Fairness in Language Testing" at the Language Testing Research Colloquium in Orlando, Florida, in 1997. Based on the opening and closing panel discussions that were held on the same topic at the conference, Kunnan (2000) edited a collection of papers on this theme. Here are two advocates of fairness who addressed the limits in different ways.[10]

Bachman (2000) directed his concerns at practitioners and their training. He asked:

> Is it fair to expect practitioners to develop, administer, and score tests when [they] have had little or no education or training in this? . . . Who is

responsible for educating practitioners about fairness issues and considerations, and providing them the tools and knowledge needed to deal with these on a practical day-to-day basis?

(pp. 39–40)

Hamp-Lyons (2000) posed questions regarding her own stance on fairness issues:

Was I fair to the students who took the *ELTS*, when I didn't let their voices speak in my dissertation? Was I fair to those who would take the *Access*, when I remained associated with it after I learned the unethical ways it was to be used? Was I fair to freshman students at Michigan, when I kept silent about the fact that transfer students [have] a special statistical advantage on the test (*MELAB*)? Was I fair to teachers in the *TOEFL* preparation courses around the world, when I didn't publish a revision of my book on the *Test of Written English*, after I knew how it really worked?

(p. 34)

Conclusion

Despite the efforts of many individuals, organizations, and governments and their guidelines, frameworks and legislations, unfairness and injustice prevails in the world today. One location that unfairness and justice is still entrenched is the contexts of educational, workplace and immigration and citizenship assessment. This book makes a case for formal evaluations of all language assessments so that all stakeholders have the information necessary to evaluate assessments and assessment practice. In order to do this, two questions are posed: (1) What's the right thing to do to bring about fair assessments and just institutions and (2) What's the right thing to do to remove manifest unfairness and injustice?

This book calls for evaluations with specific reference to fairness and justice using a variety of research methods (both quantitative, qualitative analyses, assessments, its materials and test performance). Using Toulmin's formal argumentation model (with principles, claims, warrants and backing), various aspects of language assessments are examined with findings from different studies. In addition, a call for ethical thinking is illustrated through hypothetical scenarios so that decision-makers justify their actions.

Thus, relevant research and self-reflection among language assessment professionals and professionals-in-training should help us become advocates for fairness and justice and help us find ways of removing manifest unfairness and injustice when we confront them. If we can do this, I believe we will have fair assessments and just institutions.

I would like to end by quoting M. K. Gandhi, who wrote "You must be the change you wish to see in the world." Gandhi's view along with those of Rescher's and Hamilton's (cited at the top of the Preface), should inspire us to bring about beneficial language assessments to our communities.

Notes

1 www.gov.uk/government/organisations/ofqual/about

2 The ESLPE (at UCLA) had a arobust research program in the past, but in the last five years, its research agenda has come to a halt as the ESLPE is now run by English language programs. This unit does not seem to have any expertise in initiating research, although they continue to administer the assessment to over 2000 test takers a year.

3 Retrieved on November 20, 2016, from: http://privatewww.essex.ac.uk/~patrickp/language-origin-refugees.pdf

4 Retrieved on November 20, 2016, from: www.nytimes.com/2015/12/11/nyregion/cuomo-task-force-signals-further-retreat-from-common-core-school-standards.html?_r=0

5 See this article for the pros and cons regarding the Common Core Standards: http://teaching.about.com/od/assess/f/What-Are-Some-Pros-And-Cons-Of-The-Common-Core-Standards.htm

6 www.cgcs.org/cms/lib/DC00001581/Centricity/Domain/87/Testing%20Report.pdf

7 See www.fairtest.org/ESSA-BasisForStrongerReformMovement. The New Federal Education Law: A basis for a stronger testing resistance and assessment reform movement.

8 *Central Board of Secondary Education (appellant) vs. Bandopadhyay and others* (respondents). Civil Appeal No. 6454 of 2011 arising out of Special Leave Petition [C] No. 7526/2009. Ruling authored by Justice R. V. Raveendran. See court document for details: https://indiankanoon.org/doc/1519371/

9 Kunnan and Grabowski (2013) present a circular diagram with intersecting pathways to show how the assessment cycle is non-linear and dynamic.

10 In an extreme view, Davies (2010), in a response to Xi's (2010) "How do we go about investigating test fairness?" wrote: "I want now to explain why I think the pursuit of fairness in language testing is vain: first because it is unattainable and second because it is unnecessary (p. 171) . . . Everything Xi claims for fairness is covered by validity. To integrate fairness into validity, which is what Xi purports to do, is, at bottom, word magic: we are left no wiser about validity and expected to agree that part of what we understand to be validity should in fact be re-labeled fairness. . .The quest for fairness is then seen to be a quest for the grail. . .The search for test fairness is chimaerical" (p. 175).

References

Abedi, J., Hofstetter, C., & Lord, C. (2004). Assessment accommodations for English Language Learners: Implications for policy-based empirical research. *Review of Educational Research, 74,* 1–28.

American Educational Research Association, American Psychological Association, National Council for Measurement in Education. (2014). *Standards for educational and psychological testing.* Washington, DC: Author.

Americans with Disabilities Act. (1990). 42 U.S. Code 12101–213.

Bachman, L. F. (2000). What, if any, are the limits of our responsibility for fairness in language testing? In A. J. Kunnan (Ed.), *Fairness and validation in language assessment* (pp. 39–41). Cambridge, UK: Cambridge University Press.

Breimhorst v. Educational Testing Service. (2001). No. C-99–3387 (N.D. Cal. Jan. 24, 2001).

Central Board of Secondary Education vs. Bandopadhyay and others. Civil Appeal No. 6454 of 2011. The Supreme Court of India. Author.

Davies, A. (2010). Test fairness: A response. *Language Testing, 27,* 171–176.

Geranpayeh, A. & Kunnan, A. J. (2007). Differential item functioning in terms of age in the Certificate of Academic English exam. *Language Assessment Quarterly, 4,* 190–222.

Hamp-Lyons, L. (2000). Fairnesses in language testing. In A. J. Kunnan (Ed.), *Fairness and validation in language assessment* (pp. 30–34). Cambridge, UK: Cambridge University Press.

Hart, R., Casserly, M., Uzzell, R., Palacios, M., Corcoran, A., & Spurgeon, L. (2015). *Student testing in America's great city schools: An inventory and preliminary analysis.* Council of the Great City Schools. Washington, DC: Author.

Herman, J. L., Klein, D. C. D., & Abedi, J. (2000). Assessing students' opportunity to learn: Teacher and student perspectives. *Educational Researcher, 19,* 16–24.

Hoang, G., & Kunnan, A. J. (2016). Automated writing instructional tool for English Language Learners: A case study of "MY Access". *Language Assessment Quarterly, 13,* 359–376.

Johnstone, C. J., Moen, R. E., Thurlow, M. L., Matchett, D., Hausmann, K. E., & Scullin, S. (2007). *What do state reading test specifications specify?* Minneapolis, MN: University of Minnesota, Partnership for Accessible Reading Assessment. Retrieved from: www.cehd.umn.edu/NCEO/onlinepubs/PARA/blueprint

Koenig, J., & Bachman, L. F. (Eds.). (2004). *Keeping score for all: The effects of inclusion and accommodation policies on large-scale assessment.* Washington, DC: National Academies Press.

Kunnan, A. J. (1990). DIF in native language and gender groups in an ESL placement test. *TESOL Quarterly, 24,* 741–746.

Kunnan, A. J. (1992). An investigation of a criterion-referenced test using G-theory, factor and cluster analyses. *Language Testing, 9,* 30–49.

Kunnan, A. J. (1994). Modeling relationships among some test-taker characteristics and tests of English as a Foreign Language. *Language Testing, 11,* 225–252.

Kunnan, A. J. (Ed.). (2000). *Fairness and validation in language assessment.* Cambridge, UK: Cambridge University Press.

Liu, S., & Kunnan, A. J. (2016). Investigating the application of automated writing evaluation to Chinese undergraduate English majors: A case study of "WriteToLearn". *CALICO Journal, 33,* 71–91.

Rya, E. (2014). Assessing French. In A. J. Kunnan (Ed.), *The companion to language assessment* (pp. 1989–1998). Malden, MA: Wiley.

Rawls, J. (1971). *A theory of justice.* Cambridge, MA: Harvard University Press.

Sadanandan, S. (2014). Assessing Malayalam. In A. J. Kunnan (Ed.), *The companion to language assessment* (pp. 1823–1831). Malden, MA: Wiley.

Sankar, V. (2014). In A. J. Kunnan (Ed.), *The companion to language assessment* (pp. 1851–1862). Malden, MA: Wiley.

Sen, A. (2010). *The idea of justice.* Cambridge, MA: Harvard University Press.

Taylor, K. (2015, December 11). Cuomo panel calls for further retreat from common core standards. *The New York Times.* Retrieved from: www.nytimes.com/2015/12/11/nyregion/cuomo-task-force-signals-further-retreat-from-common-core-school-standards.html?_r=0

Thompson, K. (2014). Assessing Swahili. In A. J. Kunnan (Ed.), *The companion to language assessment* (pp. 1711–1721). Malden, MA: Wiley.

Xi, X. (2010). How do we go about investigating test fairness? *Language Testing*, 27, 147–170.

Website

www.gov.uk/government/organisations/ofqual/about

Websites for Table 10.1:

CAE, FCE: www.cambridgeenglish.org/research-and-validation/
CAEL: www.cael.ca/
CET: www.cet.edu.cn/cet_test01.htm#
IELTS: www.ielts.org/
Pearson Test of English: https://home.pearsonvue.com/Home.aspx
STEP EIKEN: www.eiken.or.jp/eiken/en/
TOEFL: www.ets.org/toefl/
TOEIC: www.ets.org/toeic
Versant: www.versanttest.com/

Websites for Table 10.2:

DELNA: www.delna.auckland.ac.nz/en.html
DELTA: http://gslpa.polyu.edu.hk/eng/delta_web/about/index.html
DUOLINGO: https://englishtest.duolingo.com/
ESLPE: http://wp.ucla.edu/wp/students/placement-exams/eslpe/
EPT: www.linguistics.illinois.edu/students/placement/
EPT: https://apling.engl.iastate.edu/english-placement-test/
ELDA: www.copetest.com/
MELAB: http://cambridgemichigan.org/about-us/research/

INDEX